REVERSING
HERMON

REVEЯSING

HERMON

ENOCH, THE WATCHERS & THE FORGOTTEN MISSION OF JESUS CHRIST

DR. MICHAEL S. HEISER

Author of the bestselling
The Unseen Realm: Recovering the Supernatural Worldview of the Bible

DEFENDER

CRANE, MO

Reversing Hermon: Enoch, the Watchers, & the Forgotten Mission of Jesus Christ
By Dr. Michael S. Heiser

Printed in the United States of America.

Scripture taken from the King James Version of the Bible unless otherwise noted.

Cover design by Jeffrey Mardis.
ISBN: 978-0-9981426-3-0

For "Booma" Miriam I. Heiser
(1903–1992)

ACKNOWLEDGMENTS

This book has been a long time in coming, both in terms of finally producing something for my friend Tom Horn, but also because no book like it exists. Readers will discover in these pages that much time and effort in high biblical scholarship has been devoted to the study of 1 Enoch (more popularly known as "the Book of Enoch") and its importance for New Testament theology. Hundreds of scholarly journal articles and doctoral dissertations have explored the literary and theological relationships between the two, but to date that research has never been collected and put forth in one volume—for either the academy or interested non-specialists. I'm thankful for Tom's encouragement to produce *Reversing Hermon* to fill that void to some degree.

Thanks are also due to my listeners at the Naked Bible Podcast. Several of the topics covered in this book were enthusiastically received as podcast episodes some time ago. The reception encouraged me to take the step and move forward with this project.

Lastly, the efforts of Kay Anderson were most appreciated. Kay worked quickly and efficiently to proofread the manuscript. Her eye for detail and thoroughness are duly noted.

Contents

Introduction. 1

SECTION PREVIEW: PART I
Genesis 6:1–4 in Its Original Ancient Contexts

CHAPTER 1
The Sons of God and the Nephilim
Taking Genesis 6:1–4 Seriously 9

CHAPTER 2
The Sin of the Watchers in 1 Enoch and Other Enochian Texts . . . 23

CHAPTER 3
The Mesopotamian Apkallu, the Watchers, and the Nephilim 37

SECTION PREVIEW: PART II
Reversing Hermon in the Gospels

CHAPTER 4
The Sin of the Watchers and the Birth of Jesus 55

CHAPTER 5
The Sin of the Watchers and the Genealogy of Jesus 71

CHAPTER 6
The Sin of the Watchers and the Ministry of Jesus. 87

SECTION PREVIEW: PART III
Reversing Hermon in the Epistles

CHAPTER 7
The Sin of the Watchers and Human Depravity 105

CHAPTER 8
The Sin of the Watchers and the
Head Covering of 1 Corinthians 11. 123

CHAPTER 9
The Sin of the Watchers and Baptism. 137

SECTION PREVIEW: PART IV
Reversing Hermon in the Book of Revelation

CHAPTER 10
The Sin of the Watchers, the Nephilim, and the Antichrist 147

CHAPTER 11
The Sin of the Watchers and the Apocalypse 163

Conclusion 181

APPENDIX I
The Question of the Inspiration of
    1 Enoch in the Early Church 183

APPENDIX II
The Dating and Manuscript Evidence for
    1 Enoch and the Book of Giants 193

APPENDIX III
Scholarly Bibliography on 1 Enoch and the Book of Giants 197

APPENDIX IV
New Testament Allusions to Books of the Pseudepigrapha 257

APPENDIX V
The Ancient Antichrist Profile
    Jew or Gentile? 257

Notes 269

INTRODUCTION

This book is about the important influence that the story of the sin of the Watchers in 1 Enoch 6–16 had on the thinking of New Testament authors. For those to whom 1 Enoch sounds unfamiliar, this is the ancient apocalyptic literary work known popularly (but imprecisely) as "the Book of Enoch."[1] Most scholars believe that 1 Enoch was originally written in Aramaic perhaps as early as the third century B.C.[2] The oldest fragments of the book were found among the Dead Sea Scrolls and dated to roughly the second century B.C. This places the book squarely in the middle of what scholars call the Second Temple Period (ca. 500 B.C.—A.D. 70), an era more commonly referred to as the "Intertestamental Period." This book will use the more academic designation ("Second Temple Period").

THE TASK

The term "Watchers" is a biblical one. The Watchers (Aramaic: *'irin*)[3] appear only in the book of Daniel in the Bible (Daniel 4:13, 17, 23), where they are also called "holy ones." In Daniel, they are therefore "good" members of God's entourage. The term occurs more frequently outside the Bible in Jewish literature composed between the Old and New Testament periods.

The Watcher story of 1 Enoch, as many readers will recall, is an expansion of the episode described in Genesis 6:1–4, in which "the sons of God (Hebrew: *beney ha-ʾelohim*) came in to the daughters of man" (Genesis 6:4, ESV). Consequently, "Watchers" is the Enochian term of choice (among others) for the divine "sons of God."[4] While the story of this supernatural rebellion occupies scant space in Genesis, it received considerable attention during the Second Temple Period. As we shall see, this attention is *not* peripheral to biblical theology.

The reason for this assertion is straightforward and will be demonstrated in detail: The Enochian version of the events of Genesis 6:1–4 preserves and transmits the original Mesopotamian context for the first four verses of the Flood account. Every element of Genesis 6:1–4 has a Mesopotamian counterpoint—a theological target that provides the rationale for why these four verses wound up in the inspired text in the first place.

Connections to that backstory can be found in the Old Testament, but they are scattered and unsystematically presented. This is not the case with Second Temple Jewish literature like 1 Enoch. Books like 1 Enoch preserve all of the Mesopotamian touchpoints with Genesis 6:1–4 when presenting their expanded retelling of the events of that biblical passage. The Enochian retelling of the story in turn finds its way into the New Testament, most transparently in the books of Peter and Jude, but, as this book will show, other New Testament writers do the same. Put another way, details in certain New Testament passages with links to the Genesis 6:1–4 episode can only be traced to 1 Enoch, and those elements in turn are quite consistent with the original Mesopotamian context of Genesis 6:1–4. This means the Enochian story not only provides important details as to how Genesis 6:1–4 should be understood, but also informs us how certain interpretations of that passage popular in both the early church and modern Christianity (e.g., the "Sethite" interpretation) fundamentally violate the original context of Genesis 6:1–4.

This is all well and good for those who already see the general incoherence of the Sethite view and other nonsupernatural interpretations. But the notion that the sin of the Watchers was a frequent theological reference point for New Testament writers will be new to most readers. It is not a novelty to scholars whose focus is the New Testament and the Second Temple Period. There is in fact a substantial amount of scholarly, peer-reviewed literature demonstrating this point. This book draws heavily on that scholarship.

If one were to ask a modern Christian, "Why is the world and all humanity so thoroughly wicked?" the chances are very high that an answer of "the Fall" would be forthcoming. We have been conditioned by church history (ancient and modern) to look only to Genesis 3 for such theology. But if you asked a Jew living in the Second Temple Period the same question, the answer would be dramatically different. Yes, the entrance of sin into God's good world occurred in Eden, but the unanimous testimony of Second Temple Judaism is that the Watchers are to blame for the proliferation of evil on the earth. The New Testament writers, being predominantly Jewish and products of the Second Temple Period, more often than not telegraphed the same outlook. We just can't see it because, frankly, we don't have Second Temple Jewish eyes. We miss what the original audience would have seen.

To narrow our focus, a number of New Testament passages say what they say because they are literary expressions of a significant theme in New Testament theology—the *reversal* of the wickedness that has permeated the human race. Many readers will recognize that Mount Hermon is the place where, according to 1 Enoch 6:6, the Watchers descended and took an oath to commit the transgression described in Genesis 6:1–4. This book's title, *Reversing Hermon,* alludes to the notion—hidden in plain sight in a surprising number of New Testament passages—that what happened in Genesis 6:1–4 had to be reversed as part of restoring the original

Edenic vision. That reversal was, is, and will be accomplished by the Messiah, Jesus of Nazareth.

My task in this book is to remove the scales of our own tradition from our eyes, at least as it relates to the importance of the Watcher story of 1 Enoch for understanding portions of the New Testament. In doing so, I'll endeavor to make serious, peer-reviewed scholarship accessible to interested readers outside the guild of academia. To that end, this is not a book filled with speculation. It is a book that provides readers with access to the best in current scholarship on 1 Enoch, other Second Temple Jewish literature (e.g., the Book of Giants found among the Dead Sea Scrolls), and their relationship to the New Testament.[5]

OBSTACLES TO THE TASK

Most Christians and Christian leaders know next to nothing about 1 Enoch. Few have read the book. Consequently, it's unreasonable to expect most Christians to have ever thought about the importance of 1 Enoch's recounting of how the Watchers' sin and corruption of humanity needed to be reversed by the Messiah. This element of New Testament theology is basically absent from popular Christian understanding of the New Testament. There are several reasons for this systemic ignorance.

First and foremost is the matter of canonicity. A handful of important early Christian writers such as Tertullian, Irenaeus, Origen, and Clement either advocated 1 Enoch as worthy of canonical status or considered it authoritative on certain matters of truth and doctrine. The book was assigned full canonical recognition only in the Ethiopian Church.[6]

A book that isn't considered inspired by most of Christianity, many are told, isn't valuable for biblical understanding. Consequently, unlike Peter and Jude, whose New Testament contributions show a close knowledge of 1 Enoch, many Christians not only never read 1 Enoch, but are discouraged from doing so. I don't consider the book of 1 Enoch to be inspired and canonical, but that is no excuse for neglecting it in the study of Scripture. Frankly, this entire book is testimony to the folly of this inattention.

The assumption that uninspired ancient books aren't valuable for understanding Scripture is deeply flawed. Biblical writers in both testaments show detailed knowledge of ancient writings now known to the modern world. That this material wasn't inspired didn't bother biblical writers. It is well known among scholars, for example, that Old Testament covenants follow the structure of different types of ancient Near Eastern treaties,[7] that prophets and psalmists quote from the Baal Cycle (e.g., *KTU* 1.5.I; Psalm 74:13), and that Solomon borrowed material from the Wisdom of Amenemope for Proverbs 22:17–23:11. In the New Testament, Paul's quotations of Greek poets are well known (Acts 17:28, Epimenides and Aratus; 1 Corinthians 15:33, Euripedes or Menander; Titus 1:2, Epimenides) as is the use of the apocryphal ("deutero-canonical" to Roman Catholics) *Wisdom of Solomon* in Hebrews 1:2 (Wisdom of Solomon 7:26). These are far from the only instances.

A second factor is that the reputation of 1 Enoch has been sullied by misguided thinking about the nature of the modern collection of books into which it has been grouped by scholars: the Pseudepigrapha. The following is representative: "The Pseudepigrapha books are those that are distinctly spurious and unauthentic in their overall content" and "no such formula as 'it is written' or 'the Scriptures say' is connected with these citations."[8] These assertions are incoherent. With respect to the first, the fact that Peter and Jude embrace content that is demonstrably from 1 Enoch means that the content of that book, though not canonical, cannot be thought of as entirely inauthentic. Regarding the second, some early church writers do indeed cite 1 Enoch with formulaic phrases like "For Scripture says" and "For it is written."[9]

As noted above, 1 Enoch is part of a grouping of ancient works known to scholars collectively as the Pseudepigrapha. The term does *not* mean "false writings" in the sense that the content of these books is to be regarded as wholly spurious. Rather, the term refers to the practice of producing written works and then assigning their authorship to someone (real or imagined) other than the actual author. This practice was common in the ancient world and is to be distinguished from literary forgeries. Well-known New Testament scholar D. A. Carson writes:

> A literary forgery is a work written or modified with the intent to deceive. All literary forgeries are pseudepigraphical, but not all pseudepigrapha are literary forgeries. There is a substantial class of pseudepigraphical writings that, in the course of their transmission, somehow became associated with some figure or other. These connections between a text and an ancient figure, however fallacious, were judgments made with the best will in the world.[10]

The motivation for writing under a pseudonym or a *nom de plum* varied, whether well-intentioned or disreputable. For our purposes, the work of 1 Enoch cannot be regarded with suspicion merely because it is certain that the biblical figure of Enoch didn't write the book.[11] Canonical books named after biblical figures for which no evidence exists that their namesake did any of the writing include Job, 1 and 2 Samuel, and Joshua. Lack of evidence for a namesake's authorship of a book bearing his name is no measurable invalidation of a work's worth or value. During the Second Temple Period, pseudepigraphical literature was quite common. The practice didn't discourage faithful Jews from reading such books.[12] Peter and Jude are obvious examples.

As this book will demonstrate, Peter and Jude were not alone. The New Testament writers took the story of the Watchers in 1 Enoch 6–16 seriously. While several specific statements in the epistles of Peter and Jude can be traced directly to the book, 1 Enoch informs other New Testament writers in profound ways and, therefore, it influences the theological content of what they wrote under inspiration as well.

Section Preview

Part I

Genesis 6:1–4 in Its Original Ancient Contexts

It won't seem unusual that we begin our study in Genesis 6:1–4. After all, that's the passage behind the story of the sin of the Watchers in 1 Enoch. But it is perhaps unexpected that we'll also be spending a good deal of time looking at ancient Mesopotamia. As we'll see, Genesis 6:1–4 and the story of the Watchers have deep roots in Mesopotamian literature. This is a fact with which scholars of 1 Enoch are well-acquainted, but which most lay readers are not.[13]

More specifically, the story of the sons of God and the Nephilim in Genesis 6:1–4 is framed by the Mesopotamian story of the seven pre-Flood wise, divine sages—the *apkallu*. The Mesopotamian material has explicit, unmistakable point-for-point parallels to Genesis 6:1–4. These parallels show that the Genesis passage was written as a theological polemic—a refutation of Mesopotamian religious interpretation of pre- and post-Flood events. Understanding the close relationship between the apkallu saga and Genesis 6:1–4 is crucial for understanding the Watcher story of 1 Enoch for several reasons:

(1) The Watcher story is an expansion of Genesis 6:1–4;
(2) Several of the elements added to Genesis 6:1–4 in 1 Enoch are not

found anywhere in the Old Testament—but are present in both the Mesopotamian material *and the New Testament*;

(3) The above show us that the writer of 1 Enoch knew and preserved the original Mesopotamian context of Genesis 6:1–4;

(4) This preservation demands that we take the Watcher story seriously, even though it is not in the canon, and that we interpret Genesis 6:1–4 supernaturally, understanding the sons of God (the Watchers) as being divine, and their offspring, the Nephilim, as men—but not merely men;

(5) This context and its preservation help us understand how the Watcher story of 1 Enoch influenced the thinking of Peter, Jude, and other New Testament writers and, therefore, how considering the Watcher story as a backdrop is necessary for interpreting certain New Testament passages.

The Sons of God
and the Nephilim
Taking Genesis 6:1–4 Seriously[14]

G enesis 6:1–4 is one of the most marginalized passages in the
Bible. Many pastors and Bible students do all they can to avoid
taking it at face value, opting for "safe" interpretations that allow
it to be shelved. Second Temple Judaism gave it a prominent, almost central, role in understanding God's activity in history. This book seeks to
demonstrate that it deserves that status. Genesis 6:1–4 is actually one of
the most important, serving an important role in biblical theology. Consequently, discussing how it should be—and shouldn't be—interpreted is
where we need to begin.

> [1]When man began to multiply on the face of the land and daugh-
> ters were born to them, [2]the sons of God saw that the daughters of
> man were attractive. And they took as their wives any they chose.
> [3]Then the Lord said, "My Spirit shall not abide in man forever,
> for he is flesh: his days shall be 120 years." [4]The Nephilim were on

the earth in those days, and also afterward, when the sons of God came in to the daughters of man and they bore children to them. These were the mighty men who were of old, the men of renown.

Few Bible passages raise as many questions as this one. Who are the sons of God? Are they divine or human? Who were the Nephilim? Before we start tackling these questions and others, we need to learn how *not* to interpret this passage.

THE SETHITE INTERPRETATION

The so-called Sethite interpretation refuses to take the passage at face value, with the sons of God as divine beings ("angels") and their offspring as giants. This view has been the consensus Christian position since the late fourth century A.D. It is still the predominant approach to Genesis 6:1–4 in modern evangelical churches.[15]

In this approach, the sons of God are merely human beings, men from the line of Seth, Adam and Eve's son who was born after Cain murdered Abel (Genesis 4:25–26; 5:3–4). Presumably, these four verses describe forbidden intermarriage between the godly men of Seth's lineage ("sons of God") and the ungodly women of Cain's line ("daughters of humankind"). In this reading, everyone who lived on earth ultimately came from these two lines, both of them descended from Adam and Eve's children.[16] In this way, the Bible distinguished the godly from the ungodly. Part of the rationale for this view comes from Genesis 4:26, where, depending on the translation, we read that either Seth or humankind "began to call on the name of the Lord" (NIV). The line of Seth was to remain pure and separate from evil lineage. The marriages of Genesis 6:1–4 erased this separation and incurred the wrath of God in the Flood.

The Sethite view of Genesis 6:1–4 is deeply flawed. First, Genesis 4:26 never states that the only people who "called on the name of the

Lord" were men from Seth's lineage. That idea is imposed on the text. Second, as we'll see in the next chapter, the view fails miserably in explaining the Nephilim. Third, the text never calls the women in the episode "daughters of Cain." Rather, they are "daughters of humankind." There is no actual link in the text to Cain. This means that the Sethite view of the text is supported by something *not* present in the text, which is the very antithesis of exegesis. Fourth, there is no command in the text regarding marriages or any prohibition against marrying certain persons. There are no "Jews and Gentiles" at this time.[17] Fifth, nothing in Genesis 6:1–4 or anywhere else in the Bible identifies people who come from Seth's lineage with the descriptive phrase "sons of God." That connection is purely an assumption through which the story is filtered by those who hold the Sethite view.

A close reading of Genesis 6:1–4 makes it clear that a contrast is being created between two classes of individuals, one human and the other divine. When speaking of how humanity was multiplying on earth (v. 1), the text mentions only daughters ("daughters were born to them"). The point is not literally that every birth in the history of the earth after Cain and Abel resulted in a girl. Rather, the writer is setting up a contrast of two groups. The first group is human and female (the "daughters of humankind"). Verse 2 introduces the other group for the contrast: the sons of God. That group is not human, but divine.

There are more deficiencies in this viewpoint than I will take time here to expose, but the point is evident. The Sethite hypothesis collapses under the weight of its own incoherence.

DIVINIZED HUMAN RULERS

Another approach that argues the "sons of God" in Genesis 6:1–4 are human suggests that they should be understood as divinized human rulers. A survey of the academic literature arguing this perspective reveals that it springs from the following: (1) taking the phrase "sons of the Most High" in Psalm 82:6 as referring to humans, then reading that back into Genesis 6:1–4; (2) noting language where God refers to humans as His sons (Exodus 4:23; Psalm 2:7), which, it is argued, is parallel to ancient Near Eastern beliefs that kings were thought to be divine offspring;[18] and (3) arguing that the evil marriages condemned in the verses were human polygamy on the part of these divinized rulers.

As with the Sethite interpretation, this view makes assumptions that render it invalid when tested. First, the text of Genesis 6 never says the marriages were polygamous. That idea must be read into the passage. Second, ancient parallels restrict divine sonship language to kings. Consequently, the idea of a group of sons of God lacks a coherent ancient Near Eastern parallel. The precise plural phrase refers to divine beings elsewhere in the Old Testament, not kings (Job 1:6; 2:1; 38:7; Psalm 29:1; 82:6 [cf. 82:1b]; 89:6 [Hebrew: 89:7]).[19] Third, the broad idea of "human divine kingship" elsewhere in the Old Testament is not a coherent argument against a supernatural view of Genesis 6. It was God's original design for His human children to be servant rulers over the earth under His authority as His representatives—in the presence of His glory. Restoring the loss of the Edenic vision eventually involves creating a people known as Israel and giving them a king (David), who is the template for Messiah. In the final eschatological outcome, the Messiah is the ultimate Davidic king, and all glorified believers share that rule in a new, global Eden. But it is flawed hermeneutics to read either ancient kingship or the glorification of believers back into Genesis 6. The reason is obvious: the marriages in Genesis 6:1–4 corrupt the earth in the prelude to the Flood story. A biblical theology of divinized human rulership in the restored Eden would not be corruptive and evil.

In summary, the plurality of the phrase "sons of God" and the heavenly contexts of its use elsewhere show us there is no exegetical reason to exclude the occurrences of the phrase in Genesis 6:2, 4 from the list of supernatural beings. What drives this choice is apprehension about the supernatural alternative.

SIDING WITH PETER AND JUDE

Peter and Jude embraced a supernatural view of Genesis 6:1–4. Two passages are especially relevant.

2 PETER 2:1–10:

[1]But there were also false prophets among the people.... [3]And in greediness they will exploit you with false words, whose condemnation from long ago is not idle, and their destruction is not asleep. [4]For if God did not spare the angels who sinned, but held them captive in Tartarus with chains of darkness and handed them over to be kept for judgment, [5]and did not spare the ancient world, but preserved Noah, a proclaimer of righteousness, and seven others when he brought a flood on the world of the ungodly, [6]and condemned the cities of Sodom and Gomorrah to destruction, reducing them to ashes, having appointed them as an example for those who are going to be ungodly, [7]and rescued righteous Lot, worn down by the way of life of lawless persons in licentiousness [8](for that righteous man, as he lived among them day after day, was tormenting his righteous soul by the lawless deeds he was seeing and hearing), [9]then the Lord knows how to rescue the godly from trials and to reserve the unrighteous to be punished at the day of judgment, [10]and especially those who go after the flesh in defiling lust and who despise authority.

JUDE 5–7:

[5]Now I want to remind you, although you know everything once and for all, that Jesus, having saved the people out of the land of Egypt, the second time destroyed those who did not believe. [6]And the angels who did not keep to their own domain but deserted their proper dwelling place, he has kept in eternal bonds under deep

gloom for the judgment of the great day, [7] as Sodom and Gomorrah and the towns around them indulged in sexual immorality and pursued unnatural desire in the same way as these, are exhibited as an example by undergoing the punishment of eternal fire.

Scholars agree that the passages are about the same subject matter. [20] They describe an episode from the time of Noah and the Flood when "angels" sinned. [21] That sin, which precipitated the Flood, was sexual in nature; it is placed in the same category as the sin that prompted the judgment of Sodom and Gomorrah. The transgression was interpreted by Peter and Jude as evidence of despising authority and the boundaries of "proper dwelling" for the parties concerned. All of those elements are transparent in Genesis 6:1–4. There is simply no other sin in the Old Testament that meets these specific details—and no other "angelic" sin at all in the Old Testament that might be the referent. [22]

The punishment for the transgression, however, is not mentioned in Genesis 6:1–4. Peter has the divine sons of God held captive in "Tartarus" in chains of darkness until a time of judgment. [23] Jude echoes the thought and clarifies the judgment as the day of the Lord ("the great day"; cf. Zephaniah 1:1–7; Revelation 16:14). These elements come from Jewish literature written between our Old and New Testaments (the Second Temple Period) that retell the Genesis 6 episode. The most famous of these is 1 Enoch. That book informed the thinking of Peter and Jude; it was part of their intellectual worldview. [24] The inspired New Testament writers were perfectly comfortable referencing content found in 1 Enoch and other Jewish books to articulate their theology.

These observations are important. Jewish tradition before the New Testament era overwhelmingly took a supernatural view of Genesis 6:1–4. In other words, they were in line with 2 Peter and Jude. The interpretation of the passage, at least with respect to its supernatural orientation, was not an issue until the late fourth century A.D., when it fell out of favor with some influential church fathers, especially Augustine. [25]

But biblical theology does not derive from the church fathers. It derives from the biblical text, framed in its own context. Scholars agree that the Second Temple Jewish literature that influenced Peter and Jude shows intimate familiarity with the original Mesopotamian context of Genesis 6:1–4. For the person who considers the Old and New Testaments to be equally inspired, interpreting the Genesis passage "in context" means analyzing it in light of its Mesopotamian background as well as 2 Peter and Jude, whose content utilizes supernatural interpretations from Jewish theology of their own day.[26] Filtering Genesis 6:1–4 through Christian tradition that arose centuries after the New Testament Period cannot honestly be considered interpreting it in context.

THE NEPHILIM

One of the great debates over Genesis 6:1–4 is the identity of the Nephilim, a question that is inextricably related to the meaning of the term. As we'll discover in chapter 3, the role of the ancient Mesopotamian context for why Genesis 6:1–4 is even in the Bible is crucial to the correct understanding of the Nephilim. Jewish thinkers in the Second Temple Period understood that original Mesopotamian context, which is why they overwhelmingly viewed the Nephilim of divine sons of God as giants. This perspective includes the translation of the Hebrew term with *gigas* ("giant") in the Septuagint, the Greek translation of the Hebrew Old Testament.[27]

It might seem obvious to some readers that Nephilim ought to be understood as "giants." But many commentators resist the rendering, arguing that it should be read as "fallen ones" or "those who fall upon" (a battle expression). These options are based on the idea that the word derives from the Hebrew verb *n-p-l* (*naphal,* "to fall"). More importantly, those who argue that Nephilim should be translated with one of these expressions rather than "giants" do so to avoid the quasi-divine nature of the Nephilim. That in turn makes it easier for them to argue that the sons of God who produced the Nephilim were human.

In reality, it doesn't matter whether "fallen ones" is the translation. The Nephilim and the Anakim/Rephaim who descend from them (Numbers 13:33; Deuteronomy 2:20–21; 3:1–11) are still described as unusually tall. Consequently, insisting that the name means "fallen" produces no escape from a supernaturalist interpretation.[28]

Despite the uselessness of the argument, I'm not inclined to concede the point. The term Nephilim does not mean "fallen ones."[29] Jewish writers and translators (e.g., the Septuagint) habitually think "giants" when they use or translate the term. There are good reasons for that.

Explaining my own view of what the term means involves Hebrew morphology, the way words are spelled or formed in Hebrew. That discussion gets technical very quickly, but we need to devote some attention to it here.

The spelling of the word "Nephilim" provides a clue to what root word the term is derived from. "Nephilim" is spelled two different ways in the Hebrew Bible: *nephilim* and *nephiylim*. The difference between them is the "y" in the second spelling. Hebrew originally had no vowels. All words were written with consonants only. As time went on, Hebrew scribes started to use some of the consonants to mark long vowel sounds. English does this with the "y" consonant—sometimes it's a vowel. Hebrew does that with its "y" letter, too (the *yod*).

The takeaway is that the second spelling (*nephiylim*) tells us that the root behind the term had a long-i (y) in it before the plural ending (-im) was added. That in turn helps us determine that the word does not mean "those who fall." If that were the case, the word would have been spelled *nophelim*. A translation of "fallen" from the verb *naphal* is also weakened by the "y" spelling form. If the word came from the verb *naphal*, we'd expect a spelling of *nephulim* for "fallen."

However, there's another possible defense for the meaning "fallen." Instead of coming from the verb *naphal*, the word might come from a noun that has a long-i vowel in the second syllable. This kind of noun is called a *qatiyl* noun by Hebrew grammarians. Although there is no such noun as *naphiyl* in the Hebrew Bible, the hypothetical plural form would be *nephiylim*, which is the long spelling we see in Numbers 13:33.

This option solves the spelling problem, but it fails to explain everything else: the original Mesopotamian context, the Second Temple Jewish recognition of that context, the connection of the term to Anakim giants (Numbers 13:33; Deuteronomy 2–3), and the fact that the Septuagint translators translated the word as "giants," not "fallen ones."

So where does the spelling *nephiylim* come from? Is there an answer that would simultaneously explain the spelling and why the translators were consistently thinking "giants"? There is indeed.

Recall that the Old Testament tells us that Jewish intellectuals were taken to Babylon. During those seventy years, the Jews learned to speak Aramaic. They later brought it back to Judah. This is how Aramaic became the primary language in Judea by the time of Jesus. My view is that the Jewish scribes adopted an Aramaic noun: *naphiyla*—which means "giant." When that word is pluralized in Hebrew, you get *nephiylim*, precisely what we see in Numbers 13:33. This is the only explanation for the meaning of the word that accounts for all the contexts and all the details.

THE ORIGIN OF THE NEPHILIM

There are two possible approaches to the origin of the Nephilim in Genesis 6:1–4 that are consistent with the supernatural understanding of the sons of God in the Israelite worldview.[30] The first and most transparent is that divine beings came to earth, assumed human flesh, cohabited with human women, and spawned unusual offspring known as Nephilim. Naturally, this view requires seeing the giant clans encountered in the conquest as physical descendants of the Nephilim (Numbers 13:32–33).[31]

The primary objection to this approach is the sexual component. The modern enlightened mind simply can't tolerate it. Appeal is usually made to Matthew 22:23–33 in this regard, under the assumption that verse 30 teaches that angels cannot engage in sexual intercourse:

> [23]The same day Sadducees came to him, who say that there is no resurrection, and they asked him a question, [24]saying, "Teacher, Moses said, 'If a man dies having no children, his brother must marry the widow and raise up offspring for his brother.' [25]Now there were seven brothers among us. The first married and died, and having no offspring left his wife to his brother. [26]So too the second and third, down to the seventh. [27]After them all, the woman died. [28]In the resurrection, therefore, of the seven, whose wife will she be? For they all had her." [29]But Jesus answered them, "You are wrong, because you know neither the Scriptures nor the power of God. [30]For in the resurrection they neither marry nor are given in marriage, but are like angels in heaven. [31]And as for the resurrection of the dead, have you not read what was said to you by God: [32]'I am the God of Abraham, and the God of Isaac, and the God of Jacob'? He is not God of the dead, but of the living.'" [33]And when the crowd heard it, they were astonished at his teaching.

The text does not say angels cannot have sexual intercourse; it says they *don't*. The reason ought to be obvious. The context for the statement is the resurrection, which refers either broadly to the afterlife or, more precisely, to the final, renewed global Eden. The point is clear in either option. In the spiritual world, the realm of divine beings, there is no need for procreation. Procreation is a necessity for perpetuating the human population. Life in the perfected Edenic world also does not require maintaining the human species by having children—everyone has an immortal resurrection body. Consequently, there is no need for sex in the resurrection, just as there is no need for it in the nonhuman spiritual realm. Genesis 6 doesn't have the spiritual realm or the final Edenic world as its context. The analogy breaks down completely. The passage in Matthew is therefore useless as a commentary on Genesis 6:1–4.

Despite the flawed use of this Gospel passage, Christians still balk at this interpretive option for Genesis 6:1–4. The ancient reader would have had no problem with it. But for moderns, it seems impossible that a divine being could assume human flesh and do what this passage describes.

The objection is odd, since this interpretation is less dramatic than the incarnation of Yahweh as Jesus Christ. How is the virgin birth of God as a man more acceptable? What isn't mind-blowing about Jesus having both a divine and human nature fused together? For that matter, what doesn't offend the modern scientific mind about God going through a woman's birth canal and enduring life as a human, having to learn how to talk, walk, eat with a spoon, be potty-trained, and go through puberty? All these things are far more shocking than Genesis 6:1–4.

That angels—and even God—can have true corporeality is evident in the Bible. For example, Genesis 18–19 is quite clear that Yahweh Himself and two other divine beings met with Abraham in physical flesh. They ate a meal together (Genesis 18:1–8). Genesis 19:10 informs us that the two angels had to physically grab Lot and pull him back into his house to avoid harm in Sodom, something that would be hard to do if the two beings were not truly physical. Another example is Genesis 32:22–31, where we read that Jacob wrestled with a "man" (32:24), whom the text also describes as *elohim* twice (32:30–31). Hosea 12:3–4 refers to this incident and describes the being who wrestled with Jacob as *elohim* and *mal'ak* ("angel"). This was a physical struggle, and one that left Jacob injured (32:31–32).

While visual appearances in human form are more common, the New Testament also describes episodes in which angels are best understood as corporeal. In Matthew 4:11, angels came to Jesus after He was tempted by the devil and "ministered" to Him (cf. Mark 1:13). Surely this means more than floating around before Jesus' face. Angels appear and speak (Matthew 28:5; Luke 1:11–21, 30–38), instances that presume actual sound waves being created. If a merely auditory experience was meant, one would expect the communication to be described as a dream-vision (Acts 10:3). Angels open doors (Acts 5:19) and hit disciples to wake them up (Acts 12:7). This particular episode is especially interesting, because the text has Peter mistakenly thinking the angel was only a vision.

There is a second supernaturalist approach to Genesis 6:1–4 that takes the sexual language as euphemistic, not literal. In this perspective, the language of cohabitation is used to convey the idea that divine beings who are rivals to Yahweh are responsible for producing the Nephilim, and therefore are responsible for the later giant clans.

This approach uses Yahweh's relationship to Abraham and Sarah as an analogy.[32] While there is no suggestion of a sexual relationship between an embodied Yahweh and Sarah to produce Isaac and, therefore, the Israelites, it is nonetheless true that the Israelites came about through supernatural intervention. In that sense, Yahweh "fathered" Israel. The means God used to enable Abraham and Sarah to have a child are never described in the Bible, but Scripture is clear that divine intervention of some sort was necessary.[33] The Bible's silence on the nature of the supernatural intervention opens the door to the idea that other rival gods produced offspring to oppose Yahweh's children.

Both approaches therefore presume that the Nephilim and the subsequent giant clans had a supernatural origin, but they disagree on the means.[34]

NEPHILIM AFTER THE FLOOD

Genesis 6:4 pointedly informs readers that the Nephilim were on earth before the Flood "and also afterward." The phrase looks forward to Numbers 13:33, which says with equal clarity that the oversized descendants of Anak "came from the *nephilim*."[35] The sons of Anak, the Anakim, were one of the giant clans described in the conquest narratives (e.g., Deuteronomy 2:10–11, 21; Joshua 11:21–22; 14:12, 15). The text clearly links them to the Nephilim, but how is this possible given the account of the Flood?[36]

The problem is one that has puzzled interpreters since antiquity. Some Jewish writers presumed the answer was that Noah himself had been fathered by one of the sons of God and was a Nephilim giant.[37] But Genesis 6:9 clearly wants to distance Noah from the unrighteousness that precipitated the Flood, so this explanation doesn't work.

There are two alternatives for explaining the presence of giants after the Flood who descended from the giant Nephilim: (1) the Flood of Genesis 6–8 was a regional, not global, catastrophe; (2) the same kind of behavior described in Genesis 6:1–4 happened again (or continued to happen) after the Flood, producing other Nephilim, from whom the giant clans descended.

The first option, a localized Flood, naturally depends on the coherence of the arguments in defense of a local Flood, especially those arguments dealing with the wording in the biblical text that seems to suggest the deluge was worldwide. Many biblical scholars, scientists, and other researchers have marshaled the evidence in favor of this reading.[38] For our purposes, this option would allow human survival somewhere in the regions known to the biblical authors (Genesis 10), specifically the ancient Near East, the Mediterranean Sea, and the Aegean Sea.[39]

The second option is a possibility deriving from Hebrew grammar. Genesis 6:4 tells us there were Nephilim on earth before the Flood "and also afterward, when the sons of God went into the daughters of humankind." The "when" in the verse could be translated "whenever," thereby suggesting a repetition of these pre-Flood events after the Flood. In other words, since Genesis 6:4 points forward to the later giant clans, the phrasing could suggest that other sons of God fathered more Nephilim after the Flood.[40] As a result, there would be no survival of original Nephilim, and so the post-Flood dilemma would be resolved. A later appearance of other Nephilim occurred by the same means as before the Flood.

The purpose of this brief survey of the interpretive issues presented by Genesis 6:1–4 is simple enough—to demonstrate that familiar non-supernaturalist views of the passage are evasive and unsatisfactory for many reasons. They fail to take the passage seriously for what it says. The next two chapters will reinforce the need to let the passage say what it says, but, more importantly, they will demonstrate that the Enochian expansion of Genesis 6:1–4 actually preserves the original context for the passage. This is why a supernaturalist approach to Genesis 6:1–4 is not only the right approach, but is an essential one for understanding why the New Testament writers took the material in Enoch so seriously.

2

The Sin of the Watchers in
1 Enoch and Other Enochian Texts

Now that we know how to approach (or not) the biblical story of Genesis 6:1–4, we need to see how Jewish writers of the Second Temple Period understood the story. The exercise will not only be instructive—and perhaps new to some readers—but will serve to provide a solid introduction to the key touchpoint for the present book: the story of the sin of the Watchers. By the end of this chapter, readers will see quite clearly that Second Temple Jews did not attempt to strip the supernatural elements from Genesis 6:1–4; rather, they affirmed them. This in turn will prepare us for chapter 3, where we will go back in time to the original Mesopotamian context for Genesis 6:1–4. At that point, the reader will be able to grasp a crucial fact for our study: Second Temple Jewish writers understood and preserved the original supernaturalist backstory from Mesopotamia. This literary inheritance explains why these Jewish authors wrote about Genesis 6:1–4 the way they did. Since New Testament writers were a product of this theological and intellectual environment, it makes complete sense that they looked at the sin of Watchers the same way and that parts of the New Testament are best understood with this in mind.

A BROAD OVERVIEW OF 1 ENOCH

Since many readers will have never read 1 Enoch, it is advisable to get a feel for the whole book before drilling down into the story about the sin of the Watchers. As I noted in the introduction, the term "Watcher" is a biblical one, appearing in Daniel 4:13, 17, 23.[41] The term is qualified by "holy one" (Daniel 4:13, 23), and so "Watcher" is not by default a term for an evil divine being.[42] In 1 Enoch, the term is one of several used in place of "sons of God" in its retelling of the episode of Genesis 6:1–4.

The book of 1 Enoch as we know it today is actually a composite literary work whose parts can be dated to different periods.[43] The distinct sections are:

The Book of the Watchers (chapters 1–36)
The Book of Parables (chapters 37–71), or the "Similitudes"
The Book of the Luminaries (chapters 72–82), or the
     "Astronomical Book"
The Book of Dreams (chapters 83–90)
The Apocalypse of Weeks (chapter 91:11–17)
The Epistle of Enoch (chapter 91:1–10, 92–105)
The Birth of Noah (chapters 106–107)
Another Chapter of Enoch (chapter 108)

With respect to the first section, the Book of the Watchers (1 Enoch 1–36), the first five chapters basically serve as an introduction to the entire section. Our chief focus in this book, the story of the sin of the Watchers, is found in chapters 6–16. John C. Collins describes the flow of the story this way:

Chapters 6–16 tell the story of the Watchers, in which two stories seem to be woven together. In one, the leader of the fallen angels is named Asael (Azazel in the Ethiopic text), and the primary sin is improper revelation; in the other the leader is Shemihazah, and the primary sin is marriage with humans and procreation of giants…. The Watchers beget giants on earth by their union with human women. Out of these giants come evil spirits that lead humanity astray (1 Enoch 15:11–12; this motif is elaborated further in Jubilees). In the short term, the crisis of the Watchers is resolved when God sends the flood to cleanse the earth.

Enoch is introduced in chapter 12 as a scribe whom the Watchers ask to intercede for them. Enoch ascends to heaven on a cloud and comes before the heavenly throne in chapter 14, in a passage that is important for the history of Jewish mysticism. His intercession, however, is rejected. The Watchers abandoned heaven for the attraction of the flesh. Enoch represents the opposite tendency: He is a human being who is taken up to heaven to live with the angels.[44]

The rest of the Book of the Watchers (chapters 17–36) describes Enoch being taken on a cosmic tour to the ends of the earth by angels. It is on this heavenly journey that Enoch sees the places where the spirits of the dead are kept inside a mountain in three compartments (chapter 22) and Gehenna (chapters 26–27). In chapter 32, Enoch sees the Garden of Eden and the Tree of the Knowledge of Good and Evil from which Adam and Eve ate. Interestingly, while this section of the Book of the Watchers notes the sin of Adam, it considers it of lesser significance when compared to the sin of the Watchers.

The next major section, 1 Enoch 37–71, is called the Book of Parables. It is also known as the Similitudes of Enoch. This is the only portion of the book for which there is no manuscript evidence from Qumran. The book includes three lengthy "parables" (1 Enoch 38–44, 45–57, and 58–69). As Collins notes, "The main theme is the coming judgment, 'when the Righteous One appears before the chosen righteous whose works are weighed by the Lord of Spirits' (1 Enoch 38:2). Then the rulers of the earth will be dumbfounded and humbled. The Righteous One is also called the Chosen One and 'that Son of Man' who accompanies the 'Head of Days' as in Daniel 7 (1 Enoch 46:1–2)."[45]

The third section (1 Enoch 72–82) is referred to by scholars as the Astronomical Book since its content deals with astronomical observations that are given a theological interpretation (particularly eschatological). In terms of manuscript data, it may be the oldest portion of what we now know as 1 Enoch.

The so-called Book of Dreams (1 Enoch 83–90) is the next section. Its content mirrors certain passages in Jeremiah (23, 31, 33, 50), Ezekiel (34, 37), and Daniel (2, 7–8, 10). Collins summarizes the visions:

> 1 Enoch 83–90 consists of two apocalypses. The first, in chapters 83–84, is a simple vision of cosmic destruction. The second, known as the Animal Apocalypse, is a complex allegory in which people are represented by animals. Adam is a white bull. Cain and Abel are black and red bullocks; Israel is sheep. In the period after the exile, the sheep are given over to seventy shepherds, representing the angelic patrons of the nations. The reign of these shepherds is divided into four periods, which are allotted twelve, twenty-three, twenty-three, and twelve shepherds, respectively. At the end of the third period, we are told that "small lambs were born from these white sheep, and they began to open their eyes" (1 Enoch 90:6). This is generally taken to refer to the Hasidim who supported Judas Maccabus [sic]. Judas is represented by a great horn that grew on one of the sheep. Eventually God comes down and sets up His throne for judgment. The Watchers and the seventy shepherds are destroyed, but so are the "blind sheep," or apostate Jews. Those who had been destroyed are brought back, presumably by resurrection, and all are transformed into "white bulls"—the condition of Adam and the early patriarchs. This apocalypse was evidently written at the time of the Maccabean revolt by people who supported the Maccabees.[46]

The very short Apocalypse of Weeks (91:11–17) follows. Its similarity to Daniel 9:24–27 is obvious. The short portion records "what Enoch saw in a heavenly vision and understood from the tablets of heaven."[47] The vision explains how future history will be divided into ten "weeks" (presumably weeks of years as in Daniel 9:24–27). The weeks describe the time of the end and the judgment of the Watchers.

The Epistle of Enoch (91:1–10, 92–105) is something of a sermonic exhortation. Deferring once again to Collins:

> The bulk of the epistle is taken up with woes against sinners and exhortations for the righteous. The sinners are condemned mainly for social offenses. They "build their houses with sin" (1 Enoch 94:8) and "trample upon the humble through your power" (1 Enoch 96:5). The reward of the righteous, however, has ultimately an otherworldly character. They will "shine like the lights of heaven and be associates of the host of heaven" (1 Enoch 104:2–6). They are also promised some more mundane gratification. The wicked will be given into their hands, and they will cut their throats (1 Enoch 98:12).[48]

The last two sections are quite brief: The Birth of Noah (chapters 106–107) and Another Chapter of Enoch (chapter 108). The former portion narrates how "Noah's miraculous birth foreshadowed his role as the preserver of the human race. Placed at the end of the corpus, the story promises salvation for the righteous, who will survive the great judgment that was prefigured in the deluge."[49] The final chapter is little more than an appendix that "alludes to earlier journey traditions and provides a last word that assures the salvation of the righteous and the damnation of the sinners."[50]

THE STORY OF THE SIN OF THE WATCHERS: 1 ENOCH 6–16

Understanding the sin of the Watchers in 1 Enoch is fairly straightforward. One needs only to read 1 Enoch 6–16 to see how the writer expands upon

Genesis 6:1–4. For that reason, I'm going to reproduce a good bit of this portion of the Book of the Watchers in what remains of this chapter. The translation is that produced by Nickelsburg in his scholarly commentary on 1 Enoch.[51] The most salient chapters are 1 Enoch 6–8, and so we begin with them in their entirety:

> 1 Enoch 6: [1]And when the sons of men had multiplied, in those days, beautiful and comely daughters were born to them.[2]And the watchers, the sons of heaven, saw them and desired them. And they said to one another, "Come, let us choose for ourselves wives from the daughters of men, and let us beget for ourselves children." [3]And Shemihazah, their chief,[52] said to them, "I fear that you will not want to do this deed, and I alone shall be guilty of a great sin." [34]And they all answered him and said, "Let us all swear an oath, and let us all bind one another with a curse, that none of us turn back from this counsel until we fulfill it and do this deed." [5]Then they all swore together and bound one another with a curse. [6]And they were, all of them, two hundred, who descended in the days of Jared onto the peak of Mount Hermon.[53] And they called the mountain "Hermon" because they swore and bound one another with a curse on it.[54] [7]And these are the names of their chiefs: Shemihazah—this one was their leader; Arteqoph, second to him; Remashel, third to him; Kokabel, fourth to him; Armumahel, fifth to him; Ramel, sixth to him; Daniel, seventh to him; Ziqel, eighth to him; Baraqel, ninth to him; Asael, tenth to him; Hermani, eleventh to him; Matarel, twelfth to him; Ananel, thirteenth to him; Setawel, fourteenth to him; Samshiel, fifteenth to him; Sahriel, sixteenth to him; Tummiel, seventeenth to him; Turiel, eighteenth to him; Yamiel, nineteenth to him; Yehadiel, twentieth to him. [8]These are their chiefs of tens.
>
> 1 Enoch 7: [1]These and all the others with them took for themselves wives from among them such as they chose. And they began to go in to them, and to defile themselves through them,

and to teach them sorcery and charms, and to reveal to them the cutting of roots and plants. [2]And they conceived from them and bore to them great giants. And the giants begat Nephilim, and to the Nephilim were born Elioud.[55] And they were growing in accordance with their greatness.[56] [3]They were devouring the labor of all the sons of men, and men were not able to supply them. [4]And the giants began to kill men and to devour them. [5]And they began to sin against the birds and beasts and creeping things and the fish, and to devour one another's flesh. And they drank the blood. [6]Then the earth brought accusation against the lawless ones.

1 Enoch 8: [1]Asael[57] taught men to make swords of iron and weapons and shields and breastplates and every instrument of war. He showed them metals of the earth and how they should work gold to fashion it suitably, and concerning silver, to fashion it for bracelets and ornaments for women. And he showed them concerning antimony and eye paint and all manner of precious stones and dyes. And the sons of men made them for themselves and for their daughters, and they transgressed and led astray the holy ones.[58] [2]And there was much godlessness upon the earth, and they made their ways desolate. [3]Shemihazah taught spells and the cutting of roots.

Hermani taught sorcery for the loosing of spells and magic and skill.

Baraqel taught the signs of the lightning flashes.

Kokabel taught the signs of the stars.

Ziqel taught the signs of the shooting stars.

Arteqoph taught the signs of the earth.

Shamsiel taught the signs of the sun.

Sahriel taught the signs of the moon.

And they all began to reveal mysteries to their wives and to their children.

[4](And) as men were perishing, the cry went up to heaven.

What of the rest of the story? In 1 Enoch 9, four archangels (Michael and Sariel and Raphael and Gabriel) see the terrible events unfolding on earth and approach God for a solution. The souls of humankind demand: "Bring in our judgment to the Most High, and our destruction before the glory of the majesty, before the Lord of all lords in majesty" (1 Enoch 9:3). The four archangels say to God (1 Enoch 9:11):

> You know all things before they happen, and you see these things and you permit them and you do not tell us what we ought to do to them with regard to these things.

God responds in 1 Enoch 10:1–3 with news that should sound familiar to biblical readers:

> [1]Then the Most High said, and the Great Holy One spoke. And he sent Sariel to the son of Lamech, saying, [2]"Go to Noah and say to him in my name, 'Hide yourself.' And reveal to him that the end is coming, that the whole earth will perish; And tell him that a deluge is about to come on the whole earth and destroy everything on the earth. [3]Teach the righteous one what he should do, the son of Lamech how he may preserve himself alive and escape forever. From him a plant will be planted, and his seed will endure for all the generations of eternity."

1 Enoch 10–11 describes how the archangels do as God commanded, and also round up the offending Watchers and bind them. One portion reads:

> …until the day of their judgment and consummation, until the eternal judgment is consummated. Then they will be led away to the fiery abyss, and to the torture, and to the prison where they will be confined forever.... And at the time of the judgment, which I shall judge, they will perish for all generations. Destroy all

the spirits of the half-breeds and the sons of the watchers, because they have wronged men. (1 Enoch 10:12–15)

Kvanvig summarizes the rest of the material relation to the sin of the Watchers (1 Enoch 12–16) aptly:

The second section (Enoch 12–16) introduces Enoch, who is not mentioned in the first. He is situated in heaven among the Watchers and holy ones. There are clear correspondences between this description of Enoch and the one we find in Genesis 5:18–24. Enoch was sent to the Watchers on earth to pronounce judgment because their sexual union with the women had corrupted the earth. The Watchers were seized with fear and asked Enoch to write a petition on their behalf and bring it back to the supreme God. Enoch went to the waters of Dan, southwest of Mount Hermon. There he fell asleep and saw a dream vision. In the vision, he was brought back to heaven, to the temple of the supreme God. God recalled for him the Watcher incident once more and the judgment He had decided. Here, new information is added: From the dead bodies of the giants the evil spirits would arise. They would haunt mankind until the final judgment. Enoch was then sent back to the Watchers with the message that ends the story: "You will not have peace."

THE SIN OF THE WATCHERS:
A SUMMARY

Having read the excerpts from 1 Enoch, we can summarize the story for the purposes of reference throughout the rest of our study. Annette Yoshiko Reed does this nicely, especially as it will relate to the trajectory of this book:

The birth of the Giants is explored in terms of the mingling of "spirits and flesh" (15:8). Angels properly dwell in heaven, and humans properly dwell on earth (15:10), but the nature of the Giants is mixed. This transgression of categories brings terrible results: after their physical death, the Giants' demonic spirits "come forth from their bodies" to plague humankind (15:9, 11–12; 16:1). According to 1 En[och] 16, the angelic transmission of heavenly knowledge to earthly humans can also be understood as a contamination of distinct categories within God's orderly Creation. As inhabitants of heaven, the Watchers were privy to all the secrets of heaven; their revelation of this knowledge to the inhabitants of the earth was categorically improper as well as morally destructive.[59]

The Watchers, then, are clearly celestial (nonhuman) beings whose actions are regarded not only as morally evil, but spiritually destructive. While human rebellion first appeared in Eden, it is the actions of the Watchers that served as a catalyst to spread wickedness among humanity like a spiritual contagion. They are held responsible for teaching humans a variety of things that engender lust, warfare, astrology, occult practices, etc.

For the present purposes, readers should have it fixed in their minds that the story of the sin of the Watchers not only informed the mass of Jews in the Second Temple Period about the meaning and significance of Genesis 6:1–4, but it also informed New Testament writers who were a part of that period and community. We've already seen how Peter and Jude were informed by 1 Enoch when it came to "the angels that sinned." The Watcher story lurks behind all sorts of New Testament passages. Demonstrating this fact is the purpose of this book.

Lest this thought be troubling—seeming as it is out of place with Christian tradition—two things can be said. First, biblical theology by definition comes from the biblical text (or ought to), not from Christian history or the writings of Christians about the Bible. We must be committed to the biblical text, read and interpreted in its own ancient context—not a later context—for our theology. Second, there is solid evidence that in the earliest Christian traditions, this reading of Genesis 6:1–4 was known and embraced. Stuckenbruck writes:

In particular [we] see the Christian *Testament of Solomon* 5:3; 17:1. In 5:3 (within the section 5:1–11), the author reinterprets the demon Asmodeus—this is a deliberate reference to the Book of Tobit which follows the longer recension (cf. Codex Sinaiticus at 3:7–8,17; 6:14–15,17; 8:2–3; 12:15)—one born from a human mother and an angel. In the latter text (in the passage 17:1–5) the demonic power thwarted by Jesus (in an allusion to M[ar]k 5:3) is identified as one of the giants who died in the internecine conflicts. Similarly, in the *Pseudo-Clementine Homilies* 8.12–18 refers to the giants, which are designated as both "bastards" (18; cf. 15) and "demons" (14; 17) in the ante-diluvian phase of their existence. Here they are said to have survived the deluge in the form of disembodied "large souls" whose post-diluvian activities are proscribed through "a certain righteous law" given them through an angel…. Furthermore, one may consider Tertullian's *Apology* 22, a passage deserving more detailed analysis, in which the offspring of the fallen angels are called a "demon-brood" who "inflict…upon our bodies diseases and other grievous calamities…." [In] the *Instructions* by the 3rd century North African bishop Commodianus (ch. 3)…the disembodied existence of the giants after their death is linked to the subversion of "many bodies." The implications of the giants traditions for concepts of demonology at the turn of the Common Era have until now been insufficiently recognised.[60]

By way of a specific example, the beloved early church authority Irenaeus clearly looked at Genesis 6:1–4 the way the writer of 1 Enoch did. In his article, "The Origin of Sin in Irenaeus and Jewish Pseudepigraphical Literature," D. R. Schultz writes:

It is well known that Satan appears in the writings of Irenaeus as the "tempter" of Adam. However, Irenaeus often bypasses Adam in his treatment of Satan and angels, so that this evil spirit world directly brings about mankind's sinful condition. In effect, then, Irenaeus sometimes attributes the origin of sin directly to Satan and his forces in terms strongly reminiscent of 1 Enoch, Jubilees, and other late Jewish pseudepigraphical writings…. [T]he role of Satan in man's sinfulness is a prominent one for Irenaeus, as (Satan) takes on many different titles. He is referred to as the "strong man," the devil, and the apostate angel. It becomes evident that Irenaeus uses all of these names to signify a single creature who is angelic in nature and the chief adversary of God. Sin is directly related to angelic powers and principally to the leader of these powers, Satan. He is the first to sin against God and later lead others to that sin or apostasy…. Thus, the apostasy reaches from Satan to other angels who follow his lead in sin, transgression, and revolt. Moreover, the apostasy which began with Satan and continued through the apostate angels also extends to the whole of mankind. Irenaeus, speaking of all those whom God should punish in the eternal fires, lists "the angels who transgressed and became apostates, together with the ungodly, and unrighteous, and wicked, and profane among men" (citing Irenaeus, *Against Heresies,* 1,10,1 [1,2])…. Irenaeus definitely understands that there exists a causal relationship between Genesis 6:1–4 and the wickedness that follows in Genesis 6:5…. Further clarification is achieved through an examination of the manner in which Satan's apostasy is extended to mankind. Irenaeus has two different descriptions of the angels defiling mankind. One description is concerned with "unlawful unions" of angels with offspring from the daughters of men. This "unlawful union" produces "giants" upon the earth which cause man's sinfulness; and these giants, which Irenaeus calls the "infamous race of men," performed fruitless and wicked deeds. (citing

Irenaeus, *Proof of the Apostolic Preaching*, 18 and *Against Heresies* 11.4,36,4 [4,58,4])[61]

Irenaeus famously describes these "wicked deeds" in terms that have clear counterparts to the Watcher story: "The virtues of roots and herbs, and dyeing and cosmetics, and discoveries of precious materials, love philtres, hatreds, amours, passions, constraints of love, the bonds of witchcraft, every sorcery and idolatry, hateful to God."[62]

These thought trajectories will be foreign to practically all those whose training in theology and ministry has followed traditional lines. But to first-century Jews, they were common—and accepted as factual.[63] Stuckenbruck comments in this regard:

Scholars have observed that in a number of early Jewish writings such angels were regarded as evil beings whose activities, whether past or even present, were inimical to God's purposes for creation.

Such an observation, however correct it may be, is often mentioned as if axiomatic; and there is, of course, ample reason for this. Traditions which refer to both evil angels and their gigantic offspring are preserved in a number of apocalyptic and sapiential writings dated mostly to the first three centuries before the Common Era, including the following documents: *1 Enoch* (*Book of Watchers* ch.'s 1–36, *Animal Apocalypse* ch.'s 85–90, and the Noahic Appendix ch.'s 106–107); *Book of Giants; Jubilees; Damascus Document*; Ben Sira; Wisdom of Solomon; *3 Maccabees; 3 Baruch*; and several fragmentary texts only preserved among the Dead Sea Scrolls (esp. 1Q20 *Genesis Apocryphon*, 4Q180–181 *Ages of Creation*, 4Q370 *Exhortation Based on the Flood*, 4Q444 *Incantation*, 4Q510–511 *Songs of the Sage*, and 11Q11 *Apocryphal Psalms*). For all the apparently one-sided emphasis of these writings with respect to their interpretation of "the sons of God" and their progeny as evil, nothing in Genesis 6 itself unambiguously prepares for such an understanding…. [I]t is thus remarkable how uniformly the ambiguous Genesis 6:1–4 was being read as a story about irreversibly rebellious angels and giants.[64]

Stuckenbruck is of course correct that a number of details of 1 Enoch's Watcher story are not unambiguously present in Genesis 6:1–4. But, as we shall see in our next chapter, they *are* present in the Mesopotamian story of the apkallu that prompted the writing of Genesis 6:1–4. When one reads these four short verses in light of the Mesopotamian religious propaganda they were designed to rebut, there is no room for any other interpretation of Genesis 6:1–4 than a supernaturalist approach.

3

THE MESOPOTAMIAN APKALLU, THE WATCHERS, AND THE NEPHILIM

Until very recently, the Mesopotamian backstory to Genesis 6:1–4 was unknown to all but a handful of scholars.[65] This means that what follows will not be found in the writings of any modern denominational founder (Calvin, Luther, Wesley, etc.), nor any commentary on Genesis (to date), nor on the lips of any favorite preacher or Bible teacher.[66] Without the knowledge of this backstory, interpreters fail to interpret Genesis 6:1–4 in its own context. Insisting on nonsupernatural interpretations like the Sethite hypothesis, where the sons of God are merely men from the line of Seth, violates the passage's original intent and meaning.

INTRODUCING THE APKALLU

Greenfield's brief summary of the apkallu states:

In Mesopotamian religion, the term *apkallu* (Sumerian: abgal) is used for the legendary creatures endowed with extraordinary wisdom. Seven in number, they are the culture heroes from before the Flood.... In the myth of the "Twenty-one Poultices" the "seven *apkallu* of Eridu," who are also called the "seven *apkallu* of the Apsu," are at the service of Ea (Enki).... A variety of wisdom traditions from the antediluvian period were supposedly passed on by the *apkallu*.... The tradition of the *apkallu* is preserved in the *bīt-mēseri* ritual series and also by Berossus. The seven sages were created in the river and served as "those who ensured the correct functioning of the plans of heaven and earth." Following the example of Ea, they taught mankind wisdom, social forms and craftsmanship. The authorship of texts dealing with omens, magic and other categories of "wisdom" such as medicine is attributed to the seven *apkallu*.[67]

Readers familiar with the Watchers episode in 1 Enoch will be able to see a clear parallel to the Watcher story from even this cursory summary. The apkallu were divine beings bestowing special knowledge to humankind. This is precisely what the Watchers were blamed for in 1 Enoch. But there is much more. Several other specific links to Genesis 6:1–4 will be evident as we proceed.

As Greenfield's summary noted, the seven apkallu were thought to have been created in "the river" and were assigned "the correct functioning of the plans of heaven and earth." The "river" is actually a reference to the primeval deep in Mesopotamian thought.[68] This watery abode was located under the earth (hence, "underworld") and was part of (or equivalent to, depending on the text) the Abyss (called the *Apsu* or *Abzu* by Mesopotamians) or realm of the dead. Readers will recall the same sort of conception for the realm of the dead in biblical material (e.g., Job 26:5–6). This means that, for Mesopotamians, the apkallu came from the Abyss and were responsible for maintaining the correct balance between heaven and earth that was the will of the greater gods. As such, the apkallu were thought to possess knowledge from the divine world that "made heaven and earth tick," so to speak.

Over time, the apkallu had dealings with humanity. Mesopotamian literature presents them as the great antediluvian ("pre-Flood") sages, "culture-heroes who brought the arts of civilization to the land. During the time that follows this period, nothing new is invented, the original revelation is only transmitted and unfolded."[69] This process of civilizing the world of men is viewed positively in Mesopotamian thought, so much so that "claims of both the physical ancestry and equality to antediluvian figures were important for Mesopotamian kings and scholars alike."[70] This was especially the case with respect to the apkallu, for such associations meant that humans could claim access to knowledge held only by the gods in the Mesopotamian divine council, an idea that would have been used to legitimize status, power and influence.[71]

It is difficult to do justice to the importance of the idea that the knowledge that made Mesopotamian civilization great—particularly in the case of Babylon—came from a divine source. It is a subject with immediate ties to Genesis. Cuneiform scholar Amar Annus writes:

> There was a broad tradition in the Babylonian scribal milieu that the seventh antediluvian figure, a king or a sage, ascended to heaven and received insights into divine wisdom. The seventh antediluvian king according to several lists was Enmeduranki, the king of Sippar, who distinguished himself with divine knowledge from the gods Adad and Shamash. Biblical scholars generally agree that the religious-historical background of the figure of Enoch, the seventh antediluvian patriarch in Gen[esis] 5:23–24 and subsequently the apocalyptic authority in Enochic literature, lies in the seventh Mesopotamian antediluvian king Enmeduranki.

As this excerpt demonstrates, the connection back to Genesis is Enoch. Jude 14 notes that Enoch was the seventh from Adam. Enoch was the father of Methuselah and the great-grandfather of Noah (Genesis 5:21–30). Enoch was the first to be taken to heaven, joining God and the divine council as a man (Genesis 5:24).[72] The correlation with Enmeduranki is interesting because of how the Mesopotamian stories regard the transmission of divine knowledge from before the Flood to those who survived the Flood. This is specifically the role of the apkallu.

THE TRANSMISSION OF DIVINE KNOWLEDGE VIA THE APKALLU

The scribes of Babylon living after the Flood took great pains to establish the notion that their knowledge—and so the greatness of Babylon and the greatness of its king—was directly inherited from the divine realm. But how did they make that argument? One scholar whose focus is Mesopotamian beliefs about secret knowledge explains:

> The learned scribes received their secret texts in the same manner that all scribes received texts from before their own time: they inherited copies of them from other scribes. But how did they inherit copies *from the gods*? This is where another of Ea's associations assisted the scholars in their construction of secret corpora by providing a mechanism of reception. Ea from very early times was associated with the seven mythological sages called the *apkallu* who lived before the flood. The scholars created a mythology in which the members of their guild became the professional continuation of the position of the ancient *apkallu*.[73]

Amar Annus goes on to describe how the scholarly writings of the scribes were specifically linked to the apkallu by a literary tactic. Scribes would title their treatises with names given to the apkallu.

> Giving to the antediluvian sages names resembling titles of scientific treatises served the purpose of establishing the explicit connection between contemporary and primeval scholarship.... As the Mesopotamian conception of knowledge was

pre-eminently associated with pragmatic kinds of it, the term "wisdom" denotes the realms of technologies and handicraft skills as well. In some royal inscriptions of first-millennium Mesopotamia, references occur to royal craftsmen (*umma nu*), "who know the secret." Such capable craftsmen as the carpenter Ninildu, the lapidary Ninzadim, the metal worker Ninagal, the stone-cutter Ninkurra and the goldsmith Kusigbanda were the patron deities of smiths, manifestations of the god Ea, and also identified with antediluvian apkallus.[74]

Francesca Rochberg adds:

This gets to the root of the Mesopotamian scribal notion of knowledge, which is what unites divination, horoscopy, and astronomy in the learned cuneiform tradition. And this way of identifying the elements of knowledge, i.e., systematized, even to some extent codified knowledge, was connected with the gods from whom it was claimed such scholarly knowledge was derived in the days before the Flood.[75]

It is no understatement that, for Mesopotamians, the entire repository of knowledge that was to prove indispensable for civilization—and thus their own greatness—"was traced back to the wisdom of apkallus in its entirety."[76] This role is a precise parallel to the Watchers of 1 Enoch, who taught humanity forbidden knowledge by which they became wicked and depraved (1 Enoch 8:1–4; 10:7–8).

But how did the knowledge of the pre-Flood apkallus survive the Flood?

THE LINEAGE OF THE APKALLU

A well-known tablet from Uruk dating to the Seleucid period (W.20030, 7) plots out this transmission of divine knowledge on both sides of the

Flood.[77] It lists seven pre-diluvian kings, each of them accompanied by an assisting apkallu, the divine sage who gave the king the knowledge necessary for civilization. The list reads as follows, with the name of the apkallu on the left and the king on the right (in the cuneiform text the signs for the apkallu are part of the names on the left):

U'an: Aialu
U'anduga: Alalgar
Enmeduga: Ammelu'anna
Enmebulugga: Enme'ušumgalanna
Anenlilda: Dumuzi
Utu'abzu: Enmeduranki

Following these names, one post-Flood apkallu is mentioned with his corresponding king: Nungalpiriggal (Enmekar).[78] Other Mesopotamian texts actually provide evidence for four post-Flood apkallu. These individuals are the key players in understanding why Genesis 6:1–4 was ever written in Scripture. The four post-Flood apkallu are said in one cuneiform tablet to be "of human descent."[79] The fourth post-Flood apkallu is further described as being only "two-thirds apkallu."[80]

The implication of these sources is that the post-Flood apkallu were the result of sexual intercourse with human women. In her short essay on the apkallu, Anne Kilmer draws this same conclusion, and sees its relationship to the Nephilim of Genesis 6:1–4 quite clearly:

Humans and apkallu could presumably mate since we have a description of the four post-flood apkallu as "of human descent," the fourth being only "two-thirds apkallu" as opposed to pre-flood pure apkallu and subsequent human sages (*ummanu*).[81]

Unfortunately, Kilmer did little more in her short essay other than to identify the post-Flood hybrid offspring with the biblical Nephilim. The work of Amar Annus is an altogether different case. His work in 2010 has laid out the parallels between the story of the Mesopotamian apkallu and Genesis 6:1–4 in greater detail and with more care than anyone to date.

Unlike Kilmer, Annus took note of the observation that the pre-Flood apkallu were fully divine but the post-Flood apkallu were hybrid beings. The result is that "apkallu" is a term for both fully divine beings before the Flood and quasi-divine hybrid beings after the Flood. This is precisely how 1 Enoch uses the term "Watcher" for both the fully divine sons of God who cohabited with human women in Genesis 6:1–4 and the spirits of the giant offspring produced by the forbidden union (1 Enoch 6–7). The former is readily understandable, as the Watchers who descended to earth were fully divine. The term "Watcher" was applied to the latter because the immaterial nature of the giants (their spirits) were not human but divine. Consequently, this is why the spirits of dead giants in the Enochian story were considered evil and, thus, the origin of demons (1 Enoch 15:8–12).[82]

THE APKALLU UNDER JUDGMENT AS EVIL SPIRITS

The apkallu from before the Flood were heroes to Mesopotamians. But is there evidence that the post-Flood apkallu of Mesopotamia were perceived to be giants and evil spirits? There is indeed.

Annus has a lengthy discussion of how apkallu were also associated with evil. He writes in part:

> It is a little known fact that apkallu are occasionally depicted as malevolent beings in Mesopotamian literature, who either angered the gods with their hubris, or practiced witchcraft…. The post-diluvian sages in particular were attributed some malicious deeds, as the translation of the latter part of the *Bit Meseri* text shows…. It is explicitly said in [one] passage that two of the four post-diluvian sages angered the gods. Piriggalnungal angered the storm-god, who caused draught on earth for three years…. The

apkallus occur at least twice in the anti-witchcraft series *Maqlû* as witches, against whom incantations are directed.... From many references in Mesopotamian literature we can learn that the fish-like sages were thought to have been created and also reside in Apsu.... The fact that apkallu are born and often reside in Apsu is not evidence that points to their exclusively positive character, since demonic creatures were also often thought to have their origin in the depths of the divine River. For example, in the Mesopotamian myth about slaying the dragon Labbu by god Tishpak, the monster is called "offspring of River." This river, where the representations of witches and the models of evil omen carriers were cast for the purpose of purification, also had an epithet and aspect of deluge.[83]

In the Babylonian version of the Flood story, of which the apkallu were important characters, the great god Marduk is not kindly disposed toward either humans or the apkallu who cohabit with them, thereby preserving human civilization. In *The Erra Epic* (I.147–162), Marduk speaks about what he had done with the apkallu after the Flood:

I sent craftsmen down to Apsu, I ordered them not to come up. I changed the location of *mēsu*-tree and *elmešu* stone, and did not show it to anybody.

Where is the *mes*-tree, the flesh of the gods, the emblem of the king of the universe, the pure tree, august hero, perfect for lordship, whose roots reach a hundred leagues through the vast sea to the depth of the underworld, whose crown brushed [Anu's] heaven on high? Where is Ninildum, great carpenter of my supreme divinity, wielder of the glittering hatchet, who knows that tool, who makes [it] shine like the day and puts it in subjection at my feet? Where is Kusig-banda, fashioner of god and man, whose hands are consecrated? Where is Ninagal, wielder of the upper and lower millstone, who grinds up hard copper like hide and who forges to[ols]? Where are the choice stones, created by the vast sea, to ornament my diadem? Where are the seven [sa]ges of the depths, those sacred fish, who, like Ea their lord, are perfect in sublime wisdom, the ones who cleansed my body?[84]

Annus notes that the "craftsmen," a term we saw earlier that was applied to the apkallu, were "apparently done away by Marduk during the flood, just as God punished the Watchers with the deluge…like the Watchers, the Mesopotamian apkallus were punished by a flood according- ing to the *Erra Epic.*"[85] Annus is cautious about presuming that Marduk sent the apkallu away to the abyss because they violated the divine order of the cosmos, but given the fact that, as Greenfield noted earlier, the apkallu were responsible for maintaining the correct balance between heaven and earth, it seems reasonable to conclude that their behavior with humanity in the Flood episode may be in view.

That transgression of the divine order does in fact seem to be in view is further suggested by Marduk's comment that "I changed the location of *mēsu*-tree and *elmešu* stone," thereby preventing access to both by the apkallu. Annus gives us important details, but doesn't quite put the pieces together:

Relocation of a tree and stones is also a motif in the *Erra Epic*, where Marduk during the flood 'changed the location of *mēsu*- tree and *elmešu*-stone', in the context of sending the sages down to Apsu (I 147–48). The garden with trees and precious stones in the second dream is comparable to the garden in the end of the hero's journey in the Gilgamesh epic (IX 173–90), with the trees bearing jewels and precious stones.

It is impossible to miss in these words Ezekiel's language of Eden— the original earthly garden where heaven met earth. Ezekiel's literary con- text is, tellingly, Babylon (Ezekiel 1:13). Ezekiel 28:11–14 combines the garden imagery, the cosmic mountain imagery, and the lustrous precious stones associated with the radiance of divine presence in his description of Eden. Eden of course had the tree of life. Ezekiel 31:1–9 is also famous for its enigmatic description of the "garden of God" (31:8) with massive trees. The point is that the imagery from Marduk's comments about what he had done to the apkallu in effect points to the banishment of the apkallu from his presence—his abode, the place of council, the place where cosmic order was maintained. This is precisely how the Watchers were punished. They are cast away from God and forsaken. They no longer have a role in the divine council to participate with God in the affairs of heaven and earth. The parallels to 1 Enoch's description of how God dealt with the Watchers is unmistakable:

> As apkallus are sent down to Apsu, the Watchers and their sons "will be led away to the fiery abyss, and to the torture, and to the prison where they will be confined forever" in [1 Enoch] 10.13. The prison, where the spirits of the fallen angels are kept, is a chasm like Apsû, an abyss containing fiery pillars, and it is situated at the "end of the great earth" according to the Greek version of 1 En[och] 18.10, or "beyond the great earth" following the Ethiopic. The expression "great earth" is highly unusual in both languages, but it becomes explicable in the light of Mesopotamian mythology. The "great earth" is a name for the netherworld in Mesopotamian texts, *ki-gal* in Sumerian, whence the Akkadian *kigallu* was borrowed. The expression is found in the name of Mesopotamian queen of the underworld, Ereshkigal.... [T]he Aramaic fragment 4Q530 from Qumran, which belongs to the Book of Giants…contains in a broken context the reference to "gardeners" (*gnnyn*) at work, nurturing and protecting the trees (2 ii 7), which connotes the Watchers prior to their apostasy. This reference to "gardeners" is to be compared to Jub[ilees] 5.6, where God sent the angels to earth, and 4.15 further specifies the reason: "in order to instruct human beings and to act (with) jus-

tice and righteousness upon earth." According to Jubilees, only after the Watchers' arrival and sojourn among human beings were they corrupted and led astray by the irresistible beauty of mortal women.... From the comparative perspective, both the educational mission of the Watchers and likening them to "gardeners" make perfect sense. On Neo-Assyrian palace reliefs and seals, the famous apkallus as fish-cloaked men or as eagle-headed winged creatures are very often associated with the Tree of Life. The "watering of trees" by the Watchers in the Book of Giants finds many iconographic forerunners on Assyrian palace reliefs.... The Assyrian sacred tree symbolized both the divine world order and the king, who functioned as its earthly administrator. By sprinkling the tree with holy water the sages imparted to it their own sanctity, upheld the cosmic harmony, and thus "insured the correct functioning of the plans of heaven and earth."[86]

The implications of all this are straightforward. After the Flood the apkallu are judged. The only thing the Mesopotamian texts imply they did that would be contrary to the original created order was their act of cohabitation at the time of the Flood. Their knowledge lived on among humans through their hybrid offspring, produced with human women. But Marduk was not pleased.

THE APKALLU AS GIANTS AND MEN OF RENOWN

The most telling parallel to the Watchers and, thus, to Genesis 6:1–4, is that the hybrid post-Flood apkallu are giants.

Recall that the fourth of the post-Flood apkallu was described as only being two-thirds apkallu. This note comes from a section of the cuneiform *bīt mēseri* texts, incantations for protecting a house or building against invading evil spirits.[87] Annus writes:

This exactly matches the status of Gilgamesh in the post-diluvian world, as he also was "two-thirds divine, and one-third human" (I 48). Gilgamesh was remotely related to antediluvian apkallus, as he "brought back a message from the antediluvian age" (I 8). In Jewish terms, he was like one of the giant Nephilim, as exactly the Book of Giants depicts him…. There is new supporting cuneiform evidence that Gilgamesh was thought of as having a gigantic stature, his height being 11 cubits…. The reading of the passage in which the Standard Babylonian epic gives the height of Gilgamesh's giant body as 11 cubits (I 52–58), is now confirmed by the newest published evidence from Ugarit.[88]

Gilgamesh is explicitly connected to the apkallu in a cylinder that refers to him as "master of the apkallu."[89]

The parallels to Enochian material in this regard could not be more explicit. Gilgamesh is referenced by name in the Book of Giants from Qumran, another telling of the sin of the Watchers and its fallout. Other names from the Gilgamesh Epic and Mesopotamian flood stories are also present in this Second Temple Jewish book (e.g., Humbaba and Uta-napishti). All three of these names are the names of giant children of the Watchers. Annus notes that "different versions of the Jewish Book of Giants depict some giants as bird-men. [The giant] Mahaway has wings and flies in the air in the Qumran fragment 4Q530 7 ii 4."[90]

UNDERSTANDING AND HONORING THE POLEMIC OF GENESIS 6:1–4

What do the Mesopotamian data provide for the present work? Nothing less than direct ancient literary proof that:

(1) All the elements of Genesis 6:1–4 can be accounted for in Mesopotamian material relating to precisely the same context—the great Flood.

(2) These parallels were preserved in the Second Temple Jewish book known as 1 Enoch.

(3) The elements in the 1 Enoch story of the sin of the Watchers that are not found directly in Genesis 6:1–4 may nevertheless be entirely consistent with Genesis 6:1–4.

(4) New Testament writers like Peter and Jude should not be criticized for their attention to 1 Enoch in their own theological thinking.

More broadly, the Mesopotamian apkallu saga provides something biblical scholars have so long sought: a rationale for why Genesis 6:1–4 is even in the book of Genesis at all. The purpose was not to tell us about the godly human line of Seth. That interpretation is not only wholly ignorant of the original religious context but violates it at every turn. Rather, the reason Genesis 6:1–4 is in the Bible is because the writer sought to target the deeply held religious beliefs of Mesopotamia and, most pointedly, the myth of Babylonian superiority.

This is the nature of polemic argumentation, which Merriam-Webster's dictionary defines as "an aggressive attack on or refutation of the opinions or principles of another."[91] Annus' recent work on the apkallu highlights the polemic nature of Genesis 6:1–4 and the account of the sin of the Watchers in 1 Enoch. He writes:

> Varying accounts of the antediluvian history in the ancient Mesopotamian and [Second Temple] Jewish sources should be regarded as results of ancient debates. Not only direct borrowings took place, but also creative reinterpretations, especially on the Jewish side. Some of these creative reinterpretations must have occurred as *deliberate inversions* of the Mesopotamian source material. The Jewish authors often inverted the Mesopotamian intellectual traditions with the intention of showing the superiority of their own cultural foundations.[92]

The Jewish writers of the Enochian literature in fact invert every element of the apkallu tradition, linking that inversion to the sons of God and Nephilim of Genesis 6:1–4. The point was to turn the Mesopotamian belief system on its head, to make sure that Israelites and Jewish readers would know that what happened between the sons of God and the daughters of humankind was not something that bettered humanity. It was the opposite—a transgression of heaven and earth that would corrupt humankind and produce a lineage that would later be a threat to the very existence of Israel, Yahweh's portion and people (Deuteronomy 32:8–9).[93]

Annus continues, drawing attention to specific "heroic" deeds of the apkallu as perversions of divine order:

> The Mesopotamian apkallus were demonized as the "sons of God," and their sons Nephilim (Gen[esis] 6.3–4), who in later Enochic literature appear as Watchers and giants, illegitimate teachers of humankind before the flood (see 1 En[och] 6–8).... As many kinds of Mesopotamian sciences and technologies were ideologically conceived as originating with antediluvian apkallus, so both Enoch and the Watchers were depicted as antediluvian teaching powers.... By comparison, the Book of Watchers 8.1 enumerates the first set of arts forbidden to humanity—a list which consists mainly of useful crafts and technologies. This revelation of forbidden secrets was considered a transgression, because it promoted promiscuity and violence.[94]

The "wisdom" of the apkallu was not the only target. Their sexual activity with human women was also in the crosshairs of biblical and Enochian writers. Annus summarizes:

> The "sons of God" in Genesis and the Watchers in Enochic literature are fully divine, as also were the antediluvian apkallus in the Mesopotamian tradition. The four post-flood apkallus were

"of human descent," which means that apkallus could mate with humans, as the Watchers did…. This exactly matches the status of Gilgamesh in the post-diluvian world, as he also was "two-thirds divine, and one-third human" (I 48). Gilgamesh was remotely related to antediluvian apkallus, as he "brought back a message from the antediluvian age" (I 8). In Jewish terms, he was like one of the giant Nephilim, as exactly the Book of Giants depicts him…. By identifying certain traditional archenemies as descendants of Watchers, the Jewish authors once again gave a polemical thrust to the Mesopotamian concept of the ruler as "seed preserved from before the flood." This reversal of attitudes is also seen in the sexual transgressions that were ascribed to Watchers. The sexual encounters between humans and divinities had a clearly fixed place in the royal ritual of sacred marriage in Mesopotamian culture. In 1 Enoch, however, such transgression of the boundaries between human and divine is depicted as sacrilegious at the outset, and a source of irreversible corruption in the human world.[95]

Finally, Second Temple Jewish writers wanted to so clearly associate Genesis 6:1–4 with the apkallu traditions for the purpose of theological polemic that they apparently coined the term "Watcher" to do so (or at least used it to be explicit). Recalling that, for Mesopotamians, the apkallu could be good or evil, Annus explains:

Figurines of apkallus were buried in boxes as foundation deposits in Mesopotamian buildings in order to avert evil from the house. The term *maṣṣarē*, "watchers," is used of these sets of figurines in Akkadian incantations according to ritual texts. This appellation matches the Aramaic term *ʿyryn*, "the wakeful ones," for both good angels and the Watchers…. The text from Assur, KAR 298, which prescribes the making of apotropaic apkallu figurines, often quotes the first line of otherwise unknown incantation *attunu ṣalmē apkallē maṣṣarē* ("You are the apkallu-figures, the watchers," e.g., line 14).[96]

The verdict of all this is inescapable. No interpretation of Genesis 6:1–4 that does not carefully observe and interact with the original Mesopotamian context can hope to be even remotely correct. Jews of the Second Temple Period understood this context. The New Testament writers were part of that milieu. Consequently, it should be no surprise that the sin of the Watchers was in the back of their minds as they wrote about what the Messiah, Jesus of Nazareth must, did, and would reverse at His coming and return. As we'll discover from this point forward, this theme of reversing the effects of the sin of the Watchers lurks under the surface of many New Testament passages.

Section Preview

Part II

Reversing Hermon in the Gospels

As we saw in chapter 2, according to 1 Enoch, Mount Hermon was the place at which the Watchers descended to bind themselves with an oath to corrupt humanity. As such, for Jews of Jesus' day (and the era of the early church), Mount Hermon became emblematic of the transgression of the Watchers and the awful deleterious effect that had on humankind.

Each section of the remainder of this book will demonstrate how, to the New Testament writers, the theme of reversing the effects of the transgression of the Watchers was part of their theology. Only one Person could undo what the Watchers had done: the Messiah. Consequently, for New Testament writers, the coming of Jesus as Yahweh incarnate meant not only reversing the curse of death brought upon humanity by the sin of Adam, but also the undoing of depravity.

This naturally meant the return of the Edenic kingdom of God to earth—the restoration of the divine order of heaven and earth so that the presence of God could return to earth in all its immediacy and fullness. The apostles had expected this kingdom at Jesus' first coming, not only because that made sense to the Jewish psyche, but also because the plan to have the Messiah die and rise again was, to quote Paul, "the secret and hidden wisdom of God" that, had it been known to the powers of darkness, they would never have crucified the Lord (1 Corinthians 2:6–8).[97]

Since the theme of reversal was tied to the appearance and work of the Messiah, our study of the reversal theme will obviously begin with the first advent. The three chapters in this section deal with, in order:

Chapter 4: How the birth of the Messiah telegraphed that part of the Messiah's arrival signaled that the sin of the Watchers or sons of God described, respectively, in 1 Enoch and Genesis 6:1–4 would be dealt with.

Chapter 5: How the genealogy of the Messiah would have led readers to expect that a reversal of the sin of the Watchers was part of the purpose of the Messiah's arrival.

Chapter 6: How certain statements and acts of Jesus would have been parsed by His first-century Jewish audience as gestures of defiance against the Watchers.

4

THE SIN OF THE WATCHERS
AND THE BIRTH OF JESUS

The notion that the birth of Jesus is somehow conceptually and theologically linked to Genesis 6:1–4 and the sin of the Watchers in 1 Enoch no doubt sounds odd to the modern Christian ear. But instead of focusing on what's familiar to us, the issue must be what was familiar to the Jews of the first century. Their intellectual and theological frame of reference can be quite foreign to our own. The right context for understanding the New Testament isn't our Christian tradition (of any variety or period). Rather, the context that produced the New Testament must guide us.

The birth of Jesus would have alerted literate first-century Jews that the Messiah's arrival would reverse the sin of the Watchers. Surprisingly, we will not discover how this was so in the birth narratives of the Gospels. This is perhaps why the connection between these two items seems so unlikely—we don't read anything in the Gospels that makes any relationship transparent. The answers are to be found elsewhere, in other New Testament passages.

PAUL, PSALM 19, AND THE KNOWLEDGE
OF THE MESSIAH'S COMING

Our starting place is Romans 10, a passage familiar to most Bible students. Many have memorized the verse, which declares that "whoever calls on the name of the Lord will be saved." But few read what follows that famous declaration.

[5]For Moses writes about the righteousness that is based on the law, that the person who does the commandments shall live by them. [6]But the righteousness based on faith says, "Do not say in your heart, 'Who will ascend into heaven?'" (that is, to bring Christ down) [7]or "'Who will descend into the abyss?'" (that is, to bring Christ up from the dead). [8]But what does it say? "The word is near you, in your mouth and in your heart" (that is, the word of faith that we proclaim); [9]because, if you confess with your mouth that Jesus is Lord and believe in your heart that God raised him from the dead, you will be saved. [10]For with the heart one believes and is justified, and with the mouth one confesses and is saved. [11]For the Scripture says, "Everyone who believes in him will not be put to shame." [12]For there is no distinction between Jew and Greek; for the same Lord is Lord of all, bestowing his riches on all who call on him. [13]For "everyone who calls on the name of the Lord will be saved." [14]How then will they call on him in whom they have not believed? And how are they to believe in him of whom they have never heard? And how are they to hear without someone preaching? [15]And how are they to preach unless they are sent? As it is written, "How beautiful are the feet of those who preach the good news!" [16]But they have not all obeyed the gospel. For Isaiah says, "Lord, who has believed what he has heard from us?" [17]So faith comes from hearing, and hearing through the word of Christ. [18]But I ask, have they not heard? Indeed they have, for "Their voice

has gone out to all the earth, and their words to the ends of the world."

Paul is clearly describing the necessity of believing in Jesus Christ for salvation (10:9–10). But in order to believe in Jesus, people must *hear* about Jesus. Paul then raises the expected objection: Not everyone has heard about Jesus. Paul gives an unexpected, fascinating answer to this objection. He asserts that they *have* heard about Jesus (Romans 10:18). Naturally, his readers would wonder, *Where? How?* Here's where things get interesting.

Paul's proof-text from the Old Testament for suggesting that people everywhere had heard about Jesus is Psalm 19:4. His quotation of the verse in Romans 10:18 comes from the Septuagint, the ancient Greek translation of the Hebrew Old Testament.[98] For Paul, everyone had heard (or should have heard) about the coming of Jesus because "their voice has gone out to all the earth, and their words to the ends of the world."

Whose voice is Paul talking about? The heavens! Let's look at the source of Paul's quotation, Psalm 19:1–4:

> [1]The heavens declare the glory of God,
> and the sky above proclaims his handiwork.
> [2]Day to day pours out speech,
> and night to night reveals knowledge.
> [3]There is no speech, nor are there words,
> whose voice is not heard.
> [4]Their voice goes out through all the earth,
> and their words to the end of the world.

There are a number of terms used in this passage to convey the idea that the heavens communicate information: The heavens "declare"; the sky "proclaims"; the cycle of days and nights "pours out speech" and "reveals knowledge"; the heavens have a "voice" and "speech" and "words" that can be heard since their message "goes out through all the earth."

A full treatment of this passage (and others) with respect to these ideas and how they fit into the context of biblical theology must be reserved for a different time. For our purposes here, this passage is one of several in the New Testament that take us into the ancient concept of astral theology, a subset of which is astral prophecy.[99] In briefest terms, and with respect to a biblical perspective (as opposed to pagan polytheism's conception), astral theology was the idea that the One who made the celestial objects in the heavens (sun, moon, stars) to be for "signs and seasons" and to mark time (Genesis 1:14) could use those objects to communicate. There is a good deal of evidence (e.g., zodiac mosaics in ancient Jewish synagogues) that faithful, theologically conservative Jews believed that divine activity that would have an impact on earthly events could be discerned in the skies—activity they were careful to attribute to the true God and no other gods.[100]

The key questions for the present chapter are, "How did Paul think the heavens communicated the coming of Jesus?" and "Is there evidence elsewhere in the New Testament that the heavens did anything like this?"

REVELATION 12 AS ASTRAL PROPHECY

Nearly all scholars who have tried to correlate the birth of the Messiah with astronomy share a crucial oversight: They start with the description of the star of Bethlehem in Matthew 2. This is a fatal flaw, one that not only overlooks Paul's astral-theological use of Psalm 19, but one that cuts off any chance of understanding how first-century Jews would have connected the birth of Jesus with the sin of the Watchers.[101]

I believe that the celestial messaging Paul had in mind in Romans 10:18 can be found in Revelation 12:1–7. This passage has several items that, if taken at face value, are astronomical signs associated with the birth of the Messiah. Considering the language of Revelation 12:1–7 in this way produces a real-time date for the birth of Jesus—a date that is laden with symbolism that first-century Jews would have understood as connecting the messianic birth to the sin of the Watchers. Revelation 12:1–7 reads as follows:

> [1]And a great sign appeared in heaven: a woman clothed with the sun, with the moon under her feet, and on her head a crown of twelve stars. [2]She was pregnant and was crying out in birth pains and the agony of giving birth. [3]And another sign appeared in heaven: behold, a great red dragon, with seven heads and ten horns, and on his heads seven diadems. [4]His tail swept down a third of the stars of heaven and cast them to the earth. And the dragon stood before the woman who was about to give birth, so that when she bore her child he might devour it. [5]She gave birth to a male child, one who is to rule all the nations with a rod of iron, but her child was caught up to God and to his throne, [6]and the woman fled into the wilderness, where she has a place prepared by God, in which she is to be nourished for 1,260 days.

It is quite clear that the signs in the heavens—where John is specifically looking (Revelation 12:1)—are indisputably astronomical: sun, moon, and stars.[102] The specific signs require attention.

1. THE WOMAN

The key figure, and logical starting point, for interpreting Revelation 12 astronomically is the woman. Since the woman gives birth to the messianic figure (Jesus) and then is persecuted and has to flee into the desert, scholars agree that verses 2–6 "reveal that this woman is a picture of the faithful community (Israel), which existed both before and after the coming of Christ."[103] Israel of course is described as the virgin of Zion in the Old Testament and produces the Messiah in fulfillment of Old Testament prophecy.[104] More specifically, of course, Mary comes to mind as the Jewish girl who gives birth to Jesus, but "Virgin Israel" best fits *both* parts of the description of the woman.[105]

Additionally, the connection to Virgin Israel is important given that the signage would have to be decipherable to Jews at the time of Jesus' birth. At that time, Mary's circumstances would have been entirely unknown. The meaning of the virgin and the twelve stars around her head is evident in Second Temple Period Jewish literature, as well as later rabbinic thought.[106]

What is John signifying when describing this woman? This much is certain: the woman in the first three verses is featured as being *in heaven* and both the sun and the moon are in association with her. Revelation 12:1 gives us clear details: the woman is "clothed" with the sun, there are twelve stars around her head, and the moon is at her feet. She is an astronomical (heavenly) sign.[107]

The idea that the woman is a constellation is made plausible when one looks closely at the text. The description that the woman was "clothed" with the sun is stock astronomical language for the sun being in the midst of a constellation. While the sun is in the woman, the moon is at her feet. For this situation to occur, the constellation of the woman must be, in astronomical language, on the ecliptic, the imaginary line in the sky that the sun and moon follow in their journey through the zodiac constellations.[108] Martin writes:

> The apostle John saw the scene when the Sun was "clothing" or "adorning" the woman. This surely indicates that the position of the Sun in the vision was located somewhere mid-bodied to the woman, between the neck and the knees. The Sun could hardly be said to clothe her if it were situated in her face or near her feet. The only time in the year that the Sun could be in a position to "clothe" the celestial woman called Virgo (that is, to be mid-bodied to her, in the region where a pregnant woman carries

a child) is when the Sun is located between about 150 and 170 degrees along the ecliptic. This "clothing" of the woman by the Sun occurs for a 20-day period each year. This 20 degree spread could indicate the general time when Jesus was born.[109]

The constellation of the Virgin giving birth to the Messiah would of course been viewed as quite coherent by the Magi, especially if they knew about Isaiah 7:14. But even if they were ignorant of this prophecy, this astro-theological linkage would still make sense to them since the sign we know as Virgo has strong associations with other ancient "mother goddess" figures who would produce divine kings.[110]

The detail that the moon was located *under* the feet of the woman (Virgo) must not be forgotten in all this. The sun must be in the Virgin constellation while the moon is simultaneously at her feet for John's vision to be accurately interpreted astronomically. Because of the moon's "behavior" relative to the ecliptic and Virgo in any given year, the twenty-day window narrows to a roughly ninety-minute period in which to astronomically pinpoint the birth of the child.

2. THE CHILD

Revelation 12:5 is very explicit that the child is Jesus, the promised Messiah: "She gave birth to a male child, one who is to rule all the nations with a rod of iron, but her child was caught up to God and to his throne." This description is an allusion to Psalm 2:7–9, which prophesied that the Messiah would defeat God's enemies and be installed as ruler over all the nations. The Psalms allusion is coupled with a description of an ascent of the child up to God and His throne—a reference to the resurrection of the child. In short, John's wording here and the immediate context is designed to create the impression that it appeared as if the devil had won the day—that the child would be killed (devoured)—but the resurrection resulted in victory (enthronement) for the Messiah. The dragon was defeated.

3. THE DRAGON

Scholars of the book of Revelation have long noted the connection of the dragon to Old Testament terminology for the sea monster that symbolized chaos.[111] As Osborne notes:

> Throughout the ancient Near East, the sea monster symbolized the war between good and evil, between the gods and chaos.... Obviously, in similar fashion to the meaning of "abyss" in 9:1–2, this builds on the fact that for the nations surrounding the Mediterranean basin, the sea meant unfathomable depths and the chaos of death. Thus, Leviathan or the "dragon" came to represent all the terrors of the sea and thus the presence of evil and death.... It also signified nations that stood against God and his people. The dragon or Leviathan is defeated both at the beginning of creation (Ps[alm] 74:13; 89:10 = Isa[iah] 51:9 ["Rahab"]; 2 Esdr. [4 Ezra] 6:49–52) and at the day of Yahweh (Isa[iah] 27:1; 2 Bar[uch] 29.4). First Enoch 60.7–10, 24 speak of the female sea monster Leviathan and the male Behemoth destroyed at the "great day of the Lord."[112]

There are two major candidates for the dragon with respect to constellations. Malina explains:

> The second sign is the fire-colored Dragon. The color red locates it in the southern sky.... The fact that the Dragon's tail sweeps (present tense) away a third of the stars of the sky further points to a location generally lacking in stars compared to other sky locations. This, again, is the south, in the region of the Abyss.... The question we might pose now is, which constellation does John label as the red Dragon, the Dragon in the south? Obviously it is not Draco, which is found at the North Pole. Boll opts for Hydra.... Immediately above Hydra and accompanying it are the constella-

tions of Corax (Raven) and Crater, which have seven and ten stars respectively. Corax with seven, corresponding to the number of heads [in Revelation 12] lies closer to Virgo…. On the other hand, Lehmann-Nitsche argues that the prototypical Dragon of the sky is really ancient Scorpio, originally a larger set of stars than the present constellation. It was truly gigantic, even by celestial zodiac standards, since it originally consisted of two [modern] zodiacal signs (Libra/Claws and Scorpio). It was only relatively recently, that is, about 237 B.C., that it was divided by the Greeks.[113]

Hydra has the advantage of matching the description of the seven heads atop the Dragon in Revelation 12:3 (cf. 13:1; 17:3, 7, 9). Hydra was also conceived as a sea serpent, imagery that matches descriptions in Revelation (13:1), which in turn come from the Leviathan material of the Old Testament (Isaiah 27:1). However, Hydra is not precisely on the ecliptic; it is adjacent and only slightly below the woman. In other words, Hydra is not positioned directly under the feet of the woman, waiting to devour the child as soon as it emerges from the woman. The ecliptic problem is resolved if ancient Scorpio is John's referent, but that said, the text of Revelation 12 only has the Dragon present ("stood before the woman"), not directly under her feet. Both options are possible correlations.

This combination of signs is not especially rare. But there are other celestial portents to consider that, although not mentioned by John in Revelation 12, were nevertheless present during the time of Jesus' birth and would have been taken as indications of the birth of a divine king to both Jews and Gentiles.

OTHER ASTRONOMICAL EVENTS OCCURRING WITH THE SIGNS IN REVELATION 12

The preceding signs are those described by John. Their occurrence together is not rare, though there were only a handful of dates in real time that can accommodate the events of New Testament chronology for the birth of Jesus. Those dates narrow to one date once other astronomical events that occurred at the same time—but which are not noted in Revelation 12—are added to the celestial profile. One of these extra events is the leading candidate for explaining the movement of the star seen by the Magi in Matthew 2.[114]

The constellation directly above the head of Virgo in the zodiac is Leo, the lion. The lion was the symbol associated with the tribe of Judah, from which the Messiah would come. The association arose from Genesis 49:9–10, where Jacob blessed him, referring to him in leonine terms while prophesying that a ruler would come from Judah's lineage:

Judah is a lion's cub;
   from the prey, my son, you have gone up.
He stooped down; he crouched as a lion
   and as a lioness; who dares rouse him?
The scepter shall not depart from Judah,
   nor the ruler's staff from between his feet,
until tribute comes to him;
   and to him shall be the obedience of the peoples.

The lion-king association is confirmed in Revelation 5:5: "And one of the elders said to me, 'Weep no more; behold, the Lion of the tribe of Judah, the Root of David, has conquered, so that he can open the scroll and its seven seals.'" The constellation Leo, then, was a royal constellation for Jewish astro-theologians.

The constellation of Leo was also important in Gentile astrology. It was the *chief* or *head* sign of the zodiac and had special importance in astrological circles.[115] Leo was considered a royal constellation since it was dominated by the star Regulus, which was known by astrologers as the "King Star."

The status of Regulus in Leo is important because on one of the possible dates for the messianic birth it came into conjunction with Jupiter.

As the largest planet, Jupiter was considered the "King Planet" in astro-theological thinking of the first century. As a result, the constellation Leo, the messianic sign of the lion of Judah to Jews who "read" the heavens, had two conjoined signs of a royal birth within it.

This combination of astronomical signs produces a unique set of circumstances that can only be accounted for by one date (and in point of fact, a ninety-minute window on that date). This date, as we will see momentarily, has dramatic significance in the Jewish calendar. According to these signs in the heavens, the date of Jesus' birth was September 11, 3 B.C.[116]

Jupiter is also important because it is the best explanation for the "star" whose movement was tracked by the Magi. Jupiter is well known for "retrograde motion," the appearance of movement back and forth in the night sky. Jupiter's first conjunction with Regulus began on September 14, 3 B.C., and continued through September 11, 3 B.C. On December 1, 3 B.C., Jupiter stopped its normal course through the fixed stars and began its annual retrogression or "backward motion." In doing so, it once again headed toward the star Regulus. Then on February 17, 2 B.C., the two were reunited. Jupiter continued on in its motion (still in retrogression) another forty days and then it reverted to its normal motion through the stars.[117] The timing is right, as the Magi embarked on their journey a year or so after Jesus was actually born.[118]

THE BIRTH OF JESUS ON SEPTEMBER 11, 3 B.C., THE DAY OF TRUMPETS, AND NOAH'S FLOOD

The astronomical context of John's description of what he saw in the heavens in Revelation 12 puts the birth of Jesus on September 11, 3 B.C. As impressive as the correlation of astronomical events with the description of Revelation 12 is, there are even more points of correlation that bear directly on the astro-theology being communicated.

The literary context of Revelation 12 is of relevance here. Immediately preceding Revelation 12, John described the heavenly appearance of the temple and the Ark of the Covenant (Revelation 11:19). The Ark was the central symbol of God's presence with Israel. The birth of the child (Jesus) in Revelation 12:1–7 was John's way of saying that the presence of God had indeed returned to earth in the form of this Child, the Messiah. New Testament scholar Greg Beale notes the significance of this juxtaposition by John:

> [A] trumpet was to be blown on Tishri 1, which in the rabbinic period came to be viewed as the beginning of the New Year. God's eschatological judgment of all people was expected to fall on this day.... The New Year trumpet also proclaimed hope in the ongoing and ultimate kingship of God, in God's judgment and reward according to people's deeds, and in Israel's final restoration.[119]

Incredibly, the astronomical reconstruction of the circumstances of Revelation 12:1–7 that produces a birth date for the Messiah of September 11, 3 B.C., was also the beginning of the Jewish New Year in 3 B.C. (*Rosh ha-Shanah*)—Tishri 1, the Day of Trumpets. The Feast of Trumpets/Tishri 1 was also the day that many of the ancient kings and rulers of Judah reckoned as their inauguration day of rule. This procedure was followed consistently in the time of Solomon, Jeremiah, and Ezra.[120] This is a powerful piece of evidence for the astronomical reading of Revelation 12:1–7 as celestial signs of the birth of the messianic king.

Jewish tradition also held that the Day of Trumpets commemorated the beginning of the world—the very first "first day" of the human calendar. As Jewish historian Theodor H. Gaster writes, "Judaism regards New Year's Day not merely as an anniversary of creation—but more importantly as a renewal of it. This is when the world is reborn."[121] Although it might sound odd, this tradition is part of a matrix of ideas that link Tishri 1 to the sin of the Watchers, the Flood of Noah, and the Nephilim.

The first step toward discerning these connections is to understand the Jewish calendar—at least insofar as it relates to our topic. The ancient

Israelite, biblical, and Jewish calendrical circumstances are like our own in that multiple calendars are in play. For example, in modern Western civilization, it is common to have a calendar that maps the seasons, a school-year calendar, and a fiscal-year calendar. All three calendars cover twelve months, but their beginning points frequently differ.

Today, the Jewish New Year (*Rosh Ha-Shanah*) "occurs on the first and second days of Tishri."[122] Anyone who is Jewish or has Jewish friends knows, however, that this New Year's Day and the New Year's Day we celebrate according to the modern Gregorian calendar (January 1) are not the same. Jewish Rosh Ha-Shanah occurs in the fall season (September–October).[123] The first month of the year is Tishri and occurs in the fall. Fall was, of course, the season of the harvest—an important idea to which we shall return in a moment.

Exodus 12:1–2, however, suggests that the first month of the Israelite calendar was not Tishri. After the Israelites escaped Egypt, the first month was aligned with the Passover (Exodus 12:3) to commemorate the new beginning of the Israelite nation after the Exodus from Egypt. The calendar of Exodus 12 detached the first season of the calendar from the agricultural harvest and instead attached it to this national rebirth. The first month of this new calendar was Nisan (Esther 3:7).

Of these two calendars, the agricultural calendar that had Tishri as the first month is the oldest in Israelite history, predating the Exodus. The biblical text contains hints of this older calendar in certain passages that describe the *ending* of the year (Exodus 23:16; 34:22). Whereas Tishri marked the fall harvest, the end of the year was marked by the Feast of Ingathering (*'āsîp*).

The important point for our purposes is that *the most ancient* Israelite calendar began with Tishri, which fell in fall season with a harvest—after the rains had produced the fall crop. This month and this harvest, as Gaster noted, were considered a memorial of creation. Why? The answer is simple: Genesis has Adam and Eve placed in a lush garden, Eden. Because of the availability of food for Adam and Eve, the creation must have begun in the harvest season—and so the earliest Hebrew calendar began the year in the harvest season. Hence, the first month, Tishri, fell in the fall harvest season. This logic produces the idea that the Israelite New Year signaled a renewal of creation.

In her fascinating scholarly essay, "The Pleiades, the Flood, and the Jewish New Year," Dr. Ellen Robbins, a lecturer at the Johns Hopkins University, details how this ancient calendrical thinking factored into the interpretation of the Flood story—including its preamble about the sons of God and the Nephilim.[124]

We must start at the way Genesis 7 describes the onset of the Flood:

[6]Noah was six hundred years old when the flood of waters came upon the earth. [7]And Noah and his sons and his wife and his sons' wives with him went into the ark to escape the waters of the flood. [8]Of clean animals, and of animals that are not clean, and of birds, and of everything that creeps on the ground, [9]two and two, male and female, went into the ark with Noah, as God had commanded Noah. [10]And after seven days the waters of the flood came upon the earth. [11]In the six hundredth year of Noah's life, in the second month, on the seventeenth day of the month, on that day all the fountains of the great deep burst forth, and the windows of the heavens were opened.

According to this passage, Noah was already 600 when the Flood began. As the waters were subsiding, just after the dove was released from the ark for the last time, Genesis 8 provides this chronological note:

[13]In the six hundred and first year, in the first month, the first day of the month, the waters were dried from off the earth. And Noah removed the covering of the ark and looked, and behold, the face of the ground was dry. [14]In the second month, on the twenty-seventh day of the month, the earth had dried out. [15]Then God said to Noah, [16]"Go out from the ark, you and your wife, and your sons and your sons' wives with you."

The math is transparent. Barely over a year after the Flood began, Noah and his family left the ark *in the second month of the year*. Noah had turned 601 by the time he left the ark.

Why is this noteworthy? Because Jewish tradition took this chronology to mean that Noah's birthday was Tishri 1. This is *the same day as the birth of the Messiah, Jesus*, if we take Revelation 12 as indicating the celestial signs present at his birth. A messiah born on Tishri 1 would inevitably have created mental and theological associations between Noah and Jesus.

There are other details about the chronology of the Flood that, given the idea that Jesus and Noah shared a birthday, would have moved ancient Jewish readers to associate the Messiah with the prologue to the Flood story, Genesis 6:1–4. The second month of the year, the month when Noah and his family emerged from the ark after the Flood had swept the earth clean of its wickedness and the awful Nephilim, was marked astronomically by the heliacal appearance of the Pleiades. A star's heliacal rising "is a phenomenon where a star is first visible in the morning sky. On this day, a star will only be briefly and barely visible, since if you had looked a day earlier, it was too close to the Sun for visibility."[125]

The cluster of stars known as the Pleiades (Hebrew term: *kima*) is mentioned three times in the Old Testament (Amos 5:8; Job 9:9; 38:31). It is always paired with Orion (Hebrew: *kesil*), since its position in the sky is close to the Orion constellation. Not surprisingly, Orion was considered a giant in the ancient world.[126] The last reference, Job 38:31, is significant in light of the Dead Sea Scrolls. In one Targum of Job (i.e., an Aramaic translation of Job) discovered at Qumran, Job 38:31 reads, "Can you bind the chains of the Pleiades (*kima*) or loose the cords of Orion (*naphila*)?"[127] This last term, the Aramaic word for Orion, is the Aramaic noun from which Nephilim derives.[128]

Recall our discussion in chapter 3 on the importance of the Mesopotamian context for Genesis 6:1–4 and its preservation in 1 Enoch and other Second Temple Jewish literature. In Mesopotamian astronomy, Orion was referred to as "the true shepherd of Anu."[129] Anu was the chief god of the heavenly realm, the sky. The shepherd motif was associated in the ancient Near East with kingship. Orion, then, was Anu's chosen king. But this *naphila* wasn't the true shepherd-king for the followers of Yahweh, the true God.

The shepherd imagery, of course, is overtly messianic:

> The king took on numerous idealized roles as leader of his people, including the idea of "royal adoption" (i.e., the deity adopts the king as his "son" [2 Samuel 7:14; cf. Psalm 89:26–27]), shepherd of the people (2 Sam[uel] 5:2; 7:7).... David became the model of the "ideal king" for Israel (cf. 2 Kings 18:3; 22:2) and the prototype of the Messiah as the ultimate "shepherd-king" (Jer[emiah] 33:15; Ezek[iel] 34:23–24; 37:24–25; cf. Rev[elation] 22:16).[130]

The theological messaging is startling. A messiah whose birth on Tishri 1 was followed in the next month by the rising of the Pleiades-Orion would have signaled the arrival of Yahweh's shepherd-king. The following month, the second month of the year when Noah and his family emerged from the ark, marked the judgment of God upon the Nephilim. But we know from Genesis 6:4 and other passages that the Flood wasn't the permanent cure for the Nephilim and the effect of the sin of the Watchers in human history. What was needed was a new Noah. And so on Tishri 1, the traditional birthday of Noah, the heavens telegraphed the identity of the better Noah, Jesus of Nazareth, born as He was from Noah's own bloodline (Luke 3:36). The permanent reversal of the ancient pact sealed on Mount Hermon had begun.

5

THE SIN OF THE WATCHERS AND
THE GENEALOGY OF JESUS

Admit it. You think genealogies are boring. While I wouldn't claim that all biblical genealogies are filled with theological insights, I can promise you that the genealogy of Jesus is different. As we'll see, it has some amazing features that link it with the expectation of a messianic reversal of the sin of the Watchers. But you have to know what you're looking at. By the time you're finished with this chapter, you will.

The scholarship on the sin of the Watchers and the genealogy of Jesus is recent.[131] The connection between these two seemingly disparate topics is related to a question that has confounded interpreters ever since the Gospel of Matthew was written: Why are there four women, possibly all Gentiles, in the bloodline of Jesus?[132]

While inclusion of women in biblical genealogies isn't unusual in itself (there are fourteen such women listed in 1 Chronicles 2, for example), the inclusion of these four women is all the more odd when one realizes that "the great Jewish female figures are missing: Sarah, Rebekah, Rachel."[133] One would think that if Matthew thought it important to include women, these women would be more logical candidates. But they aren't—*because of what Matthew wants to telegraph about the Person whose genealogy he is presenting.*

Scholars have proposed various explanations for the inclusion of Tamar, Ruth, Bathsheba ("the wife of Uriah"), and Rahab. Some theologize their inclusion as demonstrations of God's grace to sinners or, specifically, Gentiles. Others have proposed, even more abstractly, that they are present to illustrate how God's plan is mysterious.

These explanations are overly speculative and, honestly, unsatisfying. The idea put forward in this chapter is not entirely without speculation, but it has two distinct advantages: (1) textual connections back into the Old Testament narrative and Second Temple Jewish thinking, and (2) a thematic logic that not only can explain their inclusion, but correlates each woman with the rest of the women in the genealogy.

THE GENERAL THESIS: REPAIRING THE DAMAGE CAUSED BY THE WATCHERS

New Testament scholar Amy Richter believes that what she calls the "Enochic Watchers Template" is essential for understanding the women in the genealogy of Jesus. She summarizes this template early in her recent study:

> According to the Enochic watchers' template, evil came into the world when the watchers transgressed their heavenly boundary to engage in illicit sexual contact with women and teach them illicit arts. The consequences of the watchers' transgression are violence, unrighteousness, evil, idolatry, and disease. Some of these consequences come from human use of the skills taught by the watchers, skills for seduction, war-making, sorcery, and astrology.[134]

For ancient readers of Matthew's Gospel who knew the specifics of Enoch's story of the sin of the Watchers, the theological strategy of the genealogy would have been evident. Richter notes:

The writer of the Gospel according to Matthew was familiar with themes and traditions about the antediluvian patriarch Enoch, including the story of the fall of the watchers, and shows that Jesus brings about the eschatological repair of the consequences of the watchers' fall. In Matthew's Gospel, the foreshadowing of repair and then the repair itself are seen in the evangelist's genealogy and infancy narrative....

The women of the Hebrew Bible named by Matthew in his genealogy of Jesus foreshadow the reversal of the watchers' transgression. All four of them are connected with the Enochic watchers' template. They use the illicit arts, but the use of these skills leads to righteousness rather than evil. The women are also connected with other aspects of the Enochic watchers' template, including sexual interaction which connects the earthly and heavenly realms, interaction with angels, unusual aspects of their offspring, and connections with giants.

In the birth narrative, Matthew shows the birth of Jesus occurring in a way that reverses the watchers' transgression and evil in the world as it occurs in the Enochic template. Specifically, the birth of Jesus occurs through the union of a woman and a celestial being, but in contrast to the watchers' story, no sexual relations are involved. Further, in Matthew's narrative, the first humans outside of Jesus' immediate family to interact with the child Jesus are the magi who are practitioners of the illicit arts taught by the watchers and use astrological knowledge to find Jesus. In the Enochic template, the watchers bring idolatry into the world; in Matthew, the magi worship the appropriate object of worship—Jesus.[135]

Richter notes an ironic subtext to the fact that Matthew draws attention to the reversal of the sin of the Watchers through the four women: "Jesus completes what Enoch does not. That is, Jesus is able to bring about the eschatological repair of the consequences of the fall of the watchers."[136]

THE SPECIFICS OF REVERSAL TYPOLOGY
IN THE FOUR WOMEN

In what remains of this chapter, we want to examine the evidence marshaled by Richter that demonstrates how the women included in Matthew's genealogy of Jesus foreshadow the reversal of the transgression of the Watchers and, consequently, the Enochian notion of how their transgression resulted in the proliferation of evil in humankind. Richter writes:

> Transgression looms large in the stories from the now canonical Hebrew scriptures of the four women included in Matthew's genealogy (Matt[hew] 1:1–17), Tamar, Rahab, Ruth, and "the wife of Uriah" as she is called in Matthew, known from the Hebrew scriptures as Bathsheba. Aspects of the watchers' transgression and its consequences are present in the stories of each of the women named as an ancestor of Jesus. First, each woman makes use of the illicit skills and arts taught by the fallen angels in the Enochic tradition. Each of the women named in the genealogy participates in sexual activity considered suspicious at best and unrighteous at worst. Each of their stories involves use of the arts of seduction or beautification. Two of the stories, the story of Rahab and the story of the "wife of Uriah," involve both the arts of beautification and the arts of war. Each of their stories, then, includes the combination seen in the watchers' descent myth: "knowing" as sexual activity and "knowing" as understanding illicit arts. Second, each of the stories involves echoes of additional elements of the Enochic template. These elements include the following: interaction with angels, sometimes with hints of sexual activity, questions about the paternity of the women's offspring, and questions about the unusual nature of their offspring.[137]

The links between these four women and the aforementioned elements of the Enochic template are not always obvious or clear to English readers. This is due in part to dependence on English translations. In other instances, the connections are part of Second Temple Jewish readings of the biblical material that may seem foreign to modern readers. Our modern traditional perspective impedes understanding.[138]

Because of these disconnections, we need to examine the ancient biblical and Jewish material about each of these women that would have alerted first-century Jewish readers to Matthew's strategy of including them to portend a messianic reversal of the sin of the Watchers.

1. TAMAR

Tamar is the first of the four women in Matthew's genealogy (Matthew 1:3). She is known primarily from Genesis 38, where she deceives Judah, one of the twelve sons of Jacob, into an illicit sexual encounter. We need to recount the story here so the connections to the Watcher template will be decipherable.

> [1]It happened at that time that Judah went down from his brothers and turned aside to a certain Adullamite, whose name was Hirah. [2]There Judah saw the daughter of a certain Canaanite whose name was Shua. He took her and went in to her, [3]and she conceived and bore a son, and he called his name Er. [4]She conceived again and bore a son, and she called his name Onan. [5]Yet again she bore a son, and she called his name Shelah. Judah was in Chezib when she bore him.
>
> [6]And Judah took a wife for Er his firstborn, and her name was Tamar. [7]But Er, Judah's firstborn, was wicked in the sight of the Lord, and the Lord put him to death. [8]Then Judah said to Onan, "Go in to your brother's wife and perform the duty of a brother-in-law to her, and raise up offspring for your brother." [9]But Onan knew that the offspring would not be his. So whenever he went in to his brother's wife he would waste the semen on the ground, so as not to give offspring to his brother. [10]And what he

did was wicked in the sight of the Lord, and he put him to death also. [11]Then Judah said to Tamar his daughter-in-law, "Remain a widow in your father's house, till Shelah my son grows up"—for he feared that he would die, like his brothers. So Tamar went and remained in her father's house.

[12]In the course of time the wife of Judah, Shua's daughter, died. When Judah was comforted, he went up to Timnah to his sheepshearers, he and his friend Hirah the Adullamite. [13]And when Tamar was told, "Your father-in-law is going up to Timnah to shear his sheep," [14]she took off her widow's garments and covered herself with a veil, wrapping herself up, and sat at the entrance to Enaim, which is on the road to Timnah. For she saw that Shelah was grown up, and she had not been given to him in marriage. [15]When Judah saw her, he thought she was a prostitute, for she had covered her face. [16]He turned to her at the roadside and said, "Come, let me come in to you," for he did not know that she was his daughter-in-law. She said, "What will you give me, that you may come in to me?" [17]He answered, "I will send you a young goat from the flock." And she said, "If you give me a pledge, until you send it—" [18]He said, "What pledge shall I give you?" She replied, "Your signet and your cord and your staff that is in your hand." So he gave them to her and went in to her, and she conceived by him. [19]Then she arose and went away, and taking off her veil she put on the garments of her widowhood.

The rest of the story can be summarized. Judah sent the young goat by way of Hirah (v. 12), but of course Hirah found no cult prostitute, nor could the men of the town affirm that a cult prostitute (*qedēshah*) had ever been in the town. Judah consequently didn't get his items back. They turned up in Tamar's hands three months later when Judah wanted Tamar put to death for immorality, as her pregnancy by the unwitting Judah had begun to show. Tamar confronted him, and Judah acknowledged that the whole incident was caused by his unwillingness to give Tamar to his son

Shelah. Tamar would later give birth to Perez and Zerah, the former of whom is also in the genealogy of Jesus (Matthew 1:3).

There is a good deal lurking under the surface of this story. Looking more closely, we see that Judah married a Canaanite woman named Shuah (Genesis 38:2),[139] but the text does not specifically say that Tamar, the woman Judah chooses as a wife for his oldest son (Genesis 38:6), was also a Canaanite. Some scholars take the label of *qedēshah* as suggesting that Tamar was a Canaanite sacred prostitute. This overstates the data, but at the very least, the story is *cast* in such a way as to link the incident with Canaanite sacred prostitution. The important point is not whether or not Tamar is a Gentile. Rather, it is that Matthew perceives a link between Tamar and the Watchers template. That linkage most obviously derives from the illicit sexual transgression, but there is more in play than meets the eye. Richter writes:

> Tamar's deceit was not just any form of trickery. Tamar engages in the illicit arts, those, according to the Enochic template for the origins of evil in the world, which were forbidden for the watchers to share…. Specifically, Tamar uses the arts related to seduction, making herself appear as a prostitute to attract Judah's attention. While in the Hebrew she wraps herself in a veil (Gen[esis]. 38:14), the LXX[140] translates her action as "she put a covering around herself and she beautified her face." Whether by obfuscation, as in the Hebrew Bible, or beautification, as in the LXX, it is by making herself sexually attractive and available to Judah that Tamar is able to carry out her plan.[141]

Richter also establishes the interesting point that more than a few word choices in the account of Judah and Tamar can be found in either Genesis 6:1–4 or the Enochian story of the Watchers (or both):

Judah's actions, with which Genesis 38 opens, are reminiscent of the way in which the narrative of the Watchers' fall begins: "Judah <u>saw</u> there the daughter of a Canaanite man, whose name was Shua; he <u>took</u> her and

went into her, and she conceived and bore a son, and he called his name Er"
(Genesis 38:2–3, underlines added). The watchers "see" (1 Enoch 6:2) the
daughters of men; they "take" wives from among them; they "go into them"
(1 Enoch 7:1); the women "conceived" and "bore" the giants (1 Enoch 7:2).[142]

Even more telling is the name of Judah's first son: Er (Hebrew: עֵר; 'r).
Scholars have noted that the name derives from the same Semitic root
(עוּר, "to be awake") as "Watcher" (עִיר; 'îr).[143] Richter draws attention to
the connection: "Er's name thus derives from the same root as the name
of the rebel angel watchers of 1 Enoch."[144] It is also interesting that Judah
gives the disguised Tamar his signet ring as part of his pledge. Metallurgy
for jewelry was one of the illicit arts taught by the Watchers.

Lastly, though Tamar was not in reality a sacred prostitute, she is
described with the term for one: qedēshah. Though some scholars argue
that there was no such thing as sacred prostitution (offering sex as a form
of worship) and that this term has been misunderstood,[145] the Mesopotamian material is clear that the qedēshah did play the role of the goddess
Inanna in the annual act of intercourse with the king ("sacred marriage")
and participate "in exorcistic rituals and sorcery."[146] Richter observes,
"Like the Enochic watchers' transgression story, sacred marriage served
to bridge the gap between the heavenly realm and the earthly realm....
Also, as are the watchers in the Enochic story, Inanna is associated with
demons. In the story of her descent to the netherworld, she returns with a
band of demons who pose a threat to the living."[147]

2. RAHAB

Unlike Tamar, who took the guise of a prostitute to deceive Judah, Rahab
was a working prostitute (Joshua 2:1). She is one of two (cf. Ruth) unam-
biguous Gentiles among the four women, as she is a native Canaanite
living in Jericho (Joshua 2:1–2). The Enochic template element of sexual
transgression is therefore quite transparent. But, as with the Tamar episode, there is a lot more to Rahab and her story than that.

While it may sound odd to our ear, Rahab is also connected to the

Enochic template by means of warfare, giants, and angels. Richter comments on the first item as follows:

> While Rahab herself does not take up weapons of war, her actions make way for the Israelites to do so. Therefore her story is connected with the illicit arts of war. Clearly in this context, these arts are not perceived within the narrative as negative for Rahab or the Israelites who engage in them directly. Rather, they are the necessary means by which Israel enters the promised land. Rahab's story, then, makes use of two categories of illicit arts identified in 1 En[och] 8:1, arts concerned with the making of war and the beautification of women.[148]

The connection between Rahab and the giant clans is implied by what follows in the conquest of Jericho and the wars against the giant clans. Jericho was one of the cities targeted for *kherem* ("devotion to destruction"), a command patterned by the detection of the Anakim by the spies prior to the wilderness wanderings (Numbers 13:32–33).[149]

But Rahab's connection to giants seems to have entered the Jewish consciousness in another way. Matthew refers to Rahab as the mother of Boaz by a man named Salmon (Matthew 1:5). On the surface, nothing seems unusual. But Ruth 2:1 refers to Boaz as a *gibbor*, one of the terms used to describe the Nephilim offspring of the sons of God in Genesis 6:4. On its own, *gibbor* (plural: *gibborim*) does not refer to giants.[150] However, Jews in the Second Temple Period often interpreted the term that way. The Septuagint, for example, translates the term with *gigas/gigantes* ("giant"; "giants") over a dozen times whether the context supports that rendering or not.[151] The point being made here is not that Boaz was a giant. He wasn't. Rather, the point is that the description used by the author of Ruth drew the attention of Second Temple Jews—Matthew being one of them—and created a mental link between Rahab and the giant clans.[152]

What of the angel connection? This is detected in the Greek Septuagint translation of the Rahab account and the New Testament.

In the New Testament Letter of James, Rahab is paired with Abraham as an example of one "justified by works and not by faith
alone" (James 2:24). Rahab is named specifically in James 2:25:
"was not Rahab the prostitute also justified by works when she
welcomed the messengers (ἀγγέλους; ἄγγελος [aggelous; aggelos] in
the nominative singular)[153] and sent them out by another road?"
The ambiguous word ἄγγελος [aggelos], translated in many English translations of James 2:25 as "messenger," is also the word
used in the LXX for "angel." The ambiguity is present in Hebrew
as well, and in Josh 6:25 the word מלאכים [mel'akīm; "messenger, angel"] is used to explain why Joshua spared the lives of the
Canaanite Rahab and her family when the Israelites conquered
the land and committed all other Canaanite people and animals
to the ban: "But Rahab the prostitute, with her family and all
who belonged to her, Joshua spared. She lives in Israel to this
day for she hid the messengers (מלאכים) whom Joshua sent to spy
out Jericho." It is interesting that the LXX does not use ἄγγελος
[aggelos] in Josh 6:25, but κατάσκοπος (kataskopos; "spy") instead.
In other words, the writer of James is not quoting the LXX text,
but rather makes use of the ambiguous ἄγγελος [aggelos] which
may connote "messenger" or "angel," and thereby preserves the
ambiguity of the Hebrew version of Josh 6:25 with its מלאכים
[mel'akīm].[154]

It is also interesting to note that James uses both Rahab and Abraham
as models of faith—both "received messengers" (mel'akīm) hospitably (cp.
Genesis 18:1–19:1; James 2:25).[155]

3. RUTH

Like Rahab, Ruth is clearly a Gentile, being from Moab (Ruth 1:4). Richter observes:

Like Tamar, Ruth has found herself widowed with no child, and Ruth also will transgress social mores to gain security and a child.... Because she is a Moabite, Ruth is connected with three aspects of the watchers' legacy: illicit sexual intercourse, bloodshed, and idolatry. Further, Moabites share with those of illegitimate birth the status of being excluded from the assembly of the Lord. The designation of illegitimate birth is also applied at Qumran to the offspring of the watchers and the women.[156]

Readers will recall that in the story of Ruth, her Israelite mother-in-law, Naomi, comes up with a plan that, if successful, would result in Boaz redeeming Ruth through marriage, thereby ending their desperate, poverty-stricken situation.

Scholars of the Hebrew Bible have long recognized that what Ruth does at the threshing floor (Ruth 3) is overtly sexual. Ruth exposes the "feet" of Boaz while he is sleeping after he had "eaten and drunk" when "his heart was merry," and then lies down (Ruth 3:7). The Hebrew word translated "feet" (*regel*) is a well-known euphemism for genitalia in the Hebrew Bible (e.g., to "cover one's feet," meaning relieve oneself: Judges 3:24; 1 Samuel 24:4). By uncovering Boaz's "feet" (genitalia), Ruth is, in effect, offering herself as a wife to Boaz. Given the patriarchal setting of Israelite culture, this was a transgression of the way things were usually done—it was the man who would solicit marriage or take a concubine of his choice. While the text provides no evidence of a sexual encounter between the two, what Ruth did would have an illicit feel to "proper" Israelites and later Jewish readers.

For our purposes, what leads up to Ruth's offer is noteworthy:

Ruth's encounter with Boaz on the threshing floor is orchestrated by the design of Naomi, who instructs Ruth in how the night should progress. Specifically, Naomi instructs Ruth to "wash and anoint yourself, and put on your best clothes and go down to the threshing floor" (Ruth 3:3, NRSV). At its most innocuous, Naomi is merely telling Ruth to make herself presentable, to "pretty herself up" for her encounter with Boaz. However, since the intended result is to put Boaz in a position of being obligated to marry Ruth, it may be more realistic to see Naomi as encouraging Ruth to make use of the arts of seduction, specifically those named as illicit arts in the Enochic tradition. Accordingly Ruth makes use of cosmetic adornment (ointment, perfume), specifically identified as one of the illicit arts, as well as putting on her finest raiment in order to be more attractive to Boaz.... Ruth is a Moabite, a fact mentioned no less than seven times: Ruth 1:4; 1:22; 2:2, 6, 21; 4:5, 10. In Israelite tradition, Moabites were associated with idolatry and their women with sexual wantonness and seduction of Israelite men. This association comes from the episode of the worship of Baal of Peor, recorded in Numbers 25:1–5.[157]

Ruth and Boaz of course, do get married. They famously become the great-grandparents of King David (Ruth 4:18–22). Having a Moabitess in the line of David was a scandal that later rabbis felt required explanation.[158] Deuteronomy 23:2–3 was a focal point:

No one born of a forbidden union (*mamzēr*) may enter the assembly of the Lord. Even to the tenth generation, none of his descendants may enter the assembly of the Lord. No Ammonite or Moabite may enter the assembly of the Lord. Even to the tenth generation, none of them may enter the assembly of the Lord forever.

The term *mamzēr* from Deuteronomy 23:2 is significant. It is the term behind the famous designation of the giant offspring of the Watchers as "bastard spirits" in Second Temple Jewish literature, especially the Dead Sea Scrolls. David Jackson, in his scholarly work on Enochic Judaism, explains, "We find the concept of 'bastard' (ממזר; *mamzēr*), drawn from Deut[eronomy] 23:2–4 and Zech[ariah] 9:6 applied to the offspring of the angels and the women throughout the Qumran literature."[159]

Lastly, it is interesting to note that rabbinic tradition was aware of all this material and, as rabbinic interpreters often do, made it fodder for imaginative interpretation. Orpah, Ruth's sister, was believed to be the mother of Goliath and his brothers. Some rabbis presumed Orpah had giant (*Emim*) blood as a Moabitess. The Babylonian Talmud (b. *Sotah*) reads:

> It is written: "And Orpah kissed her mother-in-law but Ruth clave unto her." Let the sons of the kiss (the one who kissed) fall into the hands of the one who clave unto, as it is written; "These four were born to the giant (*ha-ra-fah*) in Gath, and fell by the hand of David." Rabba taught, because of the four tears Orpah shed on her mother-in-law she was worthy that four mighty men would come forth out of her as her offspring.[160]

This opinion is speculative for sure, but given Matthew's inclusion of Ruth in the genealogy of Jesus, Jews perhaps saw Ruth as "immune" from monstrous offspring due to her conversion to Naomi's God, or perhaps that David was a marker of messianic things to come—one who would blunt and combat the transgression of the Watchers.

4. BATHSHEBA

The sordid story of David's adultery with Bathsheba and his subsequent murder of her husband, Uriah the Hittite, is well known to Bible readers (2 Samuel 11:1–27). Two elements of the Watchers' template are clear from the outset: sexual transgression (though Bathsheba is likely best understood as a victim, not the perpetrator) and warfare. The latter is clear in that the context for Uriah's death was the siege of Rabbah

(2 Samuel 11:1). Richter summarizes how these two items work together in the story:

> Recall that in 1 Enoch Asael teaches human beings how to make weapons of war and materials for the beautification of women. The story of Bathsheba, David, and Uriah is a story that combines these elements: skills of war and a desirable woman.... The scene of David on his rooftop shares some elements with the Enochic scene of the watchers about to transgress and leave their appointed heavenly station. David looks down from his roof and sees a very beautiful woman (2 Sam[uel] 11:2) just as the watchers look down from lofty places and spy "the beautiful and comely daughters of men" (1 En[och] 6:1). The fact that David is up on his roof is mentioned twice in the verse. The woman's beauty is emphasized ("the woman was very beautiful," 2 Sam[uel] 11:2, NRSV).... In 1 Enoch, after seeing the comely women the watchers decide to "choose for ourselves wives from the daughters of men" (1 En[och] 6:1). David decides to choose for himself someone who is already the wife of a man. Shemihazah, the watcher, and David, the voyeur, share in knowing that what they do is wrong. Shemihazah knows that if he takes a human wife he "shall be guilty of a great sin" (1 En[och] 6:3). David knows that Bathsheba is already the wife of another man.... Asael taught skills for the beautification of women, the women used them, and made themselves irresistible to angels. Two aspects are present then in this strand of the tradition: the women learned skills for making their physical appearance irresistible, and angels fell for it. Once the watchers saw how beautiful the women were, they could not help themselves and were "led astray" (1 En[och] 8:1). In this telling, then, the women bear some responsibility for the angels' misdeeds.[161]

Some other items deserve attention. Uriah was one of David's *gibborim* ("mighty men"; 2 Samuel 23:39). As we saw with Ruth, being married to a *gibbor* may have made certain Jewish readers suspicious of a connection to the giants. Bathsheba would therefore be another ancestor of Jesus associated with a *gibbor*.

More interesting perhaps is the fact that Bathsheba became the *gebīrah*, the Queen Mother. This term is the feminine equivalent to *gibbor*. It is not specifically used of Bathsheba, queen wife to King David, though it is used of other Israelite queens (2 Kings 10:13; 2 Chronicles 15:16; Jeremiah 13:18; 29:2). Scholars disagree on whether the *gebīrah* had any official governmental function. There is sparse textual support for the idea. In Bathsheba's case, the only role she seems to have had was to solidify Solomon's claim on the throne (1 Kings 1). That role may have arisen *ad hoc* out of the circumstances.

Lastly, Bathsheba's name itself is of interest. In 2 Samuel 11, where readers first encounter her, she is "Bathsheba, the daughter of Eliam." In 1 Chronicles 3:5, she is given a different name: "Bath-shua, the daughter of Ammiel." In Hebrew, the first part of the name (*bat* or *bath*) means "daughter," and so the name from 1 Chronicles means "daughter of Shua." We have seen the name Shua before, back in Genesis 38:

> [1]It happened at that time that Judah went down from his brothers
> and turned aside to a certain Adullamite, whose name was Hirah.
> [2]There Judah saw the daughter of a certain Canaanite whose name
> was Shua. He took her and went in to her.

The "daughter of Shua" was Judah's unnamed wife. It was after her death (Genesis 38:12) that Judah unknowingly solicited a prostitute who wasn't a prostitute: Tamar. Since Judah's wife was clearly a Canaanite, scholars have theorized that Bathsheba was as well because of the name given to her in 1 Chronicles 3:5. This possibility would mean that Bathsheba and Uriah were not a "mixed couple," but both Gentiles. The connection back to Tamar is interesting for our purposes, because it strengthens the idea that Matthew is picking up on women with specific histories for inclusion in Jesus' genealogy.

SUMMARY

We began this chapter with the thesis, drawn largely from the work of Richter, that Matthew was familiar with the sin of the Watchers (the "Enochic template"). The Watchers were blamed for sexual transgression and corrupting humanity with forbidden knowledge. All four women in the genealogy of Jesus are connected in some way with sexual transgression, seduction, and warfare. The connections are both thematic and textual. This can hardly be a coincidence. The effect of their inclusion in the genealogy is to direct readers' attention to the One to whom the genealogy belongs: the son of Abraham, son of David, from the tribe of Judah, born as the result of a divine-human interaction approved by God for the purpose of repairing the consequences of the proliferation of sin among humankind, a proliferation laid at the feet of the Watchers.

6

THE SIN OF THE WATCHERS AND THE MINISTRY OF JESUS

At first glance one might presume that the connection between the ministry of Jesus and the sin of the Watchers is to be found in the episodes where Jesus casts out demons. While demonology and exorcism play a role in our topic, they are by no means the only connection. Our study will begin elsewhere, with a more fundamental reference point: Mount Hermon. We may not realize it, but Jesus spent some time on this mountain and in the region at its base, and what He did and said there was classic spiritual warfare.

MOUNT HERMON, MOUNTAIN OF BASHAN

It's hard to miss Mount Hermon on any visit to the Holy Land. At nine thousand feet, it is easily the tallest peak in Israel. In ancient Israel, Mount Hermon was called Sirion and Senir (Deuteronomy 3:9; 4:48).

In an earlier chapter, we learned that Mount Hermon was the location at which the Watchers bound themselves with an oath to corrupt humanity. First Enoch 6 describes the deed, connecting it explicitly to Genesis 6:1–4:

> [1]And when the sons of men had multiplied, in those days, beautiful and comely daughters were born to them. [2]And the watchers, the sons of heaven, saw them and desired them. And they said to one another, "Come, let us choose for ourselves wives from the daughters of men, and let us beget for ourselves children." [3]And Shemihazah, their chief, said to them, "I fear that you will not want to do this deed, and I alone shall be guilty of a great sin." [4]And they all answered him and said, "Let us all swear an oath, and let us all bind one another with a curse, that none of us turn back from this counsel until we fulfill it and do this deed." [5]Then they all swore together and bound one another with a curse. [6]And they were, all of them, two hundred, who descended in the days of Jared onto the peak of Mount Hermon.[162] And they called the mountain "Hermon" because they swore and bound one another with a curse on it.

The base of Mount Hermon forms the northern border of the region of Bashan, a geographical reality that helps us identify Mount Hermon with Mount Bashan of Psalm 68.

> [15]O mountain of God,[163] mountain of Bashan;
> O many-peaked mountain, mountain of Bashan!
> [16]Why do you look with hatred, O many-peaked mountain,
> at the mount that God desired for his abode,
> yes, where the Lord will dwell forever?

Since Hermon is one of many peaks in the north Bashan mountain range, some scholars are hesitant to identify Mount Hermon with Mount Bashan. Others express no such hesitation. For example, Princeton Old Testament scholar J. J. M. Roberts writes in one analysis of Psalm 68,

"Mount Hermon is rebuked for looking with envy on the mountain of Yahweh."[164] Professor John Goldingay explains the coherence of the association this way:

> Rhetorically this further section [of Psalm 68] moves in a new direction as it addresses Mount Bashan, and in content it makes for another form of link between past and present, the reality of God's dwelling.... It begins by looking across from the mountain chain running through the heartland of Ephraim and Judah to the higher and more impressive mountains on the other side of the Jordan, running south from Mount Hermon through the Golan and Gilead. Mount Hermon in particular is indeed a mighty or majestic mountain, literally, a "mountain of God." It towers into the heavens and thus suggests the possibility of or the claim to a link between heaven and earth.[165]

The association of Mount Hermon with Mount Bashan would have made sense to Second-Temple Jews familiar with 1 Enoch as well as the earlier Israelites who read Genesis 6:1–4 supernaturally, in accord with its original Mesopotamian context. English readers, centuries or millennia removed from the original readers, are largely unaware of why this is so. In a word, in Old Testament times, the whole region of Bashan was associated with giants and evil spirits—the spawn of the Watchers according to Genesis 6:1–4 and 1 Enoch.

OLD TESTAMENT BASHAN: GIANTS AND THE UNDERWORLD

We first encounter Bashan in the biblical text in the days of Israel's wanderings in the desert after the Exodus. God directs Moses to lead the people northward on the other side of the Jordan opposite the Promised Land (the "Transjordan") in preparation for taking the land he had granted to them. Readers of Deuteronomy 2–3 discover that the Transjordan was once the home of giant clans, referred to variously as Rephaim, Anakim, Emim, Zamzummin, and Amorites.[166] The Amorite reference is important. It harkens back to God's original covenantal conversation with Abraham in Genesis 15:13–16:

> [13]Then the Lord said to Abram, "Know for certain that your offspring will be sojourners in a land that is not theirs and will be servants there, and they will be afflicted for four hundred years. [14]But I will bring judgment on the nation that they serve, and afterward they shall come out with great possessions. [15]As for you, you shall go to your fathers in peace; you shall be buried in a good old age. [16]And they shall come back here in the fourth generation, for the iniquity of the Amorites is not yet complete."

As I noted in *The Unseen Realm*:

> The historical material on the Amorites is sparse.[167] Broadly speaking, the Amorite culture was *Mesopotamian*. The term and the people are known from Sumerian and Akkadian material centuries older than the Old Testament and the time of Moses and the Israelites. The word for "Amorite" actually comes from a Sumerian word ("MAR.TU") which vaguely referred to the area and population west of Sumer and *Babylon*.

The Amorites, then, are a connection back to Babylon—back to the Mesopotamian context for the biblical "giant talk" that is intimately associated with Bashan and Hermon. This helps us make sense of the prophet Amos' recollection of the conquest of the land centuries earlier. Amos specifically connected the name with giants (Amos 2:9–10):

> [9]Yet it was I who destroyed the Amorite before them,
> whose height was like the height of the cedars

and who was as strong as the oaks;
I destroyed his fruit above
and his roots beneath.
[10]Also it was I who brought you up out of the land of Egypt
and led you forty years in the wilderness,
to possess the land of the Amorite.

The terminology (Amorite, Babylonian MAR.TU) and the description (giants) convey a connection to the Nephilim (Numbers 13:32–33; Genesis 6:1–4) and its Babylonian/Mesopotamian context. All the elements of the original context of Genesis 6:14, the Mesopotamian backstory of the apkallu, and the story of the Watchers in 1 Enoch 6–15 can be nicely dovetailed with the Amorites of Bashan and Mount Bashan. These are not disparate stories; they are constituent nodes of a matrix of ideas. And we're not done.

By the time of Moses, the giant clans in the Transjordan had largely been eliminated by Abraham's line through Esau. This is why Moses was told not to harass the people of Moab and Ammon (Deuteronomy 2:9–12, 19–22). Moses' trip through the Transjordan was providentially aimed at eliminating the last vestiges of the giant clans in the northern part of the Transjordan—Bashan.

Opposition to Israel among the Amorites was led by the kings Sihon of Heshbon and Og of Bashan (Deuteronomy 3). Joshua 12:5 records that Og "ruled over Mount Hermon and Salecah and all Bashan to the boundary of the Geshurites and the Maacathites." Og was a giant, as Deuteronomy 3:11 makes clear: "only Og the king of Bashan was left of the remnant of the Rephaim. Behold, his bed was a bed of iron. Is it not in Rabbah of the Ammonites?" Nine cubits was its length, and four cubits its breadth, according to the common cubit.[168] The ancient capital of Bashan was Ashtaroth.[169] Deuteronomy 1:4 and Joshua 12:4 note that Og also lived in Edrei. These two cities had very dark spiritual associations not only for Israelites, but Canaanites. As one scholar of Canaanite religion observes:

Biblical geographical tradition agrees with the mythological and cultic data of the Ugaritic texts…. [There is an] amazing correspondence with the Biblical tradition about the seat of king Og of Bashan, "one of the survivors of the Rephaim [Ugaritic: *rpum*], who lived in Ashtarot and Edrei" (Josh[ua] 12:4 [NEB]). This place *ʿštrt* is also treated in [tablets] *KTU* 1.100:41; 1.107:17; and RS 86.2235:17 as the abode of the god *mlk*, the eponym of the *mlkm*, the deified kings, synonym of the *rpum*. For the "Canaanites" of Ugarit, the Bashan region, or a part of it, clearly represented "Hell", the celestial and infernal abode of their deified dead kings…. It is possible that this localization of the Canaanite Hell is linked to the ancient tradition of the place as the ancestral home of their dynasty, the *rpum*. The Biblical text also recalls that "all Bashan used to be called the land/earth of the Rephaim" (Deut[eronomy] 3:13 [NEB]), an ambiguous wording that could equally be translated as "the 'hell' of the Rephaim." In any case, the link between Bashan and the *rpum*/Rephaim in both traditions speaks in favour of a very old use of the two meanings of this last denomination: ancient dwellers of Northern Transjordan / inhabitants of "Hell."[170]

Some important items here need development. First, by virtue of Ashtaroth and Edrei, the region of Bashan was associated with the underworld—Canaanite hell, so to speak. Second, the Rephaim were thought to dwell in the underworld. While it is true that Canaanite literature (such as the Ugaritic texts) does not describe the Rephaim (*rpum* in Ugaritic) as giants, the biblical texts certainly do. The Old Testament also has the Rephaim in the underworld/hell. Unfortunately, English translations typically prevent us from seeing this material. Consider the following passages from the English Standard Version:

- Job 26:5–6: "The dead [rephaim] tremble under the waters and their inhabitants. Sheol is naked before God, and Abaddon has no covering."

- Psalm 88:10: "Do you work wonders for the dead? Do the departed [*rephaim*] rise up to praise you?"
- Proverbs 21:6: "One who wanders from the way of good sense will rest in the assembly of the dead [*rephaim*]."
- Isaiah 14:9–15: "Sheol beneath is stirred up to meet you when you come; it rouses the shades [*rephaim*] to greet you, all who were leaders of the earth; it raises from their thrones all who were kings of the nations. All of them will answer and say to you: 'You too have become as weak as we! You have become like us!' Your pomp is brought down to Sheol, the sound of your harps; maggots are laid as a bed beneath you, and worms are your covers. 'How you are fallen from heaven, O Day Star, son of Dawn! How you are cut down to the ground, you who laid the nations low! You said in your heart, "I will ascend to heaven; above the stars of God I will set my throne on high; I will sit on the mount of assembly in the far reaches of the north; I will ascend above the heights of the clouds; I will make myself like the Most High." But you are brought down to Sheol, to the far reaches of the pit.'"

What does all this give us? It may not be apparent, but what we've just covered is the biblical justification for the teaching of 1 Enoch that demons are the spirits of dead giants.[171] To see that's the case, we need to review some of what we learned in earlier chapters.

The connection of the Rephaim giants with the underworld, the realm of the dead, should ring a bell. In our earlier discussion (chapters 2–3) of the Mesopotamian apkallu we noted that, after the events of the Flood, "apkallu" was a term used in Mesopotamian texts for the divine sages sent to the underworld Abyss by Marduk. They were the Mesopotamian equivalent of 1 Enoch's Watchers, imprisoned in the Abyss for their transgression with human women. Those Watchers were in turn the referent for Peter and Jude's descriptions of "angels that sinned" who were "in chains in gloomy darkness" (2 Peter 2:4; Jude 6).

But "apkallu" was also the label for giants like Gilgamesh, who were "of human descent." These hybrid apkallu were the correlates to Enoch's giants. According to 1 Enoch 15:8–12, when one such giant was killed, its departed spirit (its "Watcher part") was where demons came from:

> [8]But now the giants who were begotten by the spirits and flesh— they will call them evil spirits upon the earth, for their dwelling will be upon the earth. [9]The spirits that have gone forth from the body of their flesh are evil spirits, for from humans they came into being, and from the holy watchers was the origin of their creation. Evil spirits they will be on the earth, and evil spirits they will be called. [10]The spirits of heaven, in heaven is their dwelling; but the spirits begotten in the earth, on earth is their dwelling. [11]And the spirits of the giants lead astray, do violence, make desolate, and attack and wrestle and hurl upon the earth and cause illnesses. They eat nothing, but abstain from food and are thirsty and smite. [12]These spirits (will) rise up against the sons of men and against the women, for they have come forth from them.[172]

So what's the connection with Jesus? As I noted earlier, the whole region of Bashan would have been associated by Israelites and Jews with giants and evil spirits, including the Watchers. In the days of Jesus, this region went by different names. All of what preceded is the unknown (to us) backdrop to some familiar episodes in the Gospels.

THE GATES OF HELL

The "gates of hell" incident (Matthew 16:13–20) in Jesus' ministry is familiar to most Bible students. However, the geography is unfortunately ignored, an oversight that prevents us from understanding the impact of what Jesus said and did in a region theologically tethered to the Watchers.

The events of Matthew 16:13–20 took place at Caesarea Philippi, a city located in the northern part of what had been called Bashan, at the foot of Mount Hermon.[173] Jesus asked the disciples a famous question, "Who do people say that I am?" Peter answered, "You are the Christ, the Son of the living God." Then Jesus followed with this:

> Blessed are you, Simon Bar-Jonah! For flesh and blood has not revealed this to you, but my Father who is in heaven. And I tell you, you are Peter, and on this rock I will build my church, and the gates of hell shall not be able to withstand it. (Matthew 16:17–18)

This passage is among the most controversial in the Bible, as it is a focal point of debate between Roman Catholics and Protestants. The former argue that Peter is the rock upon which the church is established and thus the passage makes Peter the leader of the original church (and the first pope). Protestants insist the rock is a reference to God on analogy of passages like 1 Corinthians 10:4.

Both of these traditional understandings are incorrect. The reference to the rock is the place where they are standing—Caesarea Philippi at the foot of Mount Hermon. The apostate King Jereboam built an idolatrous worship center there (1 Kings 12) and the city adopted the worship of Baal practiced by the Canaanites since the days of Joshua in their city Baal-Gad (Joshua 11:17; cp. Judges 3:3). In Jesus' day, Caesarea Philippi was also called Panias, having been dedicated to the worship of Pan.

When viewed from this perspective, the scene takes place on geography considered *the gates of hell* in Old Testament times, the domain of Baal, the lord of the dead, and at the mountain where the plot of the Watchers was hatched. Hell, of course, wouldn't be complete without the devil. It is well known to scholars that Baal is the Old Testament counterpart to the devil. In Ugaritic, one of Baal's titles is *ba'al zebul 'arṣ* ("Prince Baal of the Underworld"), from which the New Testament Beelzebul and Beelzebub derive.[174] This isn't about who gets to be pope (or not). It's a cosmic confrontation, with Jesus challenging the authority of the lord of the dead.

The theological messaging couldn't be more dramatic. Jesus says the "gates of hell" will not prevail against the church. We often think of this phrase as though God's people are in a posture of having to bravely fend off Satan and his demons. This simply isn't correct. Gates are defensive structures, not offensive weapons. The kingdom of God is the aggressor. Jesus goes to ground zero in biblical demonic geography to announce that Bashan will be defeated. It is the gates of hell that are under assault—and they will *not* hold up against the church. Hell has no claim on those who align themselves with Jesus. He will reverse the curse of death and His own will rise on account of Him.

CLAIMING MOUNT HERMON

Matthew, Mark, and Luke all agree that the next event in the ministry of Jesus after Peter's confession was the Transfiguration:

> [2]And after six days Jesus took with him Peter and James and John, and led them up a high mountain by themselves. And he was transfigured before them, [3]and his clothes became radiant, intensely white, as no one on earth could bleach them. [4]And there appeared to them Elijah with Moses, and they were talking with Jesus. [5]And Peter said to Jesus, "Rabbi, it is good that we are here. Let us make three tents, one for you and one for Moses and one for Elijah." [6]For he did not know what to say, for they were terrified. [7]And a cloud overshadowed them, and a voice came out of the cloud, "This is my beloved Son; listen to him." [8]And suddenly, looking around, they no longer saw anyone with them but Jesus. (Mark 9:2–8)

In early church tradition, the location of the Mount of Transfiguration was believed by many to be Mount Tabor. The earliest witness to this tradition is the fourth century A.D., not the New Testament. The Gospels themselves give no name to the mountain. Some scholars still hold to the

Tabor identification, but many have come to agree that the close proximity to Caesarea Philippi, the necessary height of the mountain in the account, and the symbolic associations make Mount Hermon the logical choice for the transfiguration:

> Mount Hermon is a strong contender for the location of Jesus' transfiguration. In all three Synoptic Gospels, the transfiguration occurs shortly after Peter's confession, and both Matthew and Mark specify a "high mountain" (while Luke refers to "the mountain"). If these sections are to be taken chronologically, then Mount Hermon is the closest location that fits.[175]

The imagery is striking. Jesus picks Mount Hermon to reveal to Peter, James, and John exactly who He is—the embodied glory-essence of God, the divine Name made visible by incarnation. The meaning is just as transparent: *I'm putting the hostile powers of the unseen world on notice. I've come to earth to take back what is mine. The kingdom of God is at hand.*

This interpretation is justified by what Paul does with Psalm 68 and Mount Bashan (Hermon). Psalm 68:18, where Yahweh leads a host of captives, may sound familiar. Paul cites the verse in Ephesians 4:

Psalm 68:18:	**Ephesians 4:8:**
You have ascended on high; you have led away captives. You have received gifts from among humankind.	Therefore it says, "When he ascended on high he led a host of captives, and he gave gifts to men."

If you look closely, there seems to be a problem. Psalm 68 gives us a standard description of conquest. The victorious captain of the army leads the enemy captives behind him. They are the human booty of war. For Paul, Psalm 68:18 was about Jesus ascending on high and *giving* gifts to humanity. Jesus is somehow the fulfillment of Psalm 68. But the Old Testament text has God ascending and *receiving* gifts.

Part of the confusion is that so many commentators have assumed that captives are being *liberated* in Ephesians 4. That isn't the case. That idea would flatly contradict the well-understood Old Testament imagery. There is no liberation; there is *conquest*.

Paul's words identify Jesus with Yahweh. In Psalm 68:18, it was Yahweh who is described as the conqueror of the demonic stronghold. For Paul it is Jesus. He conquers demonic Bashan/Hermon and puts the powers of darkness "to an open shame by triumphing over them" (Colossians 2:15). Psalm 68:18 and Ephesians 4:8 are in agreement if one sees conquest, not liberation.

What about the "receiving" and "giving" problem? Paul's adaptation of the psalm doesn't deny there was conquest. It points to the *result* of the conquest. As I noted in *The Unseen Realm:*

> In the ancient world the conqueror would parade the captives and demand tribute for himself. Jesus is the conqueror of Psalm 68, and the booty does indeed rightfully belong to him. But booty was also distributed after a conquest. Paul knows that. He quotes Psalm 68:18 to make the point that after Jesus conquered his demonic enemies, he distributed the benefits of the conquest to his people, believers. Specifically, those benefits are apostles, prophets, evangelists, pastors, and teachers (Eph[esians] 4:11).

But how is Paul getting that idea? He explains his thinking in Ephesians 4:9–10:

> Therefore it says,
>   "When he ascended on high he led a host of captives, and he gave gifts to men."
>   (In saying, "He ascended," what does it mean but that he had also descended into the lower regions, the earth? He who descended is the one who also ascended far above all the heavens, that he might fill all things.)

Here was how I explained Paul's thinking in *The Unseen Realm:*

Christ's conquest results in the dispensing of gifts to his people after ascending (in conquest) in verse 8. But that ascent was accompanied by a descent ("into the lower regions").

Paul's logic is not at all clear, at least at first. What ascent and descent is he talking about?

The key to understanding Paul's thinking is the descent. There are two possible explanations. The most common view is that, upon his death, Jesus descended into the lower regions *of the earth.* This is the way Ephesians 4:9 is worded in many translations. In this case, the language speaks both of the grave and of cosmic Sheol, the Underworld. This is possible since elsewhere in the New Testament we read that Jesus descended into the Underworld to confront the "spirits in prison"—the original transgressing sons of God from Genesis 6 (1 Pet 3:18–22). But that visitation may not be Paul's point of reference here.

The second view is reflected in the ESV, which is the translation I used for Ephesians 4. Note that instead of "lower parts of the earth" the ESV inserts a comma: "the lower regions, the earth." The effect of the comma is that Jesus descended to "the lower regions, [in other words] *the earth.*" This option fits the context better (the gifts are given to people who are of course on earth) and has some other literary advantages. If this option is correct, then the descent of verses 9–10 does not refer to Jesus' time in the grave, but rather to the Holy Spirit's coming to earth after Jesus' conquering ascension on the day of Pentecost.[176]

What this means for the theme of reversing Hermon is straightforward. When Jesus chose to go to Mount Hermon to be transfigured, *He was claiming it for the Kingdom of God.* As the Gospel chronologies tell us, these events provoked His death, the linchpin event for reversing the human predicament and ensuring the defeat of the powers of darkness.

JESUS VS. THE WATCHER SPIRITS (DEMONS)

Scholars have noted that "the ancient boundaries of Bashan, although impossible to determine exactly, appear to be the area north of Gilead, west of Salecah and the Jebel Druze Mountains…south of Mount Hermon, and east of the Jordan and the Sea of Galilee."[177] This description means that another familiar episode in Jesus' ministry occurred within the territory of Bashan: the exorcism of Legion (Mark 5).

The reader should not miss the point made earlier. For Second Temple Jews, the demons Jesus encountered and defeated were Watcher-spirits, released at the death of the ancient Nephilim/Rephaim giants. The passage from 1 Enoch 15 included above makes that quite evident, as do the Dead Sea Scroll references to the Watchers as "bastard spirits." This term quite clearly views demons as the result of the death of the hybrid ("bastard") Nephilim offspring produced in the transgression of Genesis 6:1–4, Enoch's sin of the Watchers.[178] When Jesus confronts Legion, He is facing a collective of these entities. Mark records the dramatic encounter:

[1]They came to the other side of the sea, to the country of the Gerasenes. [2]And when Jesus had stepped out of the boat, immediately there met him out of the tombs a man with an unclean spirit. [3]He lived among the tombs. And no one could bind him anymore, not even with a chain, [4]for he had often been bound with shackles and chains, but he wrenched the chains apart, and he broke the shackles in pieces. No one had the strength to subdue him. [5]Night and day among the tombs and on the mountains he was always crying out and cutting himself with stones. [6]And when he saw Jesus from afar, he ran and fell down before him. [7]And crying out with a loud voice, he said, "What have you to do with me, Jesus, Son of the Most High God? I adjure you by God, do not torment me." [8]For he was saying to him, "Come out of the man, you unclean spirit!" [9]And Jesus asked him, "What is your name?" He replied, "My name is Legion, for we are many." [10]And he begged

him earnestly not to send them out of the country. [11]Now a great herd of pigs was feeding there on the hillside, [12]and they begged him, saying, "Send us to the pigs; let us enter them." [13]So he gave them permission. And the unclean spirits came out and entered the pigs; and the herd, numbering about two thousand, rushed down the steep bank into the sea and drowned in the sea.

Prior to Mark 5, as Israel's Messiah, Jesus had restricted His ministry to a Jewish audience. His focus changed in Mark 5:1 when He intentionally entered the country of the Gerasenes—Gentile territory.[179] Mark's wording is interesting. When Legion asks, "What have you to do with me?" the question echoes that of the unclean spirits cast out by Jesus in Mark 1:24 within the Jewish territory of Galilee—with a subtle but telling difference:

- (Demons in Jewish territory): "What have you to do with us, Jesus of Nazareth?" (Mark 1:24)
- (Legion in old Bashan): "What have you to do with me, Jesus, Son of the Most High God? (Mark 5:7)

Legion identifies Jesus as "Son of the Most High," a title that reflects the Old Testament theology of cosmic geography. Recall that in Deuteronomy 32:8–9, the "Most High" had disinherited the nations of the world, assigned them to the dominion of supernatural sons of God, and then created Israel as is own inheritance from nothing.[180] Those sons of God rebelled and became corrupt (Psalm 82:1–4), throwing God's order into chaos (Psalm 82:1–5).

The exorcism of Legion is therefore more than a strange tale of suicidal swine. It's about theological messaging. Legion recognizes that Jesus is rightful Lord of the country of the Gerasenes—old Bashan now under Gentile occupation.

These familiar episodes in the ministry of Jesus occur in the darkest, most spiritually sinister places known to Old Testament Israelites and

Jewish readers of the Old Testament. Bashan and Hermon were ground zero for spiritual evil and, in particular, the Watchers of 1 Enoch. The spiritual corruption of humanity would be healed by the atonement of the cross. His resurrection meant that no member of the kingdom of God would share living space with the Watchers in the underworld Abyss, the realm of the dead. Even an army of Watchers was overmatched by the Son of the Most High. They would be lords of nothing.

Section Preview

Part III

Reversing Hermon in the Epistles

We saw in the last section that the Gospel writers sought to associate the birth, genealogy, and ministry of Jesus with the theological theme of reversing the transgression of the Watchers on Mount Hermon. It should be no surprise, then, that the sin of the Watchers was on the mind of some of the apostolic contributors to the New Testament that we know as the epistles.

This section focuses on three items discussed in the letters of Paul and Peter where the story of the sin of the Watchers from 1 Enoch is clearly lurking in the conceptual background.

First, we will revisit the notion of how, for many Jews in the Second Temple Period, the proliferation of evil throughout humanity should not be laid at the feet of Adam, but of the Watchers. Contrary to the dominant Christian tradition, the Fall of Adam is not the exclusive touch-point for the depravity of humankind. Our study will show that New Testament theology is in concert with Second Temple Judaism—that the human problem is not exclusively owed to Adam's transgression. The sin of the Watchers was also part of apostolic theology in this regard. This will surprise many readers—just as the fact that certain influential early Christian fathers believed the same thing.

Second, we will bring the Enochian Watcher story to bear on one of the more befuddling passages in Paul's epistles: his comments about the head covering in 1 Corinthians 11. Paul explicitly connects his teaching on this matter to the Enochian story by telling his readers his teaching matters "because of the angels" (1 Corinthians 11:10). If we frame Paul's discussion in the context of the sin of the Watchers and trace the meaning of "covering" (Greek: *peribalaion*) in Greco-Roman texts familiar to his Gentile readers, the enigma of the head covering disappears.

Finally, 1 Peter 3:18–22, one of the epistle's most confounding passages, comes into clear focus by reading it against the backdrop of the transgression of the Watchers in 1 Enoch. Peter's inclusion of spirits in prison, the Flood, Noah, the resurrection, and spiritual powers of darkness being subject to Christ seems nonsensical and haphazard. Quite to the contrary, Peter's theological thinking is not only clear, but powerful—if we have the Enochian story in our minds, as he did.

7

THE SIN OF THE WATCHERS
AND HUMAN DEPRAVITY

I noted in an earlier chapter that for many Jews in the Second Temple Period, the proliferation of evil throughout humanity should not be laid at the feet of Adam, but of the Watchers. That is, contrary to what nearly all Christians are taught today, a large number of people living in the first century for whom the Old Testament was the Word of God, Adam's Fall was not the exclusive touchpoint for the doctrine of depravity. In this chapter, we'll look at how New Testament thinking about sin can be read the same way—and how important early church fathers would have agreed.

TWO REASONS FOR HUMAN DEPRAVITY,
NOT JUST ONE

There are two explanations for the human condition, the ever-present propensity for people to sin against God's will. There are texts from this period that locate the sin impulse within human nature itself and others that have the catalyst for human evil being the fallen Watchers.

To illustrate the former perspective, that human sin is an intrinsic problem, two Dead Sea Scrolls will suffice:

11Q5 XXIV.11–13

[11]Remove the sin of my childhood from me and may my offences not be remembered against me.

[12]Purify me, O yhwh, from evil plague, and may it stop coming back to [me]; dry up

[13]its roots from me, may its lea[ve]s not become green in me. Glory are you, yhwh.[181]

In her doctoral dissertation on the nature of sin in Second Temple Jewish Literature, Qumran scholar Miryam Brand observed about this passage: "Here the desire to sin is not simply a tendency to commit a sinful act; it is an internal toxin: a 'condition' of sinfulness from which the human must be freed (as opposed to merely a desire to do acts of sin)."[182]

Another Dead Sea Scroll that points to the idea of humanity's intrinsic sinfulness is 1QH[a] IX.21–25:

[21]These things I know through your knowledge, for you opened my ears to wondrous mysteries although I am a creature of clay, fashioned with water,

[22]a foundation of shame and a source of impurity, an oven of iniquity and a building of sin, a spirit of error and depravity without

[23]knowledge, terrified by your just judgments. What can I say which is not known? Or declare which has not been told? Everything

[24]has been engraved before you with the stylus of remembrance for all the incessant periods and the cycles of the number of everlasting years in all their predetermined times,

[25]and they will not be hidden, and will not be lacking from before you. How will a man count his sin? How will he defend his iniquities?[183]

Brand comments on this text: "The speaker does not claim that he is guilty of particular sins. Rather, as a member of humanity, he shares in its lowly and sinful state. He is a 'creature of clay' that has been 'kneaded with water.' It is clear from this passage that the human being is not merely weak, but sinful."[184]

The well-known Second Temple Jewish thinker Philo expressed a similar thought, specifically that Adam's sin was proof of an inherently human evil inclination to God (*Opif.* 155; *Fug.* 79–80; *Det.* 122; *Mut.* 183–185).

But this of course is only one perspective. Brand introduces the other trajectory this way:

> Numerous Second Temple texts attribute human sin to the temptation of demonic forces. In attributing human sin to demons, these texts suggest a motivation significantly different from the one behind texts that reflect the "innate inclination to sin" paradigm. Attributing the principal cause of sin to demons points to individual sin not as part of the human constitution, but as the result of a forceful demonic presence, or even a demonic age.[185]

For many readers, the idea of connecting human depravity to the sin of the Watchers (the "demons" in Brand's quotation) seems strange, even in regard to Genesis 6:1–4. Traditional interpretation has human sinfulness arising from within and that alone was justification for the Flood. Genesis 6:5 is the proof text for this approach: "The Lord saw that the wickedness of man was great in the earth, and that every intention of the thoughts of his heart was only evil continually."

Genesis 6:5 is actually part of a vexing problem for biblical interpreters. Put simply, it doesn't seem to have any coherent relationship to Genesis 6:1–4. This is especially true for those who seek to strip the supernatural elements out of the passage. For anyone reading Genesis 6:1–4 without knowledge of the polemic context for those verses, it's quite understandable that the first four verses don't seem at all to lead up to Genesis 6:5.

This problem can only be solved by reading Genesis 6:1–4 in light of its original polemic context—the apkallu story. As we saw in chapter 3, the knowledge of the apkallu aligned with high precision to the knowledge taught by the Watchers that corrupted humanity before the Flood. This means that, in terms of the original purpose of Genesis 6:1–4—to take shots at Babylonian theologizing of the Flood event—the passage does in fact relate to Genesis 6:5. Without an understanding of the apkallu polemic, this connection is lost to modern readers. Brand notes in this respect:

> Biblical scholars have attempted to determine the original meaning of this story independently of its context in the biblical account. However, for Jews in the Second Temple period, the episode's importance lay in its context in Genesis 6, where it serves as an introduction to the account of the flood. As most commentators note, the location of the "sons of God" passage prior to the account of the flood implies that there is a connection between the "sons of God" story and the flood that follows. The mating of divine beings with humans is related in Gen[esis] 6:1–4 neutrally and without any indication of moral misdoing, but here the mating becomes an indication of corruption, the illicit crossing of the boundary between human and divine. In this manner the flood that follows this account is justified; it results not only from the unspecified human evil related in Gen[esis] 6:5 (and in 6:12–13), but also from a complete breakdown of the boundary between the human and divine spheres.[186]

WATCHER-SPIRITS AFTER THE FLOOD

First Enoch and other Second Temple Jewish texts are clear enough on this point—that the fallen Watchers taught human beings various points of knowledge that corrupted humanity. But that raises a specific question found in both those ancient texts and in research conducted by modern readers: If the sinning Watchers were imprisoned in the Abyss and "didn't see the light of day" after the Flood, how could their knowledge propel the spread of wickedness among humanity after the Flood?

Neither the Old Testament nor books like 1 Enoch justifies the notion that there were enough giants after the Flood to provide an explanation for human depravity. Second Temple thinking made no such direct connection to human evil in this regard. Brand articulates the problem this way:

> There is no indication that the sin of the Watchers had any lasting demonic implications for humankind beyond the flood. The forbidden mysteries that have been revealed have apparently been "cleansed" from the earth by the flood (see 1 En[och] 10:7).... Yet while sinful knowledge has apparently survived, there is no continuing demonic presence after the flood. When the flood occurs, the giants have already been completely destroyed and the Watchers have been punished.... Even in the antediluvian [pre-Flood] era, in the story as it is told in 1 En[och] 6–11 the corrupting influence of the Watchers is confined to their teachings and does not stem from ongoing activity on their part. The Watchers do not continue to actively tempt humans to sin, but have rather given them the tools to do evil. It is this forbidden knowledge that is the ongoing "source" of sin in this account, rather than continuous actions by the Watchers. This knowledge is so terrible, implies the author (or redactor), that it must have originated with evil angels.[187]

Since human evil did indeed proliferate after the Flood, some scholars see a coherence problem for linking depravity to the sin of the Watchers. They presume that there is no post-Flood connection between evil Watchers and humanity, thereby making the linkage moot. But this overlooks an important detail in the 1 Enoch story.

The answer to this question has something to do with the Nephilim, the giants produced by the sinning Watchers. It matters not that the giants were destroyed in the Flood (or, in the biblical account, thereafter). Nor does it matter that the original offending heavenly sons of God are imprisoned, where the Second Temple traditions and the books of Peter and Jude place them. Why? Because the death of the Nephilim is the point of origin for demons.

There is no indication that demons, spirit beings, were destroyed by the Flood. As we saw in chapter 2, for Second Temple Jewish theology—elements of which are evident in the Old Testament passages that have the Rephaim dead in hell/the underworld—demons were very much a part of the human experience of evil. These demons are explicitly identified as Watcher spirits in 1 Enoch. More specifically, 1 Enoch 15:8–16:1 puts forth the idea that these demonic spirits continue to corrupt humanity after the Flood:

> (15)[8]But now the giants who were begotten by the spirits and flesh—they will call them evil spirits upon the earth, for their dwelling will be upon the earth.
> [9]The spirits that have gone forth from the body of their flesh are evil spirits, for from humans they came into being, and from the holy watchers was the origin of their creation. Evil spirits they will be on the earth, and evil spirits they will be called.
> [10]The spirits of heaven, in heaven is their dwelling; but the spirits begotten in the earth, on earth is their dwelling.
> [11]And the spirits of the giants lead astray, do violence, make desolate, and attack and wrestle and hurl upon the earth and cause illnesses. They eat nothing, but abstain from food and are thirsty and smite.
> [12]These spirits (will) rise up against the sons of men and against the women, for they have come forth from them.
> (16)[1]From the day of the slaughter and destruction and death of the giants, from the soul of whose flesh the spirits are proceeding,

they are making desolate without (incurring) judgment. Thus they will make desolate until the day of the consummation of the great judgment, when the great age will be consummated. It will be consummated all at once.[188]

Nickelsburg's comments on this passage are important:

The giants' death is the prelude and presupposition for the continued violent and disastrous activity of their spirits, which goes on unpunished until the final judgment. The consequences of the watchers' sin are in keeping with the author's understanding of the nature of that sin. Since the watchers are heavenly, spiritual, and immortal, the divine spirit with which they have endowed their sons is uneradicable in the normal course of events. The death of their human side serves only to free that spirit for further activity. Moreover, as one can see from their activities, the giants have inherited the wicked, rebellious side of their fathers' nature. The freed spirits of the dead giants constitute a demonic realm that carries on the activities for which the giants were judged and punished according to chaps. 6–11.… The giants and the spirits that proceed from their dead bodies are spoken of as the same entities. The watchers' willful confusion of the created order has had its inevitable results.… Because of their dual nature, the giants are both eradicable and immortal. On the one hand, the body of their flesh can die. On the other hand, their spirits have continued existence.… Because they were begotten on earth, these spirits must remain on earth. Here they constitute an empire of evil spirits who wreak all manner of havoc on the human race.[189]

First Enoch 16:2–4 actually considers the continuity of this corruption so significant that it becomes part of the rationale for why the original now-imprisoned Watchers who cohabited with human women before the Flood will have no opportunity for redemption:

²And now (say) to the watchers who sent you to petition in their behalf, who formerly were in heaven,

³"You were in heaven, and no mystery was revealed to you;
but a stolen mystery you learned;
and this you made known to the women in your hardness of heart;
and through this mystery the women and men are multiplying evils upon the earth.'

⁴Say to them, "You will have no peace."[190]

Other Second Temple Period material makes the same theological point—the demonic Watcher spirits after the Flood played a role in human depravity. For instance, the Dead Sea Scroll 4Q 510 (4QShir^a) Fragment 1 includes the post-Flood Watchers ("bastard spirits"; line 5) in its indictment:

¹…praises. Bless[ings to the Ki]ng of glory. Words of thanksgiving in psalms of

²[splendour] to the God of knowledge, the glory of the po[werful] ones, God of gods, Lord of all the holy ones. [His] rea[lm]

³is above the powerful mighty, and before the might of his powe[r] all are terrified and scatter; they flee before the radiance of

⁴of his glorious majestic strong[hold]. *Blank* And I, a Sage, declare the splendour of his radiance in order to frighten and terr[ify]

⁵all the spirits of the ravaging angels and the bastard spirits, demons, Lilith, owls and [jackals…]

⁶and those who strike unexpectedly to lead astray the spirit of knowledge, to make their hearts forlorn. And you have been placed in the era of the rul[e of]

⁷wickedness and in the periods of humiliation of the sons of lig[ht], in the guilty periods of [those] defiled by iniquities; not for an everlasting destruction

⁸[but ra]ther for the era of the humiliation of sin. [*Blank*] Rejoice, righteous ones, in the wonderful God.

[9]My psalms are for the upright. *Blank* And for [… May] a[l]l those of perfect behaviour praise [h]im.[191]

Brand observes:

In this passage the "bastard spirits" are simply one type of the numerous demonic spirits who "strike suddenly to lead a spirit of understanding astray." The demons listed are drawn mainly from Isa[iah] 13:21and Isa[iah] 34:14, where the day of divine wrath includes the abandonment of the dwelling-places of the wicked to the unbridled forces of nature. These forces include wild animals as well as demonic figures…anarchic forces who, like other evil spirits, cause humans to transgress the divine will.[192]

THE OLD TESTAMENT LAW: ADDED BECAUSE OF WHOSE TRANSGRESSIONS?

How does the idea that the sin of the Watchers as told in 1 Enoch matter for New Testament theology? The answer is found in something Paul says about the Old Testament Law.

In his scholarly paper on the "bastard spirits" (the Watchers) and Galatians 3–4, New Testament scholar Tyler Stewart introduces us to the connection:

Paul's view of the Law has baffled scholars such that he has been accused of self-contradiction and inconsistency. While Paul praises the Law (Rom[ans] 7:12, 14) and recognizes its authority in his arguments (Rom[ans] 3:21, 31), he also makes startling claims that it is no longer relevant after the advent of Christ (Rom[ans] 10:4; 2 Cor[inthians] 3:6–9, 14–15). The difficulties of Paul's view are perhaps nowhere more pronounced than in Galatians 3–4 where the law appears almost entirely negative.

After a dense argument for the superiority of faith in Christ against "works of law" (Gal[atians] 3:1–18) Paul raises a logical question, "Why then the law? (3:19a). If the works of law do not justify (Gal[atians] 2:16; 3:11), place humanity under a curse (Gal[atians] 3:10–11), and the Law itself only added after the Abrahamic promise (Gal[atians] 3:17), then why bother at all? …Paul claims that for the Galatian believers to observe "works of the law," particularly circumcision (Gal[atians] 5:2–4; 6:12–13; also 1 Cor[inthians] 7:18) and calendar (Gal[atians] 4:10), is tantamount to rejecting Christ (Gal[atians] 5:2–4; 2:21). How can Paul make such a derogatory claim about the Torah?

Contemporary NT scholars find it nearly impossible to imagine a zealous Second Temple Jew, and a Pharisee no less (Phil[lippians] 3:5–6; Gal[atians] 1:13–14), thinking about the Law in this way. Nevertheless, subordination of Mosaic Law is not entirely unknown in Second Temple Judaism. In a rather unique parallel, subordination of Mosaic Law also appears in 1 Enoch. In fact, there are a number of striking parallels between 1 Enoch, particularly the Book of Watchers (*BW* 1 En[och] 1–36), Jubilees, and Paul's argument in Galatians 3–4. First, both 1 Enoch and Galatians subordinate the Torah as the pinnacle of revelation in similar ways. Second, there is a shared emphasis on the cosmic significance of transgressions in each text. Third, all three works are concerned with angels and their relationship to the structure of the cosmos. Tracing these parallels indicates that Paul's argument about the role of the Law in Gal[atians] 3:19–4:11 is influenced by an Enochic etiology of evil.[193]

Two items in this excerpt capture our attention: the "cosmic significance of transgressions" and how that relates to seeing how the Enochian view of evil being connected to the Watchers influenced Paul's thinking.

After Stewart devotes considerable space to showing how, for many Second Temple Jews, the revelation given to Enoch during his time in the heavens with God and His council was superior to the Law, he zeroes in on the cosmic nature of the transgressions Paul talks about.[194] He writes:

> Turning to Paul in Galatians, the significance of Mosaic Torah is, similar to Enoch literature, downplayed based on chronology and universality. In regard to chronology, Paul argues that justification by faith is prior to Torah. He connects his gospel to the promise to Abraham in Genesis 12:13.... Later he argues that the promises spoken to Abraham have priority over Torah (Gal[atians] 3:17 [Exodus 12:40–41; cf. Genesis 15:13]).... In Paul's view Sinai is ancillary to the promise given to Abraham, which he understands to be fulfilled in Christ (Gal[atians] 3:16, 19). This argument is explicit in Gal 3:19 when Paul writes: "the Law was *added*."... In addition to chronological priority, Paul is emphatic that the universal revelation of the gospel cannot be limited to one particular people. He understands his personal calling, announcing Christ to the Gentiles, to be a *revelation* directly from God (Gal[atians] 1:1, 10–12, 16; 2:2, 7) and any threat to the universality of this revelation to be *anathema* (Gal[atians] 1:6–9; 2:14).[195]

With respect to "cosmic transgressions," the key statement is found in Galatians 3:19: "Why then the law? It was added because of transgressions, until the offspring should come to whom the promise had been made, and it was put in place through angels by an intermediary."[196] Stewart observes:

> It is common to interpret Paul arguing here that the function of the Law is to cause, produce, or provoke transgressions. This interpretation is based on the preposition χάριν ("because of") and Paul's teaching about the Law elsewhere in his letters (esp. Rom[ans] 4:15; 5:20; also Rom[ans] 3:20; 5:13; 7:5, 7–24; 1 Cor[inthians] 15:56). While this meaning is not impossible, it has been rightly challenged. One of the stronger arguments

against this interpretation is that ancient interpreters, including John Chrysostom and Clement of Alexandria, did not read Gal[atians] 3:19 describing the Law as causing transgression, but rather the prior condition that prompted God to give the law. In their interpretations the Law was given "because of transgressions," meaning <u>to restrain transgression</u>. John Riches even indicates that interpreting the Law as producing transgression was an innovation of Luther. With so much attention given to this preposition, no one asks <u>whose transgressions prompt the addition of the Law</u>?

Apparently it is assumed without comment that the transgressions are Adam's. This is not surprising since the dominant etiology of evil in contemporary Christian theology is the "Fall" of Gen[esis] 3. This is due in large part to Paul's account of sin and death resulting from Adam's transgression in Rom[ans] 5:12–21 (also 1 Cor[inthians] 15:21–22, 45–49). Surprisingly, however, apart from 4 Ezra (3:20–22; 7:116–126), 2 Baruch (54:13–22), and the Life of Adam and Eve (esp. Vit. Adae 12–17; GLAE 15–26), <u>the story of Genesis 3 was not the primary text for explaining the origin of evil in Second Temple Judaism</u>…. Certainly Paul makes explicit reference to Adam in Romans 5, but there is no indication that Paul is alluding to the Adam cycle in Galatians 3–4. <u>Moreover, Romans specifies that the singular "transgression" belongs to the "one Adam" (5:14), whereas in Galatians it is "transgressions" in the plural that prompt the addition of the Law</u>. What if Paul is working from a different etiology of evil in Galatians 3–4? The key text in the Hebrew Bible for describing the origin and effects of evil in Second Temple Judaism was not Genesis 3, but Genesis 6:1–4…. This Enochic etiology of evil, namely that angelic "Sons of God" produced illegitimate offspring with human women and thereby altered the cosmos, was pervasive in Second Temple Judaism and early Christianity.[197]

We've already seen that many Jews gave weight to the Watchers' transgression, Enoch's version of Genesis 6:1–4, as the reason for human depravity. The statement that Genesis 3 was not the chief proof text for human sin should not be as surprising as it probably is. Consider the Old Testament. Despite repeated descriptions of the sinfulness of humankind, there isn't a single citation of Genesis 3 or Adam's Fall in the entire Old Testament for an explanation of human depravity.

So, when Paul says the law "was added because of transgressions," just whose transgressions does he have in mind? Since he refers to *plural* transgressions, and not merely to Adam's Fall, the witness of Second Temple Judaism is that Paul would be utterly alone if he *wasn't* thinking of the Watchers.

This perspective would make sense in that the sin of the Watchers was viewed as the catalyst to human depravity, but also causing cosmic upheaval. In 1 Enoch 2:11 the celestial luminaries created by God "do not *transgress* their own appointed order." But tragically, the Watchers are later identified as "the stars of heaven which have transgressed the commandments of the Lord and are bound in this place until the completion of ten million years, (according) to the number of their sins" (1 Enoch 21:6; cf. 18:15).

Jude borrows this language when he compares false teachers to the angels that sinned. They are "wandering stars, for whom the gloom of utter darkness has been reserved forever" (Jude 13). Noted New Testament scholar Richard Bauckham writes of this verse:

> It is widely agreed that Jude has borrowed this image from 1 Enoch. Jewish apocalyptic thought of the heavenly bodies as controlled by angels (see, e.g., 1 Enoch 82), and inherited Oriental myths in which the apparently irregular movements of the planets were attributed to the disobedience of heavenly beings, and probably also such phenomena as comets and meteors were interpreted as heavenly beings falling from heaven (cf. Isa[iah] 14:12–15; Rev[elation] 8:10; 9:1). Thus

in 1 Enoch 18:13–16; 21:3–6, the Watchers (whose fall from heaven and judgment Jude mentioned in v 6) are represented as seven stars "which transgressed the command of the Lord from the beginning of their rising because they did not come out at their proper times" (18:15; cf. 21:6). This imagery is taken up in the later Book of Dreams (1 Enoch 83–90), which in its allegory of world history represents the fall of the Watchers as the fall of stars from heaven (86:1–3); then, in a passage corresponding to 1 Enoch 10 (which Jude quoted in v 6) the archangels cast the stars down into the darkness of the Abyss and bind them there (88:1, 3) until their judgment at the end, when they will be cast into the Abyss of fire (90:24).[198]

THE BIRTH OF THE SON OF GOD AND THE REVERSAL OF THE WATCHERS' TRANSGRESSIONS

In this perspective—that the transgressions that prompted the giving of the law were those of the Watchers—the law was added *to restrain evil.* That is, Galatians 3:19 is not to be read as though the law *produced* transgressions the way Christian tradition commonly reads it. If this be the case, then Paul is consistent in both viewing the law as something positive, but also viewing it as something inadequate. Stewart sees this clearly:

> Paul's reference to Jesus' birth in Gal[atians] 4:4 is illuminated by the Watchers narrative. Jesus' divine mission is contrasted with the angelic rebellion. The Sons of God in the *BW* rebel in heaven (1 En[och] 6:1–6) and "enter" human women on earth (7:1). In Galatians, however, when the "fullness of time has come" God sends his Son to be born "from a woman" (Gal[atians] 4:5), thus Jesus' divinely ordained mission, accomplished birth from a woman is contrasted with the rebellion of Angels entering women.

Both texts bring heaven and earth together through divine sons involved with human women.

The results of Jesus' and the Watchers' actions are also contrasted. Initially, the transgressions of the Watchers produce illegitimate offspring that destroy the earth (1 En[och] 7:1–3; 10:9–10, 15; Jub[ilees] 5:2). After the initial judgment of the Flood, the disembodied spirits of their illegitimate sons enter humans to attack them, causing disease, blindness, and destruction (1 En[och] 15:11–12; 19:1; Jub[ilees] 10:1, 8; Justin, 2 Apol 5; cf. 1 Cor[inthians] 8:4–6; 10:20–22). The Watcher's "fall" is so severe, that they must ask the human Enoch to serve as their intercessor (1 En[och] 15:2). They no longer have access to God in prayer. In parallel contrast, Jesus as the Son of God faithfully gives himself to rescue humanity from the "present evil age" (Gal[atians] 4:5; 1:4; 2:20; also Rom[ans] 5:10; 8:32). After his exaltation in resurrection, the "spirit of God's son" is sent into the hearts of believers so that they can share in his sonship (Gal[atians] 4:6; Rom[ans] 8:9–11, 15). This indwelling Spirit gives believers legitimate sonship enacted through direct prayer (Gal[atians] 4:5; Rom[ans] 8:14–15, 26–27). In both narratives the cosmos is altered and humanity affected. Just as Enoch was ironically glorified in the Watchers descent, believers are glorified in Jesus' descent and ascent.

These contrasting parallels show that the birth of God's son in Galatians offers legitimate sonship to humanity to counteract the transgression of the Watchers and their bastard sons who terrorize the earth.[199]

Reversing cosmic upheaval required something greater than the law. It required a Messiah whose atoning death would ripple throughout the cosmos, healing the entire creation. The birth, death, and resurrection of the Son of God reconciles *all things, whether on earth or in heaven* (Colossians 1:19) and holds the entire creation together (Colossians 1:16–17).

EARLY CHURCH TESTIMONY TO THE
WATCHERS AND HUMAN DEPRAVITY

Given that modern Christians are only taught one explanation for human depravity instead of the two that New Testament writers would have embraced, the fact that certain early church fathers acknowledged the role of the Watchers' transgressions in human depravity is largely unknown. Irenaeus, for example, taught both explanations for the proliferation of sin.[200] D. R. Schultz explains:

> We know that Irenaeus contrasts Adam and Christ more or less as does Paul in Romans 5 and 1 Corinthians 15. In fact, Irenaeus's use of these passages, combined with some texts of Ephesians, in this view, formed the basis upon which the early Church Father constructed his Adam-Christ typology, in which the first Adam is paralleled with the second Adam.... Also, it is well known that Satan appears in the writings of Irenaeus as the "tempter" of Adam. However, Irenaeus often bypasses Adam in his treatment of Satan and angels, so that this evil spirit world directly brings about mankind's sinful condition. In effect, then, Irenaeus sometimes attributes the origin of sin directly to Satan and his forces in terms strongly reminiscent of 1 Enoch, Jubilees, and other late Jewish pseudepigraphical writings.... Irenaeus explicitly states this about the devil, "who first became the cause of apostasy to himself and afterwards to others." The "others" and first to follow Satan in apostasy are a group of angels who revolted from a state of submission to God. Many passages [in Irenaeus] speak of the apostasy.... Irenaeus definitely understands that there exists a causal relationship between Genesis 6:1–4 and the wickedness that follows in Genesis 6:5. But he need not have come to such an understanding without some assistance, because this speculation on Genesis had already been worked out and set down in Jewish pseudepigraphical literature.[201]

Citing Irenaeus' treatises *Against Heresies* and *Proof of the Apostolic Preaching*, Schultz demonstrates how Irenaeus embraced all the main elements of 1 Enoch's story of the transgression of the Watchers—including in his doctrine of human depravity:

> Irenaeus has two different descriptions of the angels defiling mankind. One description is concerned with "unlawful unions" of angels with offspring from the daughters of men. This "unlawful union" produces "giants" upon the earth which cause man's sinfulness; and these giants, which Irenaeus calls the "infamous race of men" [who] performed fruitless and wicked deeds…. According to Irenaeus the other manner in which the angels brought about man's defilement was through evil teachings…. Irenaeus enumerates those teachings as follows: "the virtues of roots and herbs, and dyeing and cosmetics, and discoveries of precious materials, love philtres, hatreds, amours, passions, constraints of love, the bonds of witchcraft, every sorcery and idolatry, hateful to God."

Irenaeus isn't the only early church father who saw 1 Enoch's sin of the Watchers behind certain New Testament passages and apostolic theology. Tertullian is well known for having suggested that the Watchers' transgression is the explanation for Paul's enigmatic command for women to cover their heads "because of the angels" (1 Corinthians 11:10).[202] That passage requires a chapter of its own.

8

THE SIN OF THE WATCHERS AND THE HEAD COVERING OF 1 CORINTHIANS 11

1 Corinthians 11:2–16 is one of the most enigmatic passages in Paul's letters. Paul's discussion of women and public worship presents a number of exegetical challenges. With respect to the present study, one specific puzzling element of Paul's thought will draw our attention—that women should have their heads covered "because of the angels" (1 Corinthians 11:10). Several interpretations have been offered in the long history of scholarship on this phrase and the passage as a whole. This chapter will demonstrate that the most sensible alternative is that Paul had the sin of the Watchers and its supernatural reading of Genesis 6:1–4 in view.

FLAWED INTERPRETIVE OPTIONS

1 Corinthians 11:2–16 reads as follows:

> [2]Now I commend you because you remember me in everything and maintain the traditions even as I delivered them to you. [3]But

I want you to understand that the head of every man is Christ, the head of a wife is her husband, and the head of Christ is God. [4]Every man who prays or prophesies with his head covered dishonors his head, [5]but every wife who prays or prophesies with her head uncovered dishonors her head, since it is the same as if her head were shaven. [6]For if a wife will not cover her head, then she should cut her hair short. But since it is disgraceful for a wife to cut off her hair or shave her head, let her cover her head. [7]For a man ought not to cover his head, since he is the image and glory of God, but woman is the glory of man. [8]For man was not made from woman, but woman from man. [9]Neither was man created for woman, but woman for man. [10]That is why a wife ought to have a symbol of authority on her head, because of the angels. [11]Nevertheless, in the Lord woman is not independent of man nor man of woman; [12]for as woman was made from man, so man is now born of woman. And all things are from God. [13]Judge for yourselves: is it proper for a wife to pray to God with her head uncovered? [14]Does not nature itself teach you that if a man wears long hair it is a disgrace for him, [15]but if a woman has long hair, it is her glory? For her hair is given to her for a covering. [16]If anyone is inclined to be contentious, we have no such practice, nor do the churches of God. (ESV)

There are three primary scholarly proposals for what Paul is thinking with respect to his angelic warning. Loren Stuckenbruck, a scholar whose work focuses on the angelology and demonology of the New Testament and Second Temple Judaism, summarizes the options:[203]

1. Paul was simply referring to *human* ἄγγελοι (*angeloi*), messengers or envoys from other churches. Paul is concerned that they will be offended by uncovered (i.e., unveiled) women in the Corinthian church. A parallel (so this view argues) is 1 Cor 14:23 ("If, therefore, the whole church comes together and all

speak in tongues, and outsiders or unbelievers enter, will they not say that you are out of your minds").[204] An alternative to the human envoy view is that the *angeloi* were hostile, unbelieving spies in the churches.[205]

2. The angels are to be regarded as supernatural beings in God's service who are guardians of the created order. Paul fears that gender roles might be transgressed, thereby offending the angels who guard creation order.[206]

3. Paul is referring to supernatural beings thought to be present within the local church, assigned by God to ensure community purity and proper worship. The emphasis here is church order, not creation order.

There are serious flaws with each of the first three options.

In regard to the first option, while it is true that the Greek word *angelos* is used in the New Testament of human messengers (Matthew 11:10; Luke 7:24; 9:52; James 2:25), the term is not used elsewhere by Paul with this transparent meaning.[207] A greater weakness is the assumption behind the view, drawn from 1 Corinthians 14:23, that these envoys were experienced, spiritually mature believers sent to other churches for the purpose of ministry. Paul's language *in that passage* undermines the idea. Paul warns the Corinthians about "outsiders" (Greek: *idiotēs*, "untrained") and "unbelievers" (*apistoi*, "those without faith") visiting the church, not official envoys sent to minister. As Garland notes, "One is hard put, however, to figure out how a reference to human leaders in the church connects in any way to what Paul says here."[208]

The second view is hardly better than the first, as it suffers from internal inconsistency (what does cosmic order have to do with hairstyles?), and a lack of external support in Second Temple Judaism. Stuckenbruck observes:

Unquestionably, Paul is concerned with maintaining distinctions within divine order, both in 11:2–16 and in 1 Corinthians as a whole…. Angels guard this order—here the distinction between man and woman—and, presumably, would take offence at a practice which violates this order as set forth in verses 3 and 8–9. A difficulty with this interpretation is that, surprisingly, there is hardly an instance in early or rabbinic Jewish tradition in which angelic beings are specifically assigned such a role, to say nothing about what such guardian angels would have had to do with the coiffure of women.[209]

The third view is more promising than the first two, though it also had problems.[210] This view has been most forcefully put forth by Joseph Fitzmyer. However, he acknowledges: "Though many details about the wearing of the veil in antiquity, both by Jewish and Greek women, have been preserved for us, none of them bears directly on the problem of the church in Corinth. We do not know the exact nature nor the origin of the abuse Paul was trying to handle."[211]

Several Dead Sea Scrolls appear to speak to Paul's angelic theology in 1 Corinthians 11:10.[212] These texts describe a role for angels with respect to the ritual purity of the Qumran community. Stuckenbruck summarizes the idea this way:

These Qumran texts, in turn, reflect the belief, more widely attested among the Dead Sea documents, that the community (and, possibly other communities as well) related its self-understanding to the presence of angels in their midst…. Among the *Songs of the Sabbath Sacrifice,* extant mostly through the Cave 4 manuscripts from Qumran (4Q400–407; see 11Q17 and the Masada manuscript), the community describes the heavenly worship of the angels; the members of this community are said to stand in awe of the privilege they have to participate in this angelic cultus (4Q400 ii, lines 5–7). Angelic worship is thus described as exemplary, and this inspires the human community to declare about the angelic *elim:* "they are honoured among all the camps of the *elohim* and revered by human councils." Clearly, the presence of angels in the community was related, not only to its members' general sense of well-being but also represented a form of cultic worship that to which the community aspired.[213]

While I will argue below that Paul's teaching in 1 Corinthians 11:2–16 does indeed have *something* to do with creation order and order in the church, this view isolates that connection to liturgy. There is also the assumption that Paul would command *Gentile* churches to accord with the practices of the Jewish Qumran sect. Stuckenbruck senses this issue and points to a transparent inconsistency and Fitzmyer's effort to resolve it:

Of course, one glaring difference that comparison reveals is the presence of women in the Christian worshiping community. The Dead Sea documents do not envisage women as full participants in the present, heavenly, or even eschatological cultus. To the extent that Christian men and women, especially those of Jewish descent, fell heir to such traditions, they would have been aware of the new status given to the woman in the post-resurrection era, when circumcision—from which women had been excluded by definition—no longer functioned as a requirement for full admission into the participation in worship…. Paul would have instructed the women of the congregation to cover themselves, in accordance with the woman's secondary appearance in the order of creation and because her δόξα ("glory") is different from that given to men. Fitzmyer explains, in analogy to the Dead Sea texts, that the unveiled woman would have been perceived by the angels as a "bodily defect" to be excluded from the assembly. The covering would, then, be a way for compensating for this deficiency, especially so in the presence of holy angels, with whom are associated an exemplary, heavenly, and pure worship of God…. Thus, in 11:10 Paul would be seen to advocate head coverings

for women out of respect for the angels with whom the congrega-
tions' members understand themselves to be worshiping God.[214]

Despite Fitzmyer's effort, Stuckenbruck points out several difficulties
with Fitzmyer's thesis, namely that:

> It presupposes that Paul would have imagined that physical defects
> are sufficient reason for exclusion from the Christian community,
> since women are, on argument, being instructed to cover their
> heads on account of their association with other defects which,
> according to Leviticus 21:18–23 and the Dead Sea materials, are
> inadmissible to the cult.... Secondly, and more of a difficulty, the
> tradition-historical background invoked by Fitzmyer does not
> directly bear on the presence or activity of *women* in the religious
> community...[and that] it relies wholly on analogy and does not
> help to account for the head covering (and by women!) in and of
> itself.[215]

In other words, Fitzmyer's view only provides an analogy (in his
mind) for "marking" women in a religious community. It never provides
an explanation for what "covering the head because of the angels" actually
means.

A MORE PERSUASIVE ALTERNATIVE

There is a fourth alternative, one that Stuckenbruck considers workable
"despite the fact that variations of it have been so categorically dismissed
by a number of scholars."[216] This alternative is that Paul's teaching in 1
Corinthians 11:2–16 and his statements about women and their "head
covering" in particular harken back to the sin of the Watchers in 1 Enoch.
This will no doubt sound strange to many readers. In what follows, I will

contend that Paul's teaching in 1 Corinthians 11:2–16 did indeed have *something* to do with creation order and order in worship, but that something was informed by the violation of the cosmic order found in Genesis 6:1–4.[217]

Before turning our attention to what I believe is the key to connecting 1 Corinthians 11 to the transgression of the Watchers, it is worth noting how Stuckenbruck defends an Enochian view. He writes:

> Although the wearing of head coverings among men in antiquity was not uncommon, the practice among women carried with it strong sexual connotations. Apparel was, of course, one way of marking the differences—or, better, boundaries—between the sexes, that is, to keep gender categories distinct.… The notion in Graeco-Roman antiquity of female vulnerability and inferiority, assumed in many Jewish sources, and the attendant practice of prophylactic head covering fit well with the early Jewish mythological interpretations of Gen[esis] 6:1–4. With regard to this, NT scholars have customarily focused on the essentially evil character of the angels who "fell" because they were attracted by the beauty of the "human daughters." This would be much in line with the Book of Watchers of 1 Enoch (see chapters 7–8) and the Book of Giants.… [Paul's] reasons for commending head coverings are unable to break away from the deep-seated assumption that women constitute the locus where boundaries between different parts of the cosmos are most likely to be violated.… Paul's reference to the angels betrays a subtle warning that more than just social relationships between men and women are at stake; ultimately, wearing veils is a matter of maintaining the cosmic order. The head coverings are prophylactic in the sense that they protect this order by helping to draw boundaries between distinct, yet sometimes socially overlapping, spheres more clearly. These boundaries, which have structured the universe since creation,

are to be respected.... The head coverings also function to keep women distinct from the angels who, for the sake of this argument, are considered an essentially different order of creation.[218]

This perspective can be summarized as follows. The covering for women was commended to protect women from sexual scandal in society *and* supernatural violation by angels. This dual rationale focused on social boundaries and sexual vulnerability, along with the precedent of angelic violation of women in the past.

BOLSTERING THE ARGUMENT: PAUL'S VOCABULARY IN CONTEXT

The key to demonstrating the coherence of this viewpoint is careful consideration of the vocabulary for the "head covering" in the context of Greco-Roman "scientific" texts widely known in Paul's day. Once the meaning of the pertinent vocabulary is comprehended in context, it will become clear that, with respect to church order, Paul was concerned with sexual modesty and fidelity, and that the violation of Genesis 6:1–4 never reoccur.

Our discussion of the vocabulary will focus on the Greek word *peribolaion*. This term and 1 Corinthians 11:2–16 recently received focused attention in a premier scholarly journal for biblical studies. The exchange was launched by New Testament scholar Troy Martin, who put forth a controversial proposal that sounds truly bizarre but that nevertheless has profound explanatory power for this perplexing passage. Martin began his study by drawing attention to verses 13–15, in which we find the crucial Greek term:

Paul's notorious argument in 1 Cor[inthians] 11:2–16 for the veiling of women in public worship is frequently criticized for being logically convoluted and confused.... While many features of this argument in 1 Cor[inthians] 11:2–16 require explanation, the argument from nature in vv. 13–15 is particularly problematic. The rationale for the natural shame of a man with long hair is obscure (vv. 14–15a). Especially problematic is the statement that a woman's long hair is given to her instead of a covering (*anti peribolaion*) in v. 15b. As traditionally understood, this statement nullifies the previous argument that a woman should wear a covering since her long hair apparently serves that purpose. A satisfactory explanation of this argument from nature should resolve the apparent contradiction and enable this argument to support Paul's contention that women should wear the veil in public worship.... The term *peribolaion* in v. 15b provides the key for explaining this argument from nature.[219]

Martin proceeds to note that scholars have capably produced evidence that *peribolaion* is a general word that can often be well translated "covering" with reference to some article of clothing. But he quickly adds that "Even though...scholars have identified the dominant semantic domain of this word, the term *peribolaion* has a much broader semantic range."[220] He then proceeds to unload his controversial thesis:

Since *peribolaion* is contrasted with hair, which is part of the body, the physiological semantic domain of *peribolaion* in 1 Cor[inthians] 11:15b becomes particularly relevant. Euripides (*Herc fur* 1269) uses *peribolaion* in reference to a body part. He casts Hercules as complaining, "After I received [my] bags of flesh, which are the outward signs of puberty, [I received] labors about which I [shall] undertake to say what is necessary."... A dynamic translation of the first clause would be: "After I received my testicles (*peribolaia*), which are the outward signs of puberty." In this text from Euripides, the term *peribolaion* refers to a testicle.

What Martin is saying may not be clear due to its peculiarity. He is suggesting that Paul is comparing a woman's hair to a testicle. This of course sounds like absolute nonsense, but, amazingly, there is no shortage of data to support this understanding of *peribolaion*. Martin proceeds to comb through Greek medical texts by physicians like Hippocrates, the namesake of the Hippocratic oath all physicians still swear to in modern times. These texts make Martin's thesis—and its explanatory power—quite clear. Martin lays out the case:

> Ancient medical conceptions confirm this association. Hippocratic authors hold that hair is hollow and grows primarily from either male or female reproductive fluid or semen flowing into it and congealing (Hippocrates, *Nat puer* 20). Since hollow body parts create a vacuum and attract fluid, hair attracts semen…. Hair grows most prolifically from the head because the brain is the place where the semen is (78) produced or at least stored (Hippocrates, *Genit.* I). Hair grows only on the head of prepubescent humans because semen is stored in the brain and the channels of the body have not yet become large enough for reproductive fluid to travel throughout the body (Hippocrates, *Nat. puer.* 20; *Genit.* 2). At puberty, secondary hair growth in the pubic area marks the movement of reproductive fluid from the brain to the rest of the body (Hippocrates, *Nat. puer.* 20; *Genit.* I). Women have less body hair not only because they have less semen but also because their colder bodies do not froth the semen throughout their bodies but reduce semen evaporation at the ends of their hair (Hippocrates, *Nat. puer.* 20)…. According to these medical authors, men have more hair because they have more semen and their hotter bodies froth this semen more readily throughout their whole bodies (Hippocrates, *Nat. puer.* 20). The nature (Greek: *phusis*) of men is to release or eject the semen…. A man with long hair retains much or all of his semen, and his long hollow hair draws the semen toward his head area but away from his geni-

tal area, where it should be ejected. Therefore, 1 Cor[inthians] 11:14 correctly states that it is a shame for a man to have long hair since the male nature (*phusis*) is to eject rather than retain semen. In contrast, the nature (*phusis*) of women is to draw up the semen and congeal (79) it into a fetus (Hippocrates, *Genit.* 5; *Nat. puer.* 12).... This conception of hair as part of the female genitalia explains the favorite Hippocratic test for sterility in women. A doctor places a scented suppository in a woman's uterus and examines her mouth the next day to see if he can smell the scent of the suppository. If he smells the scent, he diagnoses her as fertile. If he does not smell the scent, he concludes she is sterile because the channels connecting her uterus to her head are blocked. The suction power of her hair cannot draw up the semen through the appropriate channels in her body. The male seed is therefore discharged rather than retained, and the woman cannot conceive.[221]

Martin's research produced many more examples. These citations should suffice to make the point that, strange as it may sound to our modern ears, the medical knowledge with which Paul and his readers were familiar explicitly associated a woman's hair with the conceiving of children. In fact, a woman's hair was the female counterpart to the male testicles when it came to how women became pregnant. The references to a woman's hair in 1 Corinthians 11 are, consequently, loaded with sexual inference.

UNDERSTANDING AND APPLICATION

Two questions are now relevant: What's the interpretive payoff for the passage at hand, and how does this material help us see how Paul linked his discussion of a woman's hair "given to her instead of a head covering (*peribolaion*)" to the sin of the Watchers?

Martin answers the first question for his readers:

This ancient physiological conception of hair indicates that Paul's argument from nature in 1 Cor[inthians] 11:13–5 contrasts long hair in women with testicles in men. Paul states that appropriate to her nature, a woman is not given an external testicle (peribolaion, 1 Cor[inthians] 11:15b) but rather hair instead. Paul states that long hollow hair on a woman's head is her glory (1 Cor[inthians] 11:15) because it enhances her female nature (*phusis*), which is to draw in and retain semen. Since female hair is part of the female genitalia, Paul asks the Corinthians to judge for themselves whether it is proper for a woman to display her genitalia when praying to God (1 Cor[inthians] 11:13).

Informed by the Jewish tradition, which strictly forbids display of genitalia when engaged in God s service, Paul's argument from nature cogently supports a woman's covering her head when praying or prophesying. In Isa[iah] 6:2, the seraphim who participate in the divine liturgy have six wings. Two are for flying, two cover the face for reverence, and two cover the feet for modesty. The term feet euphemistically refers to the genitals of the seraphim.[222] The priests in Yahweh's service receive special instructions for approaching the altar so that their nakedness is not exposed (Exod[us] 20:26). As a further precaution when entering the tent of meeting or approaching the altar, these priests wear "linen breeches from the loins to the thighs to cover their naked flesh" (Exod[us] 28:42–43 RSV). Again, "flesh," a euphemism, refers to the genitals (Lev[iticus] 15:2, 19; Ezek[iel] 16:26; 23:20). These breeches are for the glory and beauty of the priest (Exod[us] 28:40), while exposure of the genitals subjects the priest to guilt and death (Exod[us] 28:43).

Informed by this tradition, Paul appropriately instructs women in the service of God to cover their hair since it is part of the female genitalia. According to Paul's argument, women may pray or prophesy in public worship along with men but only when both are *decently* attired. Even though no contemporary person would agree with the physiological conceptions informing Paul's argument from nature for the veiling of women, everyone would agree with his conclusion prohibiting the display of genitalia in public worship. Since the physiological conceptions of the body have changed, however, no physiological reason remains for continuing the practice of covering women's heads in public worship, and many Christian communities reasonably abandon this practice.[223]

In summary form, the issue for Paul with respect to the practice of women and their head coverings is sexual modesty and propriety for worship. This takes us back to our earlier discussion about order in the church being a possible explanation for the phrase "because of the angels." Paul truly does have proper order in worship in mind, but his rationale isn't that angels are watching to make sure church liturgy is done correctly.

This brings us to the second question relative to how we apply all this: How is this connected to the sin of the Watchers? I would guess the answer to this second question is now fairly obvious. Paul isn't merely concerned with church order. He's concerned about cosmic boundaries.

The sexual nature of a woman's natural head covering, her hair, makes covering the hair in church worship completely understandable. But Paul had an additional concern. He wrote: "For man was not made from woman, but woman from man. Neither was man created for woman, but woman for man. That is why a wife ought to have a symbol of authority on her head, because of the angels" (1 Cor[inthians] 11:8–10).

Paul wanted women to have their hair covered as a sign that they were sexually taken, that they belonged to a man, their husbands. Why? Because of the angels. Apparently, Paul was concerned that if women didn't show this sign of sexual fidelity and "ownership," a woman could be at risk of sexual violation by angels. After all, it had happened before (Gen[esis] 6:1–4). Paul didn't want to see such a violation of cosmic order happen again.

The last two chapters of our present study have introduced us to how the sin of the Watchers, the fallen sons of God of Genesis 6:1–4, lurked in the back of Paul's mind in his letters to the Galatians and the Corinthians. But Paul wasn't alone in this regard. As we'll see next, the apostle Peter was also influenced by 1 Enoch's story of divine transgression.

9

THE SIN OF THE WATCHERS
AND BAPTISM[224]

Baptism is one of the most familiar practices in the local church. It's so familiar, in fact, that it's routine. The early church, however, associated it with the epic struggle between the children of God and the forces of darkness. This is why early baptismal formulas included a renunciation of Satan and his angels.[225] For early believers, baptism was spiritual warfare. The backdrop for this notion is the story of the sin of the Watchers in 1 Enoch. Perhaps that's the reason baptism isn't taught with this ancient perspective in mind.

Our discussion begins with 1 Peter 3:14–22, one of the more puzzling passages in the New Testament.

[14]But even if you might suffer for the sake of righteousness, you are blessed. And do not be afraid of their intimidation or be disturbed, [15]but set Christ apart as Lord in your hearts, always ready to make a defense to anyone who asks you for an accounting concerning the hope that is in you. [16]But do so with courtesy and respect, having a good conscience, so that in the things in which

you are slandered, the ones who malign your good conduct in Christ may be put to shame. [17]For it is better to suffer for doing good, if God wills it, than for doing evil.

[18]For Christ also suffered once for sins,
the just for the unjust,
in order that he could bring you to God,
being put to death in the flesh,
but made alive in the spirit,
[19]in which also he went and proclaimed to the spirits in prison, [20]who were formerly disobedient, when the patience of God waited in the days of Noah, while an ark was being constructed, in which a few—that is, eight souls—were rescued through water. [21]And also, corresponding to this, baptism now saves you, not the removal of dirt from the flesh, but an appeal to God for a good conscience through the resurrection of Jesus Christ, [22]who is at the right hand of God, having gone into heaven, with angels and authorities and powers having been subjected to him.

The overall theme of 1 Peter is that Christians must withstand persecution and persevere in their faith. That much is clear, but almost everything else in the passage has been subjected to heated academic debate.

Understanding this passage depends on comprehending two interrelated trajectories: (1) the notion of spirits being imprisoned, and (2) the literary-theological phenomenon of typology. We'll consider them in order.

SPIRITS IN PRISON, CHAINED IN GLOOMY DARKNESS

Who are "the spirits" that are "in prison"? The context associates them clearly with "the days of Noah," just before the Flood, but the association isn't adequate on its own to answer the question. Are these spirits the souls of the people who perished in the Flood? Are they the fallen "sons of God" from Genesis 6:2 (the Watchers) who sinned with human women? Are they the disembodied Watcher spirits of dead Nephilim—demons? Or is the reference to "spirits" point to all of the above?[226]

There are two important items to note in parsing out the most likely answer: the vocabulary used in 1 Peter 3:19 and the reference to imprisonment of spirits.

The word used in 1 Peter 3:19 typically translated "spirits" is *pneuma*. It frequently refers to nonhuman spirits, whether angels or evil spirits (Matthew 12:43; Mark 1:23, 26; 3:30; 5:2, 8; 7:25; 9:25a; Luke 8:29; 9:42; 11:24; Hebrews 1:14; 12:9; Revelation 18:2); the immaterial, animating force (or breath) of a human being (Matthew 27:50; Acts 7:59; Hebrews 12:23); and, one occasion in the New Testament, as the disembodied spirit of a human, a ghost (Matthew 14:26; Luke 24:37).[227] The term, then, can be used of both the human dead (infrequently) and non-human spirits (frequently).

However, one must ask if Peter's vocabulary for human beings elsewhere can be used of nonhuman spirits. In 1 Peter 3:20, one verse removed, Peter mentions "eight persons (*psychē*), were brought safely through water." This different term, *psychē*, is never used of nonhuman spirits. Rather, it speaks of the animating force of human life, the inner self or inner life of human mind, human desires or emotions, or the departed human spirit/soul.[228]

What this means is that 1 Peter 3:19–20 uses distinct vocabulary in each respective verse. Had Peter wanted readers to unambiguously conclude that the spirits in prison were human persons just like those of v. 20, it is far more likely that he would have used *psychē* in verse 19—but he didn't. Instead we find plural *pneuma* in verse 19, the term that is most commonly used for non-human spirits.[229]

The vocabulary distinction alone isn't conclusive. The second item of note must be brought to bear at this point—the reference to the spirits being in "prison" (Greek: *phylakē*).

Put simply, there is no instance in either the New Testament or 1 Enoch where disobedient human souls are said to be in an otherworldly prison. As Dalton notes:

> Nowhere in biblical literature is the world of the dead, as such, called *phylakē*. It is true that in the Syriac Peshitta version of 1 Pet[er] 3:19, *ev phylakē* is rendered by "in sheol." This is an interpretation rather than a strict translation, which derives from the later church tradition, found in Syriac writings, of Christ's "harrowing of hell." In this tradition, sheol is regarded as a prison in the keeping of Satan, from which Christ at his descent to sheol, liberated all the souls of the dead. This later, non-biblical tradition cannot be used to interpret the text of 1 Pet[er] 3:19.
>
> On the other hand, *phylakē* is used in the New Testament for the prison in which Satan is chained: "And when the thousand years are ended, Satan will be loosed from his prison." This usage is quite normal....
>
> It is important to note that, in both [1 Enoch and 2 Enoch], the fallen angels are described expressly, as being "in prison," or in equivalent terms. In 1 Enoch, they are condemned by God to prison as they await their final judgment (1 Enoch, 14:5; cf. 18:14).[230]

The reference to the spirits being imprisoned is decisive. Any literate Second Temple period Jewish reader of 1 Peter 3:19 would have understood that Peter was referring to fallen nonhuman spirits, the Watchers who sinned before the Flood (Genesis 6:2).

Michaels concurs with this assessment:

> There is agreement on virtually all sides that Jewish traditions about Enoch (occasioned by Gen[esis] 5:24), especially 1 Enoch, have influenced Peter's thought (and possibly his language) at this point. "Spirits" is used in 1 Enoch for the souls of the dead,

but always either with qualifying genitives, as in Heb[rews] 12:23 (e.g., 1 Enoch 22.3, 9, 12, 13; also 9.3, 10 in the Greek text of Syncellus), or in close dependence on preceding phrases that are so qualified (e.g., 22.6, 13). The "sons of God" who corrupted the human race (Gen[esis] 6:1–4) are customarily designated either as "angels" (e.g., 1 Enoch 6.2; cf. Jude 6; 2 Pet[er] 2:4) or as "watchers" (e.g., 1 Enoch 12.2, 4), not as "spirits," although Enoch reminds them that before they defiled themselves they had been "spiritual [Greek: spirits], living the eternal life" in heaven (15.4, 6, 7). The closest parallel in 1 Enoch to the "spirits" in 1 Peter is probably to be found in 15.8–10: "But now the giants who are born from (the union of) spirits and the flesh shall be called evil spirits upon the earth, because their dwelling shall be upon the earth and inside the earth. Evil spirits have come out of their bodies...." Although neither the original text nor the meaning of the passage is entirely clear, its apparent aim is to identify certain known demonic powers (or "evil spirits") as the indirect offspring of the ancient illicit union between originally holy and "spiritual" angels, and women of the generation before the flood. That union produced "giants" (cf. Gen[esis] 6:4 LXX) and from these giants came the "evil spirits" or demons, that continue to harass humankind.... If the authors of 1 Enoch saw the "evil spirits" of their day as offspring of the angelic "watchers," there is no reason why Peter may not have viewed the "unclean spirits" of his own Christian tradition in a similar light.[231]

Now that we've concluded that the "spirits in prison" of 1 Peter 3:19 are the imprisoned Watchers/sons of God of Genesis 6:1–4 infamy, we can proceed to the second trajectory for understanding just what 1 Peter 3:14–22 is talking about—and how all of this relates to baptism.

ENOCH, ADAM, JESUS, AND TYPOLOGY

To understand what 1 Peter 3:14–22 is communicating, we have to understand a concept that scholars have called *typology*. Typology is a kind of prophecy. Readers will of course be familiar with predictive *verbal* prophecy—when a prophet *announces* that something is going to come to pass in the future. The point is that predictive prophecy of the more familiar kind is *uttered*. Typology works differently.

Typology concerns literary types, a term that comes from the New Testament (Greek: *typos*). For example, in Romans 5:14 Paul tells us that Adam was a *typos* of Christ. This Greek word means "kind" or "mark"—something that marks or points to something else. Paul was saying that, in some way, Adam pointed to Jesus—that is, he foreshadowed or echoed something about Jesus.

A type is therefore an *unspoken* prophecy. It is an event, person, or institution that foreshadows something that will come, but that isn't revealed until after the fact. In Adam's case, that something was how his act (sin) had an effect on all humanity. Like Adam, Jesus did something that would have an impact on all humanity—His death and resurrection. Another example would be Passover, since it prefigured the crucifixion of Jesus, who was called "the lamb of God." The point is that there was some analogous connection between the type (Adam) and its echo (Jesus), called the *antitype* or "type fulfillment" by scholars.

Peter uses typology in 1 Peter 3:14–22. Specifically, he assumes that the great Flood in Genesis 6–8, especially the sons of God event in Genesis 6:1–4, *typified* or foreshadowed the gospel and the resurrection. For Peter, these events were commemorated during baptism. That needs some unpacking, since the points of correlation aren't apparent, at least to most modern readers.

In an earlier chapter, we saw the tight connections between Genesis 6:1–4 and the epistles of 2 Peter and Jude. We discovered that 2 Peter and Jude communicated something about the Flood and the sons of God that wasn't found in Genesis, but which came from the Second Temple book of 1 Enoch. Specifically, 1 Enoch 6–15 describes how the sons of God (called "Watchers" in that ancient book) who committed the offense of Genesis 6:1–4 were imprisoned under the earth for what they had done. The offending Watchers are the "spirits in prison" in 1 Peter 3:19.

Recall that the prison to which the fallen sons of God were sent was referred to as Tartarus in 2 Peter 2:4–5. The imprisonment explicitly described here doesn't come from Genesis 6:1–4, but from 1 Enoch. It is clear evidence that Peter's description was influenced by the Enochian story of the transgression of the Watchers.

Recognizing this influence is important for 1 Peter 3. In the 1 Enoch story, the Watchers appealed their sentence and asked Enoch, the biblical prophet who never died (Genesis 5:21–24), to intercede with God for them (1 Enoch 6:4). God rejected their petition and Enoch had to return to the imprisoned Watchers and give them the bad news (1 Enoch 13:1–3; 14:4–5). The point to catch is that Enoch visits the spiritual world in the "bad section of town" where the offending Watchers are being held.

Now think about these parallels and the concept of typology—*fore-shadowing*. Peter saw a theological analogy between the events of Genesis 6 and the gospel and resurrection. He considered the events of Genesis 6 to be *types* or precursors to New Testament events and ideas. Just as Jesus was the second Adam for Paul, *Jesus is the second Enoch for Peter*. Enoch descended to the imprisoned fallen angels to announce their doom. First Peter 3:14–22 has Jesus descending to these same "spirits in prison" to tell them they are *still defeated*, despite His crucifixion. God's plan of salvation and kingdom rule had not been derailed—in fact, it was right on schedule. The crucifixion actually meant victory over every demonic force opposed to God. This victory declaration is why 1 Peter 3:14–22 ends with Jesus risen from the dead and seated at the right hand of God—*above all angels, authorities, and powers*. The messaging is very deliberate, and has a supernatural view of Genesis 6:1–4 at its core. The Watchers aren't being offered salvation. They learned that their sentence is still intact and that their progeny, the Watcher spirits or demons, had not defeated the plan of God to inaugurate His rule on earth through His redeemed children.

So how does this relate to baptism? Our focus for answering that question is two terms in verse 21, that baptism is "an **appeal** to God for a good **conscience** through the resurrection of Jesus Christ."

The two boldfaced words need reconsideration in light of this Enochian backdrop. The word most often translated "**appeal**" (*eperōtēma*) in verse 21 is best understood as "pledge" here, a meaning that it has elsewhere.[232] Likewise, the word "**conscience**" (*suneidēsis*) does not refer to the inner voice of right and wrong in this text. Rather, the word refers to the disposition of one's loyalties, a usage that is also found in other contexts and Greek literature.[233]

Let's take this back to verses 19–21:

> [19][Jesus] went and proclaimed to the spirits in prison, [20]who were formerly disobedient, when the patience of God waited in the days of Noah, while an ark was being constructed, in which a few—that is, eight souls—were rescued through water. [21]And also, corresponding to this, baptism now saves you, not the removal of dirt from the flesh, but an appeal to God for a good conscience through the resurrection of Jesus Christ.

Baptism does not produce salvation in this text. Rather, it corresponds to something that does—the death of Jesus (v. 19) and the resurrection (v. 21). Baptism "saves" if one makes a decision: a pledge of loyalty to the risen Savior. In effect, *baptism in New Testament theology is a loyalty oath*, a public avowal of who is on the Lord's side in the cosmic war between good and evil. But in addition to that, it is also a visceral reminder to the defeated fallen sons of God, Enoch's Watchers.

Every baptism is therefore a reiteration of the past and future doom of the Watchers in the wake of the gospel and the kingdom of God. Early Christians understood the typology of this passage and its link back to 1 Enoch and Genesis 6:1–4. *This is why early baptismal formulas included a renunciation of Satan and his angels.* Baptism was anything but routine. It was a symbol of spiritual warfare.

Section Preview

Part IV

Reversing Hermon in the Book of Revelation

To this point in our study, we've seen that writers of the New Testament Gospels, the apostle Paul, and the apostle Peter all had 1 Enoch's story of divine transgression in mind when writing parts of their inspired content. It is no surprise that the apostle John, writing the last major portion of the New Testament, the book of Revelation, did as well.

We've in fact already seen this from John and Revelation in our discussion of the birth of Jesus in chapter 4. In this last section of our study, we return to John's thinking to discern how the transgression of the Watchers is an interpretive factor in New Testament eschatology (end-times theology). We'll be taking a look at several issues in our final two chapters.

First, what might be called "Antichrist theology" has several touchpoints with events of Genesis 6:1–4 and its story of the sin of the divine sons of God and their progeny, the Nephilim. We'll see that Second Temple Jewish expectations about the great eschatological enemy were formed in part on the basis of certain biblical passages that overlap with the content of Genesis 6:1–4.

Second, several passages in the book of Revelation are illumined by a Second Temple Enochian worldview. Specifically, the remnant of 144,000, the Abyss of Revelation 9, and the matter of Gog and Magog are informed by material in Enoch's recounting of the Watchers' transgression.

Finally, the concept of the lake of fire (Revelation 19–20), prepared for "the devil and his angels" (Matthew 25:41) has an Enochian backdrop well known to scholars, but almost totally unknown to lay Bible students.

Exploring these issues will reveal interpretive surprises. However, it is important to note that, like the preceding chapters, our emphasis here is on textual data, not speculation. Our goal will be to see how the New Testament writers were influenced by, and repurposed, not only Old Testament material, but content from 1 Enoch in their own inspired works.

10

THE SIN OF THE WATCHERS,
THE NEPHILIM, AND THE ANTICHRIST

As one might expect, the Enochian story of the transgression of the Watchers is operating in the background of certain points of New Testament eschatology. There is no direct claim in 1 Enoch or the New Testament that the Antichrist would be a descendant of the Nephilim or an incarnation of a Watcher or Satan. There are, however, a number of indications that Second Temple Jews had an "Antichrist theology" before the time of Jesus that had clear conceptual links to the sin of the Watchers and the giants.

The notion of a pre-Christian Antichrist theology understandably sounds anachronistic, but it isn't. Scholars of Second Temple Judaism have known for quite some time that there was in fact a theological profile of a great eschatological enemy of God—a profile that New Testament writers followed in their own descriptions of the Antichrist. This profile has several interesting points of contact with Genesis 6:1–4 and the story of the transgression of the Watchers from 1 Enoch.[234]

THE GREAT MESSIANIC ENEMY IN
SECOND TEMPLE JUDAISM

There are several aspects to consider with respect to how a Second Temple Jew thought about the great enemy of the Messiah—the figure that Christians would call the Antichrist, since they believed Jesus of Nazareth was in fact the Christ, the Messiah. Two aspects of this conceptual profile are Old Testament antecedents and Second Temple Jewish understandings of those Old Testament texts.

The Old Testament elements that most scholars focus upon are summarized by Horbury:

> Was an Antichrist already envisaged by Jews in the early Roman empire? They might be expected to have imagined such a figure, because biblical texts which were important in messianic hope naturally emphasize victory over enemies; see for example three passages which were all later connected with an arch-enemy of the messiah, Num[bers] 24:17 (the star from Jacob smites the corners of Moab), Isa[iah] 11:4 (with the breath of his lips he shall slay the wicked), and Ps[alm] 2:2 (the kings of the earth rise up, and the rulers take counsel together, against the Lord and against his anointed). Moreover, from the Persian period onwards it was expected that a tyrannical king would oppress Israel and the nations just before the decisive divine victory. This thought is already suggested by the placing of the prophecy of Gog of Magog in Ezek[iel] 38–9, after the prophecies of a David to come and the revival of the dry bones, and before the description of new Jerusalem; and the expectation is developed or alluded to in Dan[iel] 7:8, 24–7, 8:9–11:23–6, on the little horn which signifies a king of fierce countenance.[235]

To our eye, this picture is tenuous. Several of these passages don't point to a single tyrant (Antichrist) figure. It would be easy to argue that at least some of them require ignoring context. Nevertheless, Jewish texts of the Second Temple Period make it evident that Jewish religious leaders did produce a doctrine of a great eschatological enemy from these passages.

By way of example, in a pseudepigraphical work known as the Assumption of Moses, a work whose content shows up in the New Testament book of Jude,[236] we read the following passage (Ass. Moses 8:1–3):

> [1]And there will come upon them…punishment and wrath such as has never happened to them from the creation till that time when he stirs up against them a king of the kings of the earth who, having supreme authority, will crucify those who confess their circumcision. [2]Even those who deny it, he will torture and hand them over to be led to prison in chains. [3]And their wives will be given to the gods of the nations and their young sons will be cut by physicians to bring forward their foreskins.[237]

The interesting line here is the reference to "a king of the kings of the earth" (v. 1). The writer is clearly citing Psalm 2:2, a messianic psalm about how the kings of the Gentile nations will rise up against the Messiah, and transforms the verse to point to a *great leader* of those kings. Horbury continues:

> Jewish notions of an opponent of the messiah are commonly thought to be less well attested, or not attested at all, at the beginning of the Roman imperial period. The earliest full descriptions of Antichrist, identified by that name, are Christian, and they come from sources of the second and third centuries—Irenaeus, Tertullian, Origen, and the exegetical works attributed to Hippolytus. Moreover, the first attestations of the Greek word *antichristos* are Christian, being found—here without fuller explanation or description—in two of the three Johannine epistles of the New Testament, probably written towards the end of the first century (1 John 2:18, 22; 4:3; 2 John 7). The "antichrists" are those who

deny that Jesus is the messiah (1 John 2:18–23); their emergence fulfils the familiar teaching that "Antichrist is coming."... Accordingly, the emphasis on false teaching in these Johannine passages on Antichrist should not be sharply contrasted with the emphasis on oppressive rule in the traditions on the messianic opponent—which themselves include the motif of false teaching, in the conception of the beast with the mouth speaking great things (Dan[iel] 7:8).... Antichrist, then, was certainly an important early *Christian* conception. Nevertheless, the Christian references to him include much to suggest that, like the figure of the Christ or messiah, he derived from pre-Christian Judaism in its Greek and Roman setting. This view is consonant with the lack of explanation of the Antichrist figure in the New Testament, and it is supported by Jewish sources from the end of the Second Temple period which describe an Antichrist-like figure without using this term, naming him rather as the wicked one, Gog, or Beliar. These sources can be said to bridge the gap between the biblical passages already noted, which attest the expectations of messianic victory and of a final arch-enemy of Israel.[238]

Horbury's point is that, while a developed doctrine of Antichrist is indeed of Christian origin, the component of that Christian teaching that had the Antichrist as an imperial tyrant bent on opposing the rule of Messiah is pre-Christian and of Jewish origin.[239]

SECOND TEMPLE JEWISH DEMONOLOGY

Horbury's reference to "the wicked one, Gog, or Beliar" brings us to a third background element for this chapter's discussion of the Beast (Antichrist) of Revelation. Belial (also spelled "Beliar" in some Dead Sea Scrolls) is the leader of the powers of darkness and, as such, a parallel to both Satan and the Antichrist in New Testament theology. Torleif Elgvin provides an adequate summary:

> The NT concepts of Satan and his host are closely related to ideas that develop in the intertestamental period and are found in early Jewish literature. In their interpretation of OT passages, various books among the Pseudepigrapha and Qumran literature give different explanations to the presence of evil in the world. Some writings describe the struggle between good and evil as a cosmic-spiritual struggle and anticipate the ultimate annihilation of evil and the evil powers. In some texts, the evil powers have an angelic leader named Semihaza, Mastema, Belial or the Prince of Darkness....
>
> The earliest postbiblical source that elaborates on evil angelic forces is probably the Enochic Book of Watchers (1 Enoch 6–16; 17–36).... These chapters interpret Genesis 6:1–5: the angelic watchers cohabit with earthly women and bring magic, sin and violence to the earth. Enoch is shown the coming judgment on the angels, who in vain ask him to intercede for them. Their leader is Semihaza, but he is not portrayed as a cosmic opponent to God or the elect. 1 Enoch 10:4 reflects a variant tradition, in which Azazel is the leading angel. The watchers are bound until the final judgment (1 Enoch 10:11–12), while the offspring of the illegitimate union between angels and women become evil spirits who spread sin and destruction on earth (1 Enoch 15:8–16:1).[240]

Elgvin's overview of the data shows that, for Second Temple Period Jewish theology, the leader of the Watchers went by different names: Semihaza, Mastema, Belial, or the Prince of Darkness. The last title has obvious overlap with the way the New Testament speaks of Satan (cp. Ephesians 2:2 with Ephesians 6:12; John 12:31). While there is no explicit connection in the Bible between Satan and the transgressing sons of God of Genesis 6:1–4, it's not hard to see how Jewish thinkers would have aligned the two. The notion that Satan is some sort of divine rebel *par excellence* seems to be the rationale—followed by an assumption that it was he who gave the Watchers the idea to cohabit with human women. Again, no biblical or Second Temple Enochian text says that. The point is to show that at least some Jews made the association.

Elgvin's summary also accurately distinguishes the original offending Watchers who were bound and imprisoned until the final time of judgment and the subsequent group of evil Watcher-spirits who were released from the bodies of the Nephilim at their death. He continues:

> According to the *Damascus Document*, the watchers of heaven fell as they did not follow the precepts of God (CD 2:18). This Qumranic work attributes the rising of Moses and Aaron to the Prince of Light and their adversaries to Belial: "For in ancient times, during the first deliverance of Israel, there arose Moses and Aaron, by the hand of the Prince of Lights; and Belial, with his cunning, raised up Jannes and his brothers" (CD 5:18–19). In the present time Israel at large is subject to the dominion of Belial (CD 4:12–19). The first part of the *Rule of the Community*, prescribes a covenant ceremony to be conducted by the community "for all the days of Belial's dominion" (1QS 1:18; 2:19)—the present age is "Belial's dominion" on earth (cf. J[oh]n 12:31; 14:30; 16:11, "the prince of the world"). The liturgy has the sons of light pronounce curses against the sons of darkness, "the men of Belial's lot" (1QS 2:4–5).[241]

In this Dead Sea Scroll, the Jewish writer clearly portrays Belial the way the New Testament portrays Satan. He is set in contrast to "the Prince of Lights," whom most Qumran scholars believe is to be identified with Michael (called Israel's "prince" in Daniel 10:21; 12:1). Several Dead Sea scrolls describe a great end-times war between the messianic prince, his holy ones, and his faithful human followers and Belial and his forces, divine and human.[242]

Consider the picture that Elgvin is sketching. Certain Second Temple-Period Jewish writers saw Satan as being the catalyst behind the rebellion of the Watchers. The Watcher-spirits (demonic forces) were in turn behind opposition to people like Moses. These spirits work for Satan/Belial and help him administer his dominion in the present age. In the final battle, these spirits partner with men aligned with Satan/Belial ("men of Belial"). The assumption, then, is that Belial's army must include a human commander—the Antichrist figure.

This chain of thought is justified by passages in other books of the Pseudepigrapha. For example in Sibylline Oracles 3.63–70,[243] we read:

> Then Beliar will come from the *Sebastēnoi* and he will raise up the height of mountains, he will raise up the sea, the great fiery sun and shining moon, and he will raise up the dead, and perform many signs for men. But they will not be effective in him. But he will, indeed, also lead men astray, and he will lead astray many faithful, chosen Hebrews, and also other lawless men who have not yet listened to the word of God.

The bulk of the various books known as the Sibylline Oracles can be dated securely to ca. 150–117 B.C. via specific chronological indicators in the books. However, many of the oracles are later. As Collins notes:

> The phrase *ek* [from] *Sebastēnoi* means "from the line of the Augusti." In this case Beliar can be most plausibly identified with Nero. This interpretation is supported by two parallels. First there is the prominence of Nero as an eschatological adversary throughout the Sibylline corpus. Second, in the *Ascension of Isaiah* 4:1, Beliar is clearly said to come in the likeness of Nero ("a lawless king, the slayer of his mother"). Most probably, then, Sibylline

Oracles 3.63–74 should be taken as a reference to Nero. It was added sometime after A.D. 70 to bring this collection up to date with current eschatological expectations.[244]

This selection from the Sibylline Oracles shows us that Jews living toward the end of the Second Temple period expected Beliar to be manifest, and perhaps incarnate, as a man. This line of thought may be suggested by Nahum 1:11, 15b:

> From you came one who plotted evil against the Lord, a worthless counselor (*yō'ēṣ beliya'al*; lit. "a counselor of/to Belial").
>
> Keep your feasts, O Judah; fulfill your vows, for never again shall the worthless (*beliya'al*) pass through you; he is utterly cut off.

The phrase in the first passage could be read as we see in ESV, or taken as a proper name, "[one who] advises Belial, a demon or even Satan himself."[245] Nahum 1:15b could in turn be interpreted as a person, a "human Belial" being cut off from the land of Yahweh.

The context of these references is not the end times. Rather, the book of Nahum is clearly written as an oracle against Nineveh, the capital of Assyria (Nahum 1:1). Nevertheless, Second Temple Period Jews could (and did) see the great enemy of Messiah in these texts.

For example, another Qumran text, 4QPseudo-Ezekiel (4Q386), contains this statement:

> And yhwh said: "A son of Belial (*beliya'al*) will plot (*hashab*) to oppress my people, [4]but I will prevent him, and his dominion will not exist; but a multitude will be defiled, offspring will not remain. [5]And from the grapevine there will be no new wine, nor will the bee (?) make honey. [*Blank*] *Blank* And the [6]wicked man I will kill in Memphis and I will make my sons go out of Memphis: I will turn myself toward their re[mn]ant."[246]

The text describes a "son of Belial" who is clearly a human eschato-logical enemy. One scholar notes about 4Q386:

> We may deduce from this that the "son of Belial" is not himself one of God's people. The combination of *belîya'al* and the verb *ḥashab* ["plot"] is reminiscent of Nah[um] 1:11…. That biblical passage refers to Mesopotamia, as does 4Q386 1 iii…. What we have found in this writing is an individual who is evil, who acts tyrannically and has close connections with Satan (*belîya'al*)…. [I]t is possible that the second-century author [of 4Q386] expe-rienced his own time as pre-eschatological and portrayed the foreign ruler of his own days as a "son of Belial"… [T]he most obvious candidate is Antiochus IV Epiphanes.[247]

Second Temple Jewish demonology therefore allows us to make several observations that correlated with the military tyrant figure Jews believed would fight against the Messiah:

- Jews of this period believed that the demons, the Watcher spirits of the dead Nephilim, were part of an end-times army against the Messiah and His followers.
- The army of dark powers was led by a supernatural figure variously called Belial, Beliar, Mastema, Semihaza. The latter name is another connection to the Watchers in the minds of Second Temple Jews.
- This demonic army fought in concert with the nations of the earth, the enemies of Israel.
- The human enemies of Israel would be led by an evil tyrant, the "king of the kings of the earth" (*Ass. Moses* 8:1). Historical figures like Sennacherib of Assyria or Antiochus or a Roman emperor were all prototypes of this enemy.

These introductory concepts are important for our study. The mate-rial above illustrates how the Antichrist could have been conceived as

"Satan (Beliar) incarnate." But this isn't the only perspective of the Antichrist profile that could be entertained in Second Temple Period thought. The great end-times enemy might not be Satan incarnate, but perhaps an embodied Watcher-spirit in league with Satan.

Understanding this alternative requires recalling that, for Second Temple Jews, New Testament demons were disembodied Watcher spirits released from the bodies of Nephilim giants. That means that when writers associated the Antichrist with giants or the fallen Watchers ultimately responsible for the giants, they would *not* have been claiming the Antichrist would be a giant. Indeed, there is no claim of that nature in the ancient material. Rather, these ancient writers would have been associating the Antichrist with the demonic Watcher-spirits of the giants.

THE ANTICHRIST FIGURE, THE WATCHERS, AND THE NEPHILIM

Though a completely unlikely consideration to us, there are a number of indications that, when certain Second Temple Jews and early Christians thought about the Antichrist, the great enemy of the Messiah, they also thought about what happened in Genesis 6:1–4 and the Watcher story of 1 Enoch 6–16. Perhaps the best place to launch an exploration into this matrix of ideas is a century or so later than the Second Temple Period, the era of the early church fathers.

One of the most famous among these early Christian intellectuals, Irenaeus, famously wrote that one workable cipher for 666, number of the Beast, was *Teitan*—"Titan"—a term that would take ancient thinking back into greater antiquity to "the days of giants."[248] As Horbury explains, "Here Irenaeus clearly shares the political interpretation of the myth of the war of the Titans."[249]

The war of the Titans was the Greek tale of the revolt of the Titans against higher divine authority known to modern scholars as the *Titanomachy* ("war of the Titans"). The epic shares many details with the equally well-known *Gigantomachy* ("war of the giants"), the story of how the giants rebelled against heavenly authority, so much so that the two stories were eventually conflated in Greek literature.[250] As I have written elsewhere:

> The Titans (Gk. pl. *titanes*) were the children of the gods Uranos ("Heaven") and Gaia ("Earth"). Gaia became infuriated after Uranos cast certain of the Titans into Tartarus. Gaia successfully incited the remaining Titans (save for Oceanus) to rebel against Uranos. Gaia gave one of them, Kronos, a sickle, by which he castrated Uranos (*Theog.* 134–207). Blood from the wound fell into the soil of Earth, an impregnation of Gaia that produced the *gigantes* ("giants") along with the Eriyanes (the Roman Furies) and the ash-tree Nymphs. The Titans were later overthrown by the Olympians, led by Zeus, who cast the Titans into Tartarus. This angered Gaia once more, and she incited her children the *gigantes* to rise up against the Olympians, a conflict known as the Gigantomachy. This second conflict is preserved mainly via Apollodorus (b. ca. 180 B. C.) whose works were compiled in the 2nd cent. C.E. The Olympians defeated the *gigantes* and confined them to Tartarus.[251]

We see here that both the Titans, the classical Greek equivalent of the fallen sons of God, Enoch's Watchers, and the giants—whose origin arose from a fusion of the divine and the earthly—rebelled against heavenly authority. The punishment in both cases was imprisonment in Tartarus.

Another Second Temple Jewish connection between the Antichrist, the giants, and the Watcher transgression is the way the Septuagint (=LXX), in certain instances, renders the Hebrew term *rephaim* with *titanes* (2 Samuel 5:18, 22; 1 Chronicles 11:15).[252] Recall that the term *rephaim* was another name for the giant Anakim—descendants of the Nephilim— at the time of the conquest (e.g., Deuteronomy 2–3; Numbers 13:32–33).[253] Pearson explains:

The word in the Hebrew Bible most often translated as *gigas* ["giant"] is *gibbor,* but there is also one other group in the LXX translated with *gigas,* namely the enigmatic *rephaim.* Significantly, the *rephaim* are translated not only with *gigas,* but also with *titan* ["Titan"]—an extremely suggestive conflation of Greek mythology with the Hebrew traditions. The second of these two translations suggests the importance of another word used in the LXX, namely *Tartaros*—the place in Greek mythology in which the Titans were imprisoned after their battle with Zeus.... The use of Enochic traditions in 2 Peter 2, where the verb *tartaroo* ("cast into Tartarus") is used of the angels who sinned (v. 4), hints at the further importance of Tartarus in subsequent Christian conceptions of the underworld, mediated through the Jewish appropriation of them during the second Temple period.[254]

The parallels to Genesis 6:1–4 and 1 Enoch are obvious and undeniable. There is no guesswork in which to engage. As we saw in chapter 2, the Watchers were bound in the Abyss in 1 Enoch. That Peter and Jude knew the Enochian material well is indicated by having the "angels that sinned" chained in the underworld prison. That Peter knew the Titan story is clear from 2 Peter 2:4, where we are explicitly told that "the angels that sinned" were "sent to Tartarus." The Greek verb in the verse, *tartaroō,* could not be more clear.

An important, under-explored trajectory should also be apparent to readers at this point. Because of the Mesopotamian elements of the original context for Genesis 6:1–4 we discussed in chapter 3 that are so well preserved in 1 Enoch, it is no surprise that Second Temple Jews would also have connected the Titan and Watcher stories, complete with the giants, to Babylon. Two passages in *Pseudo-Eupolemus,* quoted by Eusebius in his *Praeparatio Evangelica,* are revealing in this respect:

[2]Eupolemus, in his work "On the Jews," states that the Assyrian city of Babylon was first founded by those who escaped the Flood. They

were giants, and they built the tower well known in history. [3]When the tower was destroyed by God's power, these giants were scattered over the whole earth.... [9]For the Babylonians hold that Belos, who is son of Kronos, lived first. Kronos begot sons named Belos and Canaan. This Canaan fathered the ancestor of the Phoenicians, whose son was Chus, called by the Greeks Asbolus. Chus was the ancestor of the Ethiopians and the brother of Mitsraim, the ancestor of the Egyptians.... These [giants] dwelt in the land of Babylonia. Because of their impiety, they were destroyed by the gods. One of them, Belos, escaped death and settled in Babylon. He built a tower and lived in it; the tower was called Belos after its builder.[255]

The passage contains several contradictions between *Pseudo-Eupolemus* and Genesis 10, not to mention quite a bit of unbiblical speculation about Abraham. Nevertheless, it is important in several respects. The key observations are that a number of Second Temple Period Jews would have believed:

- Giants—namely a giant named Belos—built the tower of Babel.
- This Belos had survived the Flood.
- Belos was the son of Kronos.[256]

Readers will recall from the earlier summary of the Titanomachy that Kronos was a Titan. The Jewish writer of Pseudo-Eupolemus sees the story of how the biblical giants had mixed parentage (divine and earthly) paralleled by the story of how Titan blood mixed with earth produced the giants.

The central point of this conceptual connection was Belos, whom many Second Temple Jews identified with Nimrod. Van der Toorn and van der Horst explain:

Here is a medley of allusions to Genesis 6 (both the motif of the giants and that of the flood) and Genesis 11 (the building of the

tower of Babel).... [T]he intermediate link is Nimrod from Genesis 10.... [W]e note the connection of Nimrod with the story
of the giants in Genesis 6 on the one hand and with the story of
the tower of Babel on the other. There are several reasons for this
connection. The offspring of the sons of God are called *gibborim*
(LXX: *gigantes*) in Gen[esis] 6:4, and Nimrod is called a *gibbor*
(LXX: *gigas*) in Gen[esis] 10:8–9. This suggested...that Nimrod
may have been one of the giants of Genesis 6. In Gen[esis] 10:10
the beginning of Nimrod's kingdom is said to have been Babel
in the land of Shinar, and in Gen[esis] 11:1–10, the people who
settled in the land of Shinar are said to have built a city there that
was called Babel (11:9). If that city was the beginning of Nimrod's
kingdom, he cannot but have been one of its builders. So Nimrod
who was one of the giants of Genesis 6 was also the one who had
built Babel.[257]

This identification of course means that certain Jews would have
believed Nimrod was descended from one of the fallen sons of God, the
Titans of the Titanomachy. While Nimrod isn't named in the Pseudo-
Eupolemus passage, his identification as the giant Belos is presumed by
means of the term *gibbor* and his biblical association with Babylon and
reputation as a builder (Genesis 10:8–12). The idea is expressed more
explicitly by the famous Second Temple Jewish writer Philo:

The earliest Jewish writer mentioning Nimrod explicitly is Philo of
Alexandria. In his writings is a clear creation of a negative image of
the hunter. Of course, in a typically Philonic way, Nimrod is alle-
gorized. In his *Quaestiones in Genesis* 2.81–82 Philo first remarks
that Ham, Nimrod's grandfather, stands for evil and that Ham's
son Cush stands for "the sparse nature of earth" and is a symbol of
unfruitfulness and barrenness. Nimrod is Cush's son because spiritual unproductiveness can only produce giants, i.e., people who
honor earthly things more than heavenly things. "For in truth

he who is zealous for earthly and corruptible things always fights against and makes war on heavenly things and praiseworthy and wonderful natures, and builds walls and towers on earth against heaven. But those things which are [down] here are against those things which are [up] there. For this reason it is not ineptly said, "a giant before (Greek: *enantion*) God," which is clearly in opposition to Deity. For the impious man is none other than the enemy and foe who stands against God.[258]

Linking the Titans and the giants back to Nimrod of Babylon would make sense when we recall that many Second Temple Period Jews understood the Mesopotamian backdrop to Genesis 6:1–4. The Babylonian apkallu would not only be the reference points for the divine sons of God and the post-Flood hybrid giants, but also the Titans and giants of classical Greece.

While the basis for a correlation (the word *gibbor*) between Nimrod and the Nephilim is exegetically weak,[259] we should remember that associating the giant clans with Babylon does not depend entirely on Genesis 6:1–4. The relationship is also signified by the term "Amorite," used of the giant clans in Amos 2:9–10 and Deuteronomy 2–3. As I wrote in *The Unseen Realm:*

> Broadly speaking, the Amorite culture was *Mesopotamian*. The term and the people are known from Sumerian and Akkadian material centuries older than the Old Testament and the time of Moses and the Israelites. The word for "Amorite" actually comes from a Sumerian word ("MAR.TU") which vaguely referred to the area and population west of Sumer and *Babylon*.... Og [was a] king of the Amorites who ruled in the region of Bashan. *Og was a giant*.... [T]he most immediate link back to the Babylonian polemic is Og's bed (Hebrew: *'eres*). Its dimensions (9 × 4 cubits) are precisely those of the cultic bed in the ziggurat called Etemenanki—which is the ziggurat most archaeologists identify

as the Tower of Babel referred to in the Bible.[260] Ziggurats functioned as temples and divine abodes. The unusually large bed at
Etemenanki was housed in "the house of the bed" (*bit erši*). It was
the place where the god Marduk and his divine wife, Zarpanitu,
met annually for ritual lovemaking, the purpose of which was
divine blessing upon the land.[261]

As I noted at the beginning of this chapter, the point being made here
is not that the Antichrist will be a giant. No biblical or Enochic text draws
such a conclusion. Rather, the material indicates that Second Temple Jewish readers of Revelation may have parsed the Antichrist as having a direct
association with the fallen Watchers, the classical Titans, and the giants.
Given the evidence that Second Temple Jews thought of the great end-
times enemy as a man in league with Satan (Belial), and that they had a
propensity to see Satan as leader of the Watchers, perceiving the Antichrist
as an embodied Watcher-spirit (demon) is understandable.

There are other theological trajectories stemming from the Watchers'
abominable progeny that factor into Second Temple Jewish "Antichrist
theology." The cosmic geography of the biblical giants—their land and
its location—has meaning for several passages in Revelation that describe
end-time events and destinies. We'll consider those next.

11

THE SIN OF THE WATCHERS
AND THE APOCALYPSE[262]

O ur study has shown how the transgression of the sons of God of Genesis 6:1–4, the Watchers of the Enochian tradition, was a major theological consideration for New Testament writers. The message of the cross was not merely that Jesus was the only hope for resolving humanity's estrangement from God caused by events in Eden, but for reversing the effects of the transgression of the Watchers as a major contributor to human corruption.

It's no surprise then that what the New Testament says about the return of Jesus would also be in part framed by the need to finally overturn the impact of the supernatural rebellion of Genesis 6:1–4. In this final chapter, our focus will be on certain features of apocalyptic events in the book of Revelation that have some connection back to the fallen Watchers and their giant progeny.[263]

THE RELEASE OF THE WATCHERS

Perhaps the passage in Revelation that most readers would readily (and correctly) identify as having something to do with the Watchers would be Revelation 9. Earlier we learned from 1 Enoch that the fate of the fallen Watchers was to be imprisoned in the Abyss for "seventy generations," or "until the day of their judgment…until the eternal judgment is consummated" (1 Enoch 10:11–13).[264] This fate is consistent with what happened to the Mesopotamian apkallu, the saga to which Genesis 6:1–4 responded in a theological polemic. It is also reflected in 2 Peter 2:4 and Jude 6, with their note that the "angels that sinned" were put "in chains of gloomy darkness" in Tartarus.

Many scholars believe that the "unlocking" of the Abyss by a "star" who is given the key (Revelation 9:1–10) is the eschatological release of the imprisoned Watchers.[265] For example, Thompson notes:

> The most suitable sequel to the time of imprisonment described in 1 Enoch 10 can be found in Rev[elation] 9 where the key to the abyss is given to a fallen star (or to the fifth, trumpet-blowing, angel?) who uses it to open the shaft to the abyss and facilitate the release of imprisoned demonic forces who emerge to terrorize earth dwellers.[266]

It is clear that there is a textual relationship between Revelation 9 and Enochian and classical material. Beale cites a number of sources in passing: "Fallen angels were said to be imprisoned in the pit to await final judgment (1 En[och] 10:4–14; 18:11–16; 19:1; 21:7; 54:1–6; 88:1–3; 90:23–26; Jubilees 5:6–14; 2 Pet[er] 2:4; cf. 4 Ezra 7:36; Prayer of Manasseh 3).[267] The bizarre description of the beings released from the Abyss as "locusts" (Revelation 9:3) that were "like horses prepared for battle: on their heads were what looked like crowns of gold; their faces were like human faces, their hair like women's hair, and their teeth like lions' teeth" (Revelation 9:7–8) does *not* undermine their identification as the fallen Watchers. Hybridized theriomorphic ("animal-shaped") descriptions applied to demonic spirits are common in ancient Jewish and classical literature.[268] If one wishes to understand Revelation 9 in its ancient literary context, the passage describes the release of the fallen Watchers before their ultimate destruction with Satan.[269]

THE 144,000 AS MIRROR REVERSAL
OF THE WATCHERS' TRANSGRESSION

Many readers will be familiar with the 144,000 introduced in Revelation 7. How it relates to the transgression of the Watchers is difficult to discern on the surface. The passage reads:

> [4]And I heard the number of the sealed, 144,000, sealed from every tribe of the sons of Israel:
> [5]12,000 from the tribe of Judah were sealed,
> 12,000 from the tribe of Reuben,
> 12,000 from the tribe of Gad,
> [6]12,000 from the tribe of Asher,
> 12,000 from the tribe of Naphtali,
> 12,000 from the tribe of Manasseh,
> [7]12,000 from the tribe of Simeon,
> 12,000 from the tribe of Levi,
> 12,000 from the tribe of Issachar,
> [8]12,000 from the tribe of Zebulun,
> 12,000 from the tribe of Joseph,
> 12,000 from the tribe of Benjamin were sealed.

Revelation 7 is not the only passage that describes the 144,000. Revelation 14:1–5 provides a key for discerning how the role of the 144,000 can be understood in light of the sin of the Watchers.

> [1]Then I looked, and behold, on Mount Zion stood the Lamb, and with him 144,000 who had his name and his Father's name

written on their foreheads. [2]And I heard a voice from heaven like the roar of many waters and like the sound of loud thunder. The voice I heard was like the sound of harpists playing on their harps, [3]and they were singing a new song before the throne and before the four living creatures and before the elders. No one could learn that song except the 144,000 who had been redeemed from the earth. [4]It is these who have not defiled themselves with women, for they are virgins. It is these who follow the Lamb wherever he goes. These have been redeemed from mankind as firstfruits for God and the Lamb, [5]and in their mouth no lie was found, for they are blameless.

It is important to note how the 144,000 are cast in this passage. They are in the *heavenly* Zion, the throne room of God, having been specially marked for close proximity to the presence of God and the service of God (v. 3). Verses 4–5 mark them as virgins—specifically, *male* virgins who "have not defiled themselves with women."

Why are the 144,000 portrayed as a heavenly priesthood? Why the specific note that they are male virgins, especially when Israelite priests could be married?

A recent scholarly study on this passage has drawn attention to the fact that this description presents the 144,000 as a *positive* analogy to the Levitical priesthood and a *negative*, reverse analogy to the sexual defilement of God's other holy ones who defiled themselves by sexual engagement with women—the fallen sons of God/Watchers of Genesis 6:1–4:

Not only are the 144,000 *positively* identified in the call and function of the Levitical system of the Old Testament; but John also employs *negative* imagery that still builds on the choice of the Levitical identification…. This is evidenced in the contrasted allusion to the *negative* qualities of the Levites that John employs from the Watcher Myth, who abandoned their calling as God's [children], and engaged in marital practices that went contrary to God's commands. John's allusion to the purity of the 144,000 is the key to him, applying the Watcher Myth as an anti-image, where the fallen angels lusted after the daughters of men and took for themselves wives, thus defiling themselves and abandoning God's order…. In terms of the commentary in 1 En[och] 15:3–12, the angels should not have taken wives from the daughters of men because (a) they have thereby defiled themselves, (b) they have thereby begotten strange children in terms of 1 En[och] 10:9, and (c) angels in any case have no need of wives since they are immortal, while men need them to perpetuate the species…. John borrows this negative imagery from the erring Enochic Levites to create an anti-image of the representative 144,000 unde-filed virgins…. [The 144,000] are…an anti-image, not only to the followers of the beast mentioned in the preceding chapter and Rev[elation] 14:6–20 (cf. Rev[elation] 17–18); but also to the fallen angels of 1 Enoch 1–36 in their ritual purity.

The theological point is that the 144,000 holy ones who fight the Beast (Antichrist) are counterpoints to the holy ones who rebelled and defiled themselves with human women. John telegraphs that these holy ones will help their earthly compatriots defeat the Beast and rectify the impurity brought to earth by the Watchers.

THE ANTICHRIST FROM DAN—BUT WHICH DAN?

We need to return to the statement that introduces the 144,000. Revelation 7:4 introduces the 144,000 as "sealed from every tribe of the sons of Israel." The statement is interesting because it is transparently *inaccurate*. A close reading of the tribes listed in the passage reveals that isn't the case. There are two tribes missing. Many tribal lists in the Old Testament do not include Joseph, for example, replacing him with the two "half tribes" of Ephraim and Manasseh, the two sons of Joseph. In Revelation 7, Manasseh and Joseph are present, but not Ephraim.

The omission that has drawn the most attention, though, is Dan. The tribe is nowhere to be found in Revelation 7.

Dan had a checkered history. The tribe forsook its allotted inheritance in the south of Canaan and migrated north, appropriating the priest of Micah the Levite, who kept household gods and an idol in his house (Joshua 19:40–48; Judges 18). The Danites eventually conquered the city of Laish and renamed it Dan (Judges 18:27, 29). This city became a cult center to Baal in later Israelite history. Earlier in Israel's history, instead of receiving a blessing from the dying Jacob like his brothers, the patriarch pronounced, "Dan shall be a serpent in the way, a viper by the path, that bites the horse's heels so that his rider falls backward" (Genesis 49:17). Deuteronomy 33:22 contains the cryptic note that "Dan is a lion's cub that leaps from Bashan."

These failures and passages associate Dan with rebellion against God, the region of Bashan, whose name in Canaanite would have been *bathan* ("serpent"),[270] and Baal worship at a location at the foot of Mount Hermon. It is no wonder that some early church writers believed that the reason Dan was omitted from Revelation 7 was because the Antichrist—the enemy of the 144,000—would come from the tribe of Dan. C. E. Hill explains:

> Our first explicit mention of a Jewish Antichrist comes in the writings of Irenaeus, where it occurs already in tandem with the opinion that he will also spring from the tribe of Dan (*AH* 5.30.2).... Somewhat surprisingly, Irenaeus brings forth but two scriptural passages in support of Antichrist's Danite origin. The first is Jer[emiah] 8: 16 (LXX) "We shall hear the voice of his swift horses from Dan; the whole earth shall be moved by the voice of the neighing of his galloping horses: he shall also come and devour the earth, and the fulness thereof, the city also, and they that dwell therein." He finds further support for this in the omission of Dan from the list of the twelve tribes of the sealed in

Rev[elation] 7:5–7.... Antichrist from the tribe of Dan...makes
his first known appearance in Irenaeus, but it is in Hippolytus
that he finds his most scrupulous and eloquent biographer. Hippolytus' copious description proceeds on the principle that "the
deceiver seeks to liken himself in all things to the Son of God."
As Jesus was the lion from the tribe of Judah—referring to Jacob's
blessing on Judah in Genesis 49:9—Antichrist will be the lion
from the tribe of Dan—referring to Moses' blessing on the tribe
of Dan in Deut[eronomy] 33:22.[271]

As readers will recall, I have argued for a Gentile template for the
Antichrist.[272] For reasons that will become apparent in this chapter, I think
too much is read into these passages about the *tribe* of Dan. However, the
northern region of Bashan associated with the *city* of Dan is meaningful for
discerning connections between the Antichrist and the Watchers' transgression. When it comes to the omission of Dan from the 144,000, their
spiritual apostasy likely played a role, but Revelation 7 says nothing about
the identity of the Antichrist. There is, in fact, something else to see in the
tribal listing that plays off Enoch's story of the Watchers.

GOG: INTERPRETIVE PITFALLS AND ERRORS

Most readers would likely presume that one of the end-times connections
leading back to the demons and the giants would be Gog of Magog,[273]
the mysterious figure of Ezekiel 38–39. While there is no *direct* exegetical
evidence that the biblical Gog is to be associated with the Watchers, the
demonic Watcher-spirits (the giant Rephaim) and Mount Hermon, Gog
is part of the matrix of ideas which includes all of those items.

The identification of Gog in Ezekiel 38–39 has proven to be one of
the more vexing problems in Old Testament study. The chaotic textual
situation in Second Temple Period sources informs us that ancient interpreters found it just as much of a conundrum.

Scholars have pursued several options for identification. Perhaps the most straightforward is the attempt to see a historical human tyrant, the leader of an ancient empire, behind the mysterious figure. Johan Lust notes in this regard:

> In an attempt to identify Gog as a historical person, attention has been drawn to a city prince Gâgi mentioned in the annals of Ashur-banipal (Cylinder B iv 2), a powerful ruler of a belligerent mountain people not far to the north of Assyria. More frequently, though, Gog is identified with Gyges (Gûgu in the Rassam-Cylinder, II 95), king of Lydia. Note, however, that the Gog of Ezekiel has the Cimmerians or Gomer as his ally, whereas the same Cimmerians appear to have attacked and defeated Gyges of Lydia. Such data suggest that Gog can hardly be identified with Gyges. Alterna-tively, Gog has been said to be the name of a country, *Gaga* or *Gagaia*, allegedly mentioned in the El Amarna Letters (*El Amarna* 1:38). It has become clear, however, that the writing *ištēn* ^kur*Ga-ga-ya* is erroneous for *ištēn* ^kur*Ga-ašga-ya*, 'one Kashkaean', so this identification must be abandoned as well.[274]

This interpretive strategy is based, in part, on an effort to associate the geographic places named in Ezekiel 38–39 (e.g., Meshech) and then combing historical sources for "tyrant candidates." At other times, histori-cal identification of Gog has been attempted by playing with the Hebrew words and creating false linguistic connections with the names of histori-cal figures. In this regard Lust observes that the Septuagint renders the phrase נְשִׂיא רֹאשׁ (*nesi' rō'sh*) as *archonta Rōs* ("commander of Ros"), and so modern readers can easily mistake the phrase as pointing to Russia.[275]

An equation with Russia is exegetically indefensible and incoher-ent. Of its many problems,[276] the most lethal is its violation of Hebrew grammar. There are two possible readings allowed by Hebrew syntax for the phrase *nesi' rō'sh*: (1) "Gog, the prince, the chief" (of Meshech and Tubal), and (2) "Gog, chief prince" (of Meshech and Tubal). Both options translate *rō'sh* as "chief" and thus eliminate understanding it as a place name. Consequently, "Russia" has no exegetical basis according to Hebrew grammar.[277]

The Septuagint (LXX) translator of Ezekiel also misunderstood the grammatical limitations of *nesi' rō'sh*, leading to several mistakes in translation.

In Numbers 24:7, part of the Balaam oracle, the traditional Masoretic Hebrew text reads, "[Jacob's] king shall be higher than Agag, and his kingdom shall be exalted." The point is that Israel's (eventual, Davidic) king will defeat the king of his enemies (in this case, a reference to Agag of the Amalekites in 1 Samuel 15). But the Septuagint—created long after the days of Samuel and Agag—does something quite surprising with this passage. Instead of "than Agag" (Hebrew: *m'gg*) the Septuagint has "his kingdom shall be higher *than Gog*." The effect is to transform the prophecy of Balaam into a remote, end-times prophecy pitting Gog against the Davidic Messiah, as opposed to an Israelite king having victory over Agag in the early days of Israel's monarchy.

How are we to understand this dramatic difference between the traditional text and the Septuagint? The LXX translation is only *textually* explainable if the Hebrew text being used by the Septuagint translator read *mgwg* instead of the Masoretic Text's *m'gg*. However, it is more likely that the Septuagint translator may have been confused by *m'gg* and invented "from Gog" as a translation solution.

The reason that confusion seems to be the best answer to the odd situation in Numbers 24:7 is that the Septuagint translator certainly blunders elsewhere with respect to Gog. Compare the traditional text with the Septuagint at the end of Amos 7:1:

Masoretic Text	Septuagint
This is what the Lord God showed me: behold, he was forming locusts when the latter growth was just beginning to sprout, and behold, it was the latter growth after the king's mowings (*gzy*).	Thus the Lord showed me and behold, an early offspring of grasshoppers coming, and behold one locust larva, Gog (*gwg*) the king.

Lust notes in regard to this verse, "In Amos' vision of the plague of locusts (7:1), the LXX translator read *gwg* for *gzy* (mowings?), focusing on Gog as the leader of a threatening army represented as a swarm of locusts."[278] It's very hard to follow the logic of the Septuagint translator. The waters get muddied a bit more when we discover that the Septuagint translator arbitrarily transforms Og of Bashan in Deuteronomy 3:1, 13 and 4:47 to "Gog" in his translation. Even more confusing is the fact that at least one Septuagint manuscript *does the reverse*—swapping in Og for Gog in Ezekiel 38:2.[279]

One certainty arises out of this messiness: At least some Second Temple Jews were comfortable associating Gog with the giant of Bashan/Hermon and the great eschatological enemy. The question is: Why?

GOG AND THE MYTHIC, SUPERNATURAL NORTH

In terms of physical geography, the region of Bashan constituted the northern limits of the Promised Land. Biblical people of course knew there were enemy cities and peoples beyond Hermon. It is of no small consequence that when enemies from these northern regions invaded the land of Israel, they came "from the north."[280] The physical north, therefore, was associated with the terror of tyrants bent on Israel's destruction.

The "tyrant from the north" factor is one of the reasons why Antiochus IV has become the prototype for the final end-times Antichrist. Antiochus IV, whose violent career tracks closely with events of Daniel 8–11, was ruler of Seleucid Syria, just north of Bashan. It was he who invaded Jerusalem in the Second Temple Period, forced Jewish priests to sacrifice unclean animals on the temple altar, and saw himself as an exalted deity. It is therefore understandable that a figure like Gog, the invader from "the uttermost parts of the north" (Ezekiel 38:6, 15; 39:2) is viewed by scholars as a foreshadowing of Antiochus.

But these observations merely scratch the surface. There's much more to see. As readers will recall, Bashan was the land of the Rephaim, the region associated with gateways to the realm of the dead, and home to the city of Dan, the central cultic site for the worship of Baal, the lord of the underworld. The foot of Mount Hermon overlapped the northern boundary of the region of Bashan. As I wrote in *The Unseen Realm*:

> The word "north" in Hebrew is *tsaphon* (or *zaphon* in some trans-literations). It refers to one of the common directional points. But because of what Israelites believed lurked in the north, the word came to signify something otherworldly. The most obvious example is Bashan. We've devoted a good deal of attention to the connection of that place with the realm of the dead and with giant clan populations like the Rephaim, whose ancestry was considered to derive from enemy divine beings. Bashan was also associated with Mount Hermon, the place where, in Jewish theology, the rebellious sons of God of Genesis 6 infamy descended to commit their act of treason. But there was something beyond Bashan—farther north—that every Israelite associated with other gods hostile to Yahweh. Places like Sidon, Tyre, and Ugarit lay beyond Israel's northern border. The worship of Baal was central in these places…. Specifically, Baal's home was a mountain, now known as Jebel al-Aqra', situated to the north of Ugarit. In ancient times it was simply known as *Tsaphon* ("north"; *Tsapanu* in Ugaritic). It was a divine mountain, the place where Baal held council as he ruled the gods of the Canaanite pantheon. Baal's palace was thought to be on "the heights of *Tsapanu/Zaphon*."… In Ugaritic texts, Baal is "lord of Zaphon" (*ba'al tsapanu*). He is also called a "prince" (*zbl* in Ugaritic). Another of Baal's titles is "prince, lord of the underworld" (*zbl ba'al 'arts*)…. It is no surprise that *zbl ba'al* becomes Baal Zebul (Beelzebul) and Baal Zebub, titles associated with Satan in later Jewish literature and the New Testament.[281]

An ancient reader would therefore not only have feared the north because of the threat of invading tyranny, but for supernatural-theological reasons. This is the conceptual grid through which Gog of Magog must be understood.

The failure to find any secure historical referent for Gog and the fact that the "far north" from which Gog hailed was so clearly associated with dark supernatural powers have led many scholars to consider Gog as a supernatural terror. This trajectory is in fact more coherent.

Several scholars have proposed that Gog could be viewed as a personification of darkness, based on the meaning of the Sumerian *gûg* ("darkness").[282] This view has found little acceptance,[283] but its detractors have offered next to nothing in the way of evidence for rebuttal. A supernatural figure of darkness actually comports well with Revelation 20:7–10, which mentions Gog and Magog along with Satan and human armies arrayed against Jerusalem (the "holy city"). It would also certainly fit with some sort of "Baal personified" figure from the cosmic north, Zaphon. As I have written elsewhere:

> The prophetic description in Ezekiel 38–39 of the invasion of "Gog, of the land of Magog" (Ezek[iel] 38:1–3, 14–15) is well known and the subject of much interpretive dispute, both scholarly and fanciful. One of the secure points is that Gog will come from "the heights of the north" (38:15; 39:2). While many scholars have focused on the literal geographic aspects of this phrasing, few have given serious thought to its mythological associations in Ugaritic/ Canaanite religion with Baal, lord of the dead. Gog would have been perceived as either a figure empowered by supernatural evil or an evil quasi-divine figure from the supernatural world bent on the destruction of God's people.... A supernatural enemy in the end times would be expected to come from the seat of Baal's authority—the supernatural underworld realm of the dead, located in the heights of the north. Gog is explicitly described in such terms.[284]

The connection to Gog as personified evil (which, as we argued in the previous chapter, is a way of talking about the antichrist) is made clear when we discover that the term "Armageddon"—which John says is Hebrew—does not refer to the city of Megiddo, but to Zion.[285] The Hebrew equivalent of "Armageddon" is actually *har mo ʻed* ("mount of assembly"), a phrase whose significance is illumined by where it appears in the Hebrew Bible. That passage is Isaiah 14:12–14, where the shining one, the son of the dawn (Hebrew: *Helel ben Shachar*; Latin Vulgate: *Lucifer*) sought to exalt himself above God and His council, the stars of God (cp. Job 38:7–8) to "be the Most High." Armageddon is about a cosmic rematch, where the original divine rebel seeks to overthrow Yahweh from Zion.

It is no coincidence that Daniel's description of the Antichrist prototype uses the same language of self-exaltation above God.

> And the king shall do as he wills. He shall exalt himself and magnify himself above every god, and shall speak astonishing things against the God of gods. He shall pay no attention to the gods of his fathers, or to the one beloved by women. He shall not pay attention to any other god, for he shall magnify himself above all. (Daniel 11:36–37)

Significantly, it is the king *of the north* being described in these verses. Gog is described in the same terms—the great destroyer from the north. As noted earlier, the immediate historical referent of Daniel 11 is the Seleucid King Antiochus IV. It was Antiochus IV who invaded Jerusalem in the Second Temple Period, desecrated the temple and its altar, and exalted himself above its God, Yahweh. Gog, the king of the north, is thus cast as an imitator or personification or agent of the lord of cosmic evil.

GOG, THE REPHAIM-TITANS, AND TYPHON

Thus far, we've not seen a specific connection between Gog and the Watchers or the giants. There is certainly data that will connect Gog to Bashan/Hermon and the Satan figure, Baal, but these other elements are wanting. What's needed is an evil, Satan-like figure who is also a Titan-giant in Second Temple Jewish thinking that can also readily be connected to crucial Antichrist passages like Daniel 7–12. Amazingly, such a figure is well known from ancient texts: Typhon.

Typhon is almost entirely unknown among Bible students. The description from the *Dictionary of Deities and Demons in the Bible* contains elements that should be familiar to readers from the previous chapter of this study, where we discussed the relationship of the Titans, Watchers, and giants:

> Typhon appears in Greek myths as the opponent of Zeus or even of all gods. He is the youngest son of Tartaros and Gaia.... The name resembles Zaphon and there seem to have been connections between Typhon and Baal-zaphon. According to Apollodorus, *Bib.* 1.41, Typhon flees to Mount Kasios, the mountain of Baal-zaphon.... Hesiod describes the struggle between Zeus and Typhon for the rule over gods and men after the defeat of the Titans. Zeus eliminates Typhon with his lightning and throws him into the Tartaros (*Theog.* 820–868).... Gradually Typhon became associated with the Giants (Hyginus, *Fab.* 151; cf. Pindar, *Pyth.* 8.17–18). From the sixth or fifth century bce onwards Typhon is identified with the Egyptian god—Seth (possibly already Pherecydes according to Origen, *Contra Cels.* 6.42; Herodotus 2.144; 156; 3.5; Diodorus Siculus, *Bibl. hist.* 1.21–22; 88; passim in Plutarch, *De Iside*).... Although Typhon is not mentioned in Dan[iel] 7–12 or Revelation it is quite possible that the typhonic type which was taken from Greek and Egyptian mythology was incorporated into passages of these apocalyptic writings in order to emphasize the appearance of foreign rulers as the tyrannical eschatological adversary. The vision in Dan[iel] 7 shows not only correspondences with Canaanite mythology, but also with texts on Seth-Typhon (especially concerning the eleventh horn). The battle against heaven and the stars in Dan[iel] 8:10–12 and

Rev[elation] 12:4; 7–9; 13:6 of the little horn, the dragon and the first beast corresponds with the role of Typhon, who according to Apollodorus, *Bib.* 1.39–40, touches the stars with his head and attacks heaven.[286]

It is crucial to realize what this short citation means. Scholars have established secure textual and conceptual links between Typhon, Daniel 7–12, a central section of the Old Testament for Antichrist typology, and Antiochus IV, whom all scholars of biblical eschatology recognize as the prototype for the Antichrist.

The major study of this material is that of van Henten, who writes:

In the Greek mythology from early authors such as Hesiod and Pindar up to and including Nonnus of Panopolis, who wrote in the fifth century A.D., Typhon figures as an appalling giant raving at gods and men.... In many texts of this group the struggle between Typhon and Zeus constitutes the central theme. In his hubris Typhon launches an attack on the Olympic gods whose uncontested leader is Zeus.... The literary character of Daniel 7 is vastly different from the mythological texts of this group. All the more striking, therefore, are the similarities to be found between the characterisation of Typhon... and the typification of the eleventh horn and its actions in Daniel 7.[287]

Van Henten goes on to introduce and illustrate numerous points of comparison, among them:

- Typhon's insolent words against Zeus and the little horn's against God (Daniel 11:36–37)
- Typhon's war against the entourage of Zeus for supremacy of heaven and the little horn's assault on God and His holy ones (Daniel 7:21–27; 11:36–37)
- The mutual contempt for existing laws (Daniel 7:25)

- The fact that Typhon, like the eleventh horn, has both human and animal features (Daniel 7:8, 20–21; 8:5–9, 21)

The point of all this is that, for Second Temple Jews, the notion that the great end-times enemy would be either the personification or the manifestation of supernatural evil associated with Bashan/Hermon and the giant offspring of the Watchers would not have sounded strange. Second Temple Period Jews would have recognized that the nature of the end-times enemy of the Messiah derived from a complex set of ideas that included these elements. Consequently, the defeat of the Antichrist signaled the final victory over the Watchers and their spawn.

THE LAKE OF FIRE—THE END OF THE WATCHERS

Matthew 25:41 tells us that the lake of fire was "prepared for the devil and his angels." The statement is unique in the New Testament. Similar passages confirm the devil ends up in the lake of fire (Revelation 20:10) and that others for whom it was not prepared end up there (Revelation 19:20; 21:8). But the idea that the lake of fire was seemingly intended or created for the devil and his angels has no apparent precedent in either the Old or New Testament.

The lake of fire is an excellent example of how New Testament writers on occasion get their theology from 1 Enoch and other Enochian texts. While the Old Testament has no account of angels being cast into the lake of fire, or that their destiny is such, 1 Enoch does. Not surprisingly, the concept is linked to the transgression of the Watchers:[288]

[9]And to Gabriel the Lord said, "Proceed against the bastards and the reprobates and against the children of adultery; and destroy the children of adultery and expel the children of the Watchers from among the people. And send them against one another (so that) they may be destroyed in the fight, for length of days

have they not. [10]They will beg you everything—for their fathers on behalf of themselves—because they hope to live an eternal life. (They hope) that each one of them will live a period of five hundred years." [11]And to Michael God said, "Make known to Semyaza and the others who are with him, who fornicated with the women, that they will die together with them in all their defilement. [12]And when they and all their children have battled with each other, and when they have seen the destruction of their beloved ones, bind them for seventy generations underneath the rocks of the ground until the day of their judgment and of their consummation, until the eternal judgment is concluded. [13]In those days they will lead them into the bottom of the fire—and in torment—in the prison (where) they will be locked up forever. [14]And at the time when they will burn and die, those who collaborated with them will be bound together with them from henceforth unto the end of (all) generations. [15]And destroy all the souls of pleasure and the children of the Watchers, for they have done injustice to man. (1 Enoch 10:9–15)

And I came to an empty place. [2]And I saw (there) neither a heaven above nor an earth below, but a chaotic and terrible place. [3]And there I saw seven stars of heaven bound together in/on it, like great mountains, and burning with fire. [4]At that moment I said, "For which sin are they bound, and for what reason were they cast in here." [5]Then one of the holy angels, Uriel, who was with me, guiding me, spoke to me and said to me, "Enoch, for what reason are you asking and for what reason do you question and exhibit eagerness? [6]These are among the stars of heaven which have transgressed the commandments of the Lord and are bound in this place until the completion of ten million years, (according) to the number of their sins." [7]I then proceeded from that area to another place which is even more terrible and saw a terrible thing: a great fire that was burning and flaming; the place had a cleavage (that extended) to the last sea, pouring out great pillars of fire; neither its extent nor its magnitude could I see nor was I able to estimate. [8]At that moment, what a terrible opening is this place and a pain to look at! [9]Then Ura'el, (one) of the holy angels who was with me, responded and said to me, "Enoch, why are you afraid like this?" (I answered and said)," [10]"I am frightened because of this terrible place and the spectacle of this painful thing." And he said unto me, "This place is the prison house of the angels; they are detained here forever [unto the age]." (1 Enoch 21:1–10)

The Watchers, bound in the Abyss until the end of days, are released and then recaptured to be thrown into the lake of fire. Readers familiar with the Enochian material on the lake of fire know that some Enochian texts single out the leader of the Watchers (who goes by various names: Asael, Azazel, Shemhazah) for special mention in these judgment texts (e.g., 1 Enoch 10:4–6). This is a very close parallel to New Testament statements and, in particular, the scene of Satan's judgment in Revelation 20:7–10. This is also why certain Christian thinkers consider Satan to be the leader of the Watchers, despite the fact that no biblical text says this, and 1 Enoch never identifies the leader of the Watchers as the original rebel of Eden.[289]

CONCLUSION

I n the introduction, I stated, "This book is about the important influence that the story of the sin of the Watchers in 1 Enoch 6–16 had on the thinking of New Testament authors," and that, "My task in this book is to remove the scales of our own tradition from our eyes, at least as it relates to the importance of the Watcher story of 1 Enoch for understanding portions of the New Testament." My hope is that the initial objective has been accomplished and that readers, now able to see parts of the New Testament more clearly for the effort, will be encouraged to learn more about 1 Enoch and other Second Temple Jewish texts.

In short, if we want to be serious about interpreting the New Testament in context, this is the sort of enterprise in which we must engage.

APPENDIX I

THE QUESTION
OF THE INSPIRATION OF
1 ENOCH IN THE EARLY CHURCH

The book we know as 1 Enoch was well known to early Christians. This isn't surprising given three transparent facts: (1) 1 Enoch is a substantially pre-Christian literary work that enjoyed readership among Jews in the Second Temple Period; (2) Christianity was born out of Second Temple Judaism; and (3) New Testament writers either presuppose or utilize its content in portions of their own writing. This heritage contributed to an understandable question among some influential early Christian writers and, one may presume, Christians in general: Should 1 Enoch be considered inspired and thus "Scripture" in the manner of other books in the Old Testament? Ultimately, Christianity at large answered this question negatively, save for the Church in Ethiopia. But the discussion is nonetheless of interest today. What follows is an abbreviated survey of how select Second Temple Jews and early Christian books and writers assessed the scriptural status of 1 Enoch.

SECOND TEMPLE JEWISH PRECURSORS[290]

THE BOOK OF JUBILEES

As I have noted elsewhere:

> *Jubilees* is presented as the account of a revelation given to Moses on Mount Sinai. The book begins in the third person with God forewarning Moses that Israel will apostasize but subsequently repent. The book then shifts to a first person accounting in the mouth of an angel. The angel speaks for God, informing Moses about all that had transpired from the beginning of creation to the Israelite arrival at Sinai. *Jubilees* is thus a rewriting of Genesis 1– Exodus 19, hence its inclusion by scholars in the "rewritten Bible" (expansions of biblical stories) genre…. The paleography of the surviving Hebrew fragments suggests a date of 125–100 b.c. for those fragments. There are reasons to suspect, however, that the original document was composed at least 50 years earlier.[291]

This ancient book is noteworthy in that "among Jubilees' additions to the biblical text are five interpolations of material from 1 Enoch and about Enoch (4:15–26; 5:1–12; 7:20–39; 8:1–4; 10:1–17)."[292] As was noted in our earlier discussion of Galatians 3–4, the figure of Enoch was regarded as a figure equal (and to some Jews, superior) to Moses. Jubilees reflects this perspective. Consequently, "for the author of Jubilees Enoch was Moses' predecessor as the writer of authoritative scripture that functions as testimony, and the content of that scripture was of major import for the readers of Jubilees."[293]

DEAD SEA SCROLLS (QUMRAN)

A number of Dead Sea Scrolls contain material known from 1 Enoch, especially the Watcher story. Nickelsburg summarizes:

The influence of the Enochic tradition at Qumran is evident also in the community's possession of (multiple copies of) texts that employ or quote from the Enochic texts. These include the *Book of Jubilees* (eight copies) and a related text (three copies), the Genesis Apocryphon (one copy), a fragmentary Hebrew text from Cave 1 that contained a form of the story of the watchers very close to 1 Enoch 6–11 (1Q19), a *pešer* on the story of the watchers (4Q180-181), a commentary or expansion on the Apocalypse of Weeks (4Q247), and the Damascus Document (eight copies), which knows the story of the rebellion of the watchers and a tradition about the giants (CD 2:16–20; see comm. on 7:2) and also appeals to the authority of the *Book of Jubilees* (CD 16:2–4).[294]

The *pesher* (*pešer*) texts are of special interest. *Pesharim* are texts that interpret (Hebrew verb: *pešer*) other texts. As Brooke notes, "the term has come to be used in modern scholarship of a literary genre of biblical commentary and the exegetical techniques used in it."[295] Producing a *pesher* text on the story of the Watchers indicates that the Enochian story was highly respected, if not considered Scripture, by whoever produced the *pesher*. Readers should recall, though, that such views cannot be considered normative within Judaism. During the Second Temple Period there was no singular Judaism. There were a variety of Judaisms. The situation is very similar to modern Christianity. Dozens of denominations and groups identify themselves as Christian, but their doctrinal perspective on just about every point of theology can vary, sometimes dramatically. Scholars generally think that the reverence for Enochian material at Qumran might indicate that the community "attracted people who prized the Enochic texts and others closely related to them, and who brought their copies of these texts with them."[296]

Early Christian Writings and Writers[297]

The Epistle of Barnabas

This ancient epistle is perhaps the earliest Christian source that cites material from 1 Enoch as Scripture. Nickelsburg writes:

> Writing ca. 135–38 c.e., probably in Egypt, the author of the *Epistle of Barnabas* paraphrases 1 Enoch 89:56, 60, 66–67 with reference to the destruction of the temple, introducing his source with the formula, "For Scripture says" (λέγει γὰρ ἡ γραφή, 16:5). To support the notion of a new temple, he quotes loosely 1 Enoch 91:13, again introducing it as Scripture ("For it is written," γέγραπται γάρ, 16:6).[298]

Justin Martyr

Justin Martyr's *Second Apology*, written between A.D. 148–161, presumes the Watchers story—that they cohabited with human women and taught humankind forbidden knowledge. Justin therefore holds them responsible for the proliferation of wickedness among humanity. Justin "recognizes the parallel between the story of the watchers and Greek myths about the amours of the gods."[299] This is of interest because Justin clearly considers the Jewish version (i.e., 1 Enoch) to be superior in its truthfulness. The opinion suggests that Justin considered 1 Enoch inspired, but we cannot be certain since it is not cited as Scripture in his work.

Irenaeus

Irenaeus was the bishop of Lyon. He lived ca. A.D. 130–200. His writings make it quite evident that he knew 1 Enoch in some detail and accepted the accuracy of the Watcher story. Of interest is what he says in the tenth chapter of *Irenaeus Against Heresies* (sec. 1):

1. The Church, though dispersed throughout the whole world, even to the ends of the earth, has received from the apostles and their disciples this faith: [She believes] in one God, the Father Almighty, Maker of heaven, and earth, and the sea, and all things that are in them; and in one Christ Jesus, the Son of God, who became incarnate for our salvation; and in <u>the Holy Spirit, who proclaimed through the prophets</u> the dispensations of God, and the advents, and the birth from a virgin, and the passion, and the resurrection from the dead, and the ascension into heaven in the flesh of the beloved Christ Jesus, our Lord, and His [future] manifestation from heaven in the glory of the Father "to gather all things in one," and to raise up anew all flesh of the whole human race, in order that to Christ Jesus, our Lord, and God, and Saviour, and King, according to the will of the invisible Father, "every knee should bow, of things in heaven, and things in earth, and things under the earth, and that every tongue should confess"[8] to Him, and that He should execute just judgment towards all; that He may send "spiritual wickednesses," <u>and the angels who transgressed and became apostates, together with the ungodly, and unrighteous, and wicked, and profane among men, into everlasting fire</u>; but may, in the exercise of His grace, confer immortality on the righteous, and holy, and those who have kept His commandments, and have persevered in His love, some from the beginning [of their Christian course], and others from [the date of] their repentance, and may surround them with everlasting glory.[300]

VanderKam notes of this passage:

It is not impossible that Irenaeus, in the wording of his lines about the angels, is thinking of 2 Pet[er] 2:4 and Jude 6, but the language he uses does not reproduce their vocabulary very closely. There is, however, some verbal similarity with 1 Enoch.... If Irenaeus is here reflecting the Watcher story, he is attributing it to the Holy Spirit's inspiration of the prophets and including it within a brief statement of the Christian faith shared throughout the scattered churches.[301]

TERTULLIAN

Tertullian was an early Christian writer from Carthage (ca. A.D. 155–240). He is famous (or infamous) for being the early church's staunchest defender of 1 Enoch's inspiration. For example, in his *On the Apparel of Women,* Book I, Chapter III, he calls 1 Enoch "Scripture" and defends its status using 2 Timothy 3:16:

> I am aware that the Scripture of Enoch, which has assigned this order (of action) to angels, is not received by some, because it is not admitted into the Jewish canon either. I suppose they did not think that, having been published before the deluge, it could have safely survived that world-wide calamity, the abolisher of all things. If that is the reason (for rejecting it), let them recall to their memory that Noah, the survivor of the deluge, was the great-grandson of Enoch himself; and he, of course, had heard and remembered, from domestic renown and hereditary tradi-tion, concerning his own great-grandfather's "grace in the sight of God," and concerning all his preachings; since Enoch had given no other charge to Methuselah than that he should hand on the knowledge of them to his posterity. Noah therefore, no doubt, might have succeeded in the trusteeship of (his) preaching; or, had the case been otherwise, he would not have been silent alike con-cerning the disposition (of things) made by God, his Preserver, and concerning the particular glory of his own house.
>
> If (Noah) had not had this (conservative power) by so short a route, there would (still) be this (consideration) to warrant our assertion of (the genuineness of) this Scripture: he could equally

have *renewed* it, under the Spirit's inspiration, after it *had* been destroyed by the violence of the deluge, as, after the destruction of Jerusalem by the Babylonian storming of it, every document of the Jewish literature is generally agreed to have been restored through Ezra.

But since Enoch in the same Scripture has preached likewise concerning the Lord, nothing at all must be rejected *by* us which pertains *to* us; and we read that "every Scripture suitable for edification is divinely inspired." By the *Jews* it may now seem to have been rejected for that (very) reason, just like all the other (portions) nearly which tell of Christ. Nor, of course, is this fact wonderful, that they did not receive some Scriptures which spake of Him whom even in person, speaking in their presence, they were not to receive. To these considerations is added the fact that Enoch possesses a testimony in the Apostle Jude.[302]

In his treatise on idolatry, Tertullian discusses certain celebrations and practices of Christians (e.g., decorating doors with lamps and wreaths) that he considers idolatrous. To make his case, Tertullian quotes Enoch's work as a product of the Holy Spirit:

But "let your works shine," saith He; but now all our shops and gates shine! You will now-a-days find more doors of heathens without lamps and laurel-wreaths than of Christians. What does the case seem to be with regard to that species (of ceremony) also? If it is an idol's honour, without doubt an idol's honour is idolatry. If it is for a man's sake, let us again consider that all idolatry is for man's sake; let us again consider that all idolatry is a worship done to men, since it is generally agreed even among their worshippers that aforetime the gods themselves of the nations were men; and so it makes no difference whether that superstitious homage be rendered to men of a former age or of this. Idolatry is condemned, not on account of the persons which are set up for worship, but on account of those its observances, which pertain to demons. "The things which are Caesar's are to be rendered to Caesar." It is enough that He set in apposition thereto, "and to God the things which are God's." What things, then, are Caesar's? Those, to wit, about which the consultation was then held, whether the poll-tax should be furnished to Caesar or no. Therefore, too, the Lord demanded that the money should be shown Him, and inquired about the image, whose it was; and when He had heard it was Caesar's, said, "Render to Caesar what are Caesar's, and what are God's to God;" that is, the image of Caesar, which is on the coin, to Caesar, and the image of God, which is on man, to God; so as to render to Caesar indeed money, to God your*self*. Otherwise, what will be God's, if all things are Caesar's? "Then," do you say, "the lamps before my doors, and the laurels on my posts are an honour to God?" *They are there* of course, not because they are an honour to God, but to him who is honoured in God's stead by ceremonial observances of that kind, so far as is manifest, saving the religious performance, which is in secret appertaining to demons. For we ought to be sure if there are any whose notice it escapes through ignorance of this world's literature, that there are among the Romans even gods of entrances; Cardea (Hinge-goddess), called after hinges, and Forculus (Door-god) after doors, and Limentinus (Threshold-god) after the threshold, and Janus himself (Gate-god) after the gate: and of course we know that, though names be empty and reigned, yet, when they are drawn down into superstition, demons and every unclean spirit seize them for themselves, through the bond of consecration. Otherwise demons have no name individually, but they there find a name where they find also a token. Among the Greeks likewise we read of Apollo Thyræus, *i.e.* of the door, and the Antelii, or Anthelii, demons, as presiders over entrances. These things, therefore, the Holy Spirit foreseeing from the beginning, fore-chanted, through the most ancient prophet Enoch, that even entrances would come into superstitious use.[303]

ORIGEN

Origen (ca. A.D. 184–254) was an early Christian scholar born in Alexandria, Egypt. As VanderKam notes, "In Origen's writings one finds evolving attitudes about the Book of Enoch, and these follow chronological lines. He alludes to the book in four of his writings, all of which can be dated fairly accurately to specific stages in his career."[304] At one point Origen considered the writings of Enoch (1 Enoch) "authentic products of the patriarch and cites them as Scripture; however, he also indicates that others in the church do not hold this opinion."[305]

The acknowledgement that some in the church did not embrace 1 Enoch as authoritative surfaces later in Origen's works. Scholars disagree as to whether Origen changed his opinion about 1 Enoch later in life. Nickelsburg writes:

> Finally, one must consider Origen's claim that the churches do not accept the books of Enoch as divine. This strongest of Origen's negative statements about Enoch seems not to be a development of Origen's previous ambivalence, but an acknowledgment of fact, which is one of several arguments that Origen uses to serve his purpose. Since his opponent cites material from Enoch, Origen emphasizes the book's questionable status "in the churches." At the same time, the words of Celsus indicate that the stories about the watchers were known and transmitted in Christian communities....
>
> I conclude the following. Origen knew parts of 1 Enoch (the Book of the Watchers, the Book of the Luminaries, and probably the Book of Parables) well enough to quote, paraphrase, and summarize an occasional passage and to recognize Celsus's misrepresentation of the material. Origen considered the texts to be authentic and Enoch to be a prophet, whose writings were "Scripture." He occasionally cited the book, quoted a passage, and even exegeted it, in order to support his exegesis of a biblical text or to

make a point that he could or would not base on a biblical text. At the same time, he acknowledged that the Enochic writings were not universally accepted as Scripture, and sometimes, with an eye to the possible skepticism of his readers, he did not invest a great deal in the probative value of these texts.[306]

APPENDIX II

THE DATING AND MANUSCRIPT EVIDENCE FOR 1 ENOCH AND THE BOOK OF GIANTS

THE DATE OF 1 ENOCH

First Enoch as we know it today is actually a composite literary work whose parts can be dated to different periods. This determination is based on internal evidence (e.g., historical reference points in 1 Enoch) and linguistic features. With the discovery of fragments of 1 Enoch among the Dead Sea Scrolls at Qumran and more intense critical study of the Ethiopic version of the book (the only complete version of all 108 chapters), the current consensus is that what we know as 1 Enoch is a composite of seven separate composed works dating to at least as early as the second century B.C. and which were complete by the end of the first century A.D.

The Book of the Watchers (chapters 1–36)
The Book of Parables (chapters 37–71)
The Book of the Luminaries (chapters 72–82)
The Dream Visions (chapters 83–90)

The Epistle of Enoch (chapters 92–105)
The Birth of Noah (chapters 106–107)
Another Chapter of Enoch (chapter. 108)

The second-century B.C. date represents the secure date of the Aramaic Qumran material. Consequently, it is obvious that the book is older than the scrolls fragments. That the book is a clear example of the apocalyptic genre known widely in Second Temple Jewish literature, most scholars are comfortable with pushing the date of significant portions of 1 Enoch another century.

MANUSCRIPTS OF 1 ENOCH

In my introduction to 1 Enoch for my employer's digital Greek Pseudepigrapha database, I summarized the manuscript and language situation for 1 Enoch as follows:

Nearly all the major sections of *1 Enoch* are witnessed in Aramaic material from Qumran. It is therefore considered likely that the original compositions were written in Aramaic. Some scholars, however, argue that the original language was Hebrew. Still others suggest that the work was written in both Hebrew and Aramaic, like the canonical book of Daniel. Since the author of the pseudepigraphical book *Jubilees* evidently draws on *1 Enoch* and the former dates to at least 170 b.c., Aramaic *1 Enoch* must predate 170 b.c. The Greek version of *1 Enoch* is older than the first century a.d. since it is quoted in the New Testament epistle of Jude (14, 15). The Greek text of *1 Enoch* derives from several manuscript sources. Between them, the Chester Beatty papyrus (4th century) and the Akhmim papyrus (6th century) preserve approximately twenty-five percent of the book. The *Chronographia* of the Byzantine chronicler George Syncellus (ca. a.d. 800) preserves two long passages as well. A number of early church fathers quote from *1 Enoch* favorably, and Clement of Alexandria, Tertullian, Origen, and Augustine all considered the work to have been written by the biblical personage. The extant data only allows dating the work to the 2nd century b.c. with any certainty, though some of the Qumran fragments may be a century earlier. The author is unknown, but may have been associated in some way with the Qumran community.[307]

Nickelsburg, in his monumental scholarly commentary on 1 Enoch, assesses the situation in a similar vein:

Since the Ethiopic version of 1 Enoch was first introduced to the West at the beginning of the nineteenth century, scholars have almost universally acknowledged that the Ethiopic version derives from a Greek translation of a Semitic original, although they have debated whether that original was in Hebrew or Aramaic. The discovery of the Qumran Aramaic Enoch mss. makes it virtually certain that Aramaic was the language in which chaps. 1–36, the Book of Giants, and chaps. 72–107 were composed, although the authors may have drawn on some Hebrew sources.[308]

With respect to English translations of this material, that is a very recent development. As I have noted elsewhere:

Much credit for the modern knowledge of *1 Enoch* must go to the Scottish traveler J. Bruce who, in 1773, brought three manuscripts of the work to Europe. It was not until 1821, however, that Richard Laurence translated the entire book into English. Laurence was also the first to publish the Ethiopic text (1838).[309]

THE BOOK OF GIANTS

The Book of Giants is not a part of 1 Enoch. The material in the Book of Giants overlaps with the content of 1 Enoch in many respects. It is, in effect, as Nickelsburg notes, "an expansion of material in 1 Enoch 6–16."[310] The book is known from Qumran from nine fragmentary Aramaic manuscripts that have been published with the rest of the Dead Sea Scrolls. Nickelsburg explains:

> The text clearly relates to parts of 1 Enoch. The most obvious point of contact is the narrative in chaps. 6–11, which turns on the giants' violent acts and their desolation of the earth. But what that narrative recounts pithily in a few sentences (7:2–6; 9:9; 10:9–10) is now subject to elaborate exposition. The stock figures of the giants come alive. They have names, they have dreams, they worry over them, discuss them, and seek to have them interpreted. In various of these respects, they recall the narratives about their fathers, the watchers, not simply in chap. 6 but also in 12:1–13:8, where the watchers interact with Enoch the scribe, petitioning him to intervene with the divine Judge…. The fragmentary condition of the Qumran mss. hinders certain conclusions about the precise relationship of this work to components of 1 Enoch…. The codicological relationship between the Book of Giants and (parts of) 1 Enoch is uncertain. Nonetheless, the nine mss. of this work at Qumran must be taken into consideration as one assesses the importance of this mythic material in the lives of the people who imported, copied, and read the texts that were deposited in the caves by the Dead Sea.[311]

APPENDIX III

SCHOLARLY BIBLIOGRAPHY ON
1 ENOCH AND THE BOOK OF GIANTS

D ue to the popularity of 1 Enoch, a number of books and studies
are available online that attract the attention of those interested
in studying this important work. These resources range from
amateurish to ridiculous. What follows are the best academic resources
for the study of 1 Enoch and the related Book of Giants. These resources
are produced by scholars and used by scholars. This bibliography may be
included in the resources provided in footnotes, but this is not a listing
of all the resources that show up in footnotes. See the notes for specific
resources on the content covered in respective chapters.

TRANSLATIONS AND CRITICAL TEXT EDITIONS

James Barr, "Aramaic-Greek Notes on the Book of Enoch I," *Journal of
Semitic Studies* 23 (1978) 184–98.
James Barr, "Aramaic-Greek Notes on the Book of Enoch II," *Journal of
Semitic Studies* 24 (1979) 179–192.

Matthew Black, *The Book of Enoch or 1 Enoch: A New English Edition with Commentary and Textual Notes in Consultation with James C. VanderKam* (SVTP 7; Leiden: Brill, 1985).

Matthew Black, *Apocalypsis Henochi Graece* (Pseudepigrapha Veteris Testamenti Graece 3; Leiden: Brill, 1970).

R. H. Charles, *The Book of Enoch, or 1 Enoch: Translated from the Editor's Ethiopic Text, and edited with the introduction notes and indexes of the first edition wholly recast, enlarged and rewritten; together with a reprint from the editor's text of the Greek fragments* (Oxford: Clarendon, 1912).

R. H. Charles, "Book of Enoch," *The Apocrypha and Pseudepigrapha of the Old Testament*, volume 2 (ed. R. H. Charles; Oxford: Clarendon, 1913) 163–281.

Ephraim Isaac, "1 (Ethiopic Apocalypse of) Enoch," in *Old Testament Pseudepigrapha*, vol 1 (ed. James H. Charlesworth; Garden City, N. Y.: Doubleday, 1983–85) 5–89.

Michael A. Knibb, *The Ethiopic Book of Enoch: A New Edition in the Light of the Aramaic Dead Sea Fragments* (2 vols; Oxford: Clarendon, 1978).

Michael A. Knibb, "1 Enoch," in *The Apocryphal Old Testament* (ed. H. F. D. Sparks; New York: Oxford University Press, 1984) 169–319.

J. T. Milik, *The Books of Enoch: Aramaic Fragments of Qumrân Cave 4* (Oxford: Clarendon, 1976).

George W.E. Nickelsburg and James C. VanderKam, *1 Enoch: A New Translation; Based on the Hermeneia Commentary* (Fortress Press, 2004). This is the best and most recent English translation of 1 Enoch.

Michael Sokoloff, "Notes on the Aramaic Fragments of Enoch from Qumran Cave 4," *Maarav* 1 (1978–79) 197–224.

Loren Stuckenbruck, *The Book of Giants from Qumran: Text, Translation, and Commentary* (Texte und Studien zum antiken Judentum 63; Tübingen: Mohr Siebeck, 1997).

Loren Stuckenbruck, Portions of the Book of Giants in *Discoveries in the Judaean Desert* 36 (Oxford: Clarendon, 2000), 8–94.

Charles C. Torrey, "Notes on the Greek Texts of Enoch," *Journal of the American Oriental Society* 62 (1942) 52–60.

James C. VanderKam, "The Textual Base for the Ethiopic Translation of 1 Enoch," in *Working with No Data: Studies in Semitic and Egyptian Presented to Thomas O. Lambdin* (ed. D. M. Golomb; Winona Lake, Ind.: Eisenbrauns, 1987) 247–62.

COMMENTARIES, MONOGRAPHS, AND JOURNAL ARTICLES

William Adler, *Time Immemorial: Archaic History and Its Sources in Christian Chronography from Julius Africanus to George Syncellus* (Dumbarton Oaks Studies 26; Washington, D.C.: Dumbarton Oaks Research Library and Collection, 1989).

Amar Annus, "On the Origin of Watchers: A Comparative Study of the Antediluvian Wisdom in Mesopotamian and Jewish Traditions," *Journal for the Study of the Pseudepigrapha* 19:4 (2010): 277–320.

Angela Kim Harkins, Kelley Coblentz Bautch, and John C. Endres, eds., *The Watchers in Jewish and Christian Traditions* (Minneapolis: Fortress Press, 2014).

Martha Himmelfarb, "A Report on 1 Enoch in the Rabbinic Literature," in *Society of Biblical Literature Seminar Papers* 18, 2 vols (ed. Paul J. Achtemeier; Missoula, Mont.: Scholars Press, 1978) 1:259–69.

Jack P. Lewis, *A Study of the Interpretation of Noah and the Flood in Jewish and Christian Literature* (Leiden: Brill, 1968).

George W. E. Nickelsburg, "1 Enoch and Qumran Origins: The State of the Question and Some Prospects for Answers," in *Society of Biblical Literature Seminar Papers* 25 (ed. Kent Harold Richards; Atlanta: Scholars Press, 1986) 341–60.

George W. E. Nickelsburg, *1 Enoch: A Commentary on the Book of 1 Enoch* (Hermeneia—a Critical and Historical Commentary on the Bible; ed. Klaus Baltzer; Minneapolis, MN: Fortress, 2001).

George W. E. Nickelsburg and James C. VanderKam, *1 Enoch 2: A Commentary on the Book of 1 Enoch, Chapters 37–82* (Hermeneia—a Critical and Historical Commentary on the Bible; ed. Klaus Baltzer; Minneapolis, MN: Fortress, 2012).

George W. E. Nickelsburg, "Scripture in 1 Enoch and 1 Enoch as Scripture," in *Texts and Contexts: Biblical Texts in Their Textual and Situational Contexts: Essays in Honor of Lars Hartman* (ed. Tord Fornberg and David Hellholm; Oslo: Scandinavian University Press, 1995) 333–54.

Annette Yoshiko Reed, *Fallen Angels and the History of Judaism and Christianity* (Cambridge University Press, 2005).

John C. Reeves, *Jewish Lore in Manichaean Cosmology: Studies in the Book of Giants Tradition* (Monographs of the Hebrew Union College 14; Cincinnati: Hebrew Union College Press, 1992).

Michael E. Stone, "The Book of Enoch and Judaism in the Third Century B.C.E.," *Catholic Biblical Quarterly* 40 (1978) 479–92.

James C. VanderKam, "1 Enoch, Enochic Motifs, and Enoch in Early Christian Literature," in *The Jewish Apocalyptic Heritage in Early Christianity* (ed. James C. VanderKam and William Adler; Compendia rerum iudaicarum ad Novum Testamentum 3/4; Minneapolis: Fortress Press, 1996) 32–101.

James C. VanderKam, *Enoch: A Man for All Generations* (Columbia, S.C.: University of South Carolina Press, 1995).

James C. VanderKam, *Enoch and the Growth of an Apocalyptic Tradition* (Catholic Biblical Quarterly Monograph Series 16; Washington, D.C.: Catholic Biblical Association of America, 1984).

James C. VanderKam, "Some Major Issues in the Contemporary Study of 1 Enoch: Reflections on J. T. Milik's *The Books of Enoch: Aramaic Fragments of Qumrân Cave 4,*" *Maarav* 3 (1982) 85–97.

Pieter G. R. de Villiers, ed., *Studies in 1 Enoch and the New Testament* (= *Neotestamentica* 17; Stellenbosch: University of Stellenbosch Press, 1983).

Archie T. Wright, *The Origin of Evil Spirits: The Reception of Genesis 6.1-4 in Early Jewish Literature* (Tübingen: Mohr-Siebeck, 2005).

APPENDIX IV

NEW TESTAMENT ALLUSIONS TO BOOKS OF THE PSEUDEPIGRAPHA

This collection of allusions to various books in what scholars now refer to as the Pseudepigrapha was compiled by Kevin P. Edgecomb.[312] His collection is used here by permission. His original collection, posted online, included allusions to the Apocrypha. Since the present book focuses on 1 Enoch, the listing below is restricted to that and other books now known as the Pseudepigrapha.

Sources for the collection of citations include the indices from the United Bible Societies' *The Greek New Testament* and the Nestle-Aland *Novum Testamentum Graece* (27th ed.), as well as:

Charlesworth, James H., ed. *The Old Testament Pseudepigrapha*. 2 vols. New York: Doubleday, 1983, 1985.
Metzger, Bruce M., ed. *The New Oxford Annotated Bible*. 2nd ed. New York: Oxford University Press, 1994.

Additionally, Edgecomb writes:

I have added some few items, which are marked at the head of the line with an asterisk. Those entries which appear only in the UBS4 are marked at the head of the line with [UBS4].... The translations of Pseudepigrapha are those included in Charlesworth's *Old Testament Pseudepigrapha*.

Naturally, what constitutes an allusion varies in the opinions of scholars. The purpose here is not to argue for or against any definition. Rather, it is to provide a reference resource for establishing the extent to which New Testament writers were exposed to the pseudepigraphical books known today, and how content of the New Testament reflects that earlier (or contemporary) material. As this present book establishes, however, the influence of the Pseudepigrapha extends beyond allusions. New Testament writers can (and did) write with Enochian (pseudepigraphical) content in mind to make a theological point. That is, sometimes what we encounter in the New Testament is best understood with pseudepigraphical content (such as the Watcher story) in mind as backstory.

Citations are numbered consecutively under each book followed by the New Testament verse(s).

1 ENOCH

1. **1.2:** And Enoch, the blessed and righteous man of the Lord, took up (his parable) while his eyes were open and he saw, and said, "(This is) a holy vision from the heavens which the angels showed me: and I heard from them everything and I understood. I look not for this generation but for the distant one that is coming."

    1 Peter 1.12: It was revealed to them that they were serving not themselves but you, in regard to the things that have now been announced to you through those who brought you good news by the Holy Spirit sent from heaven—things into which angels long to look!

2. 1.9: Behold, he will arrive with ten million of the holy ones in order
    to execute judgment upon all. He will destroy the wicked ones and
    censure all flesh on account of everything that they have done, that
    which the sinners and the wicked ones committed against him.
    Jude 14–15: It was also about these that Enoch, in the seventh genera-
    tion from Adam, prophesied, saying, "See, the Lord is coming with ten
    thousands of his holy ones, to execute judgment on all, and to convict
    everyone of all the deeds of ungodliness that they have committed in
    such an ungodly way, and of all the harsh things that ungodly sinners
    have spoken against him."

3. 5.4: But as for you, you have not been long-suffering and you have
    not done the commandments of the Lord, but you have transgressed
    and spoken slanderously grave and harsh words with your impure
    mouths against his greatness. Oh, you hard-hearted, may you not find
    peace!
    Jude 16: These are grumblers and malcontents; they indulge their
    own lusts; they are bombastic in speech, flattering people to their own
    advantage.

4. 5.7: But to the elect there shall be light, joy, and peace, and they shall
    inherit the earth. To you, wicked ones, on the contrary, there will be
    a curse.
    Matthew 5.5: Blessed are the meek, for they will inherit the earth.

5. 9.4: And they said to the Lord of the potentates, "For he is the Lord of
    lords, and the God of gods, and the King of kings, and the seat of his
    glory stands throughout all the generations of the world. Your name is
    holy, and blessed, and glorious throughout the whole world."
    Revelation 15.3: And they sing the song of Moses, the servant of God,
    and the song of the Lamb: "Great and amazing are your deeds, Lord
    God the Almighty! Just and true are your ways, King of the nations!"

Revelation 17.14: They will make war on the Lamb, and the Lamb will conquer them, for he is Lord of lords and King of kings, and those with him are called and chosen and faithful.

[UBS4] **Revelation 19.16:** On his robe and on his thigh he has a name inscribed, "King of kings and Lord of lords."

6. **9.5:** You have made everything and with you is the authority for everything. Everything is naked and open before your sight, and you see everything; and there is nothing which can hide itself from you.

Hebrews 4.13: And before him no creature is hidden, but all are naked and laid bare to the eyes of the one to whom we must render an account.

7. **9.10:** And now behold, the Holy One will cry, and those who have died will bring their suit up to the gate of heaven. Their groaning has ascended into heaven, but they could not get out from before the face of the oppression that is being wrought on earth.

1 Peter 3.19: in which also he went and made a proclamation to the spirits in prison.

8. **10.4–5:** And secondly the Lord said to Raphael, "Bind Azaz'el hand and foot and throw him into the darkness!" And he made a hole in the desert which was in Duda'el and cast him there; he threw on top of him rugged and sharp rocks. And he covered his face in order that he may not see light.

2 Peter 2.4: For if God did not spare the angels when they sinned, but cast them into hell and committed them to chains of deepest darkness to be kept until the judgment.

***Matthew 22.13:** Then the king said to the attendants, "Bind him hand and foot, and throw him into the outer darkness, where there will be weeping and gnashing of teeth."

9. **10.6:** and in order that he may be sent into the fire on the great day of judgment.

Jude 6: And the angels who did not keep their own position, but left their proper dwelling, he has kept in eternal chains in deepest darkness for the judgment of the great day.

Revelation 19.20: And the beast was captured, and with it the false prophet who had performed in its presence the signs by which he deceived those who had received the mark of the beast and those who worshiped its image. These two were thrown alive into the lake of fire that burns with sulfur.

10. **10.11–14:** And to Michael God said, "Make known to Semyaza and the others who are with him, who fornicated with the women, that they will die together with them in all their defilement. And when they and all their children have battled with each other, and when they have seen the destruction of their beloved ones, bind them for seventy generations underneath the rocks of the ground until the day of their judgment and of their consummation, until the eternal judgment is concluded. In those days they will lead them into the bottom of the fire—and in torment—in the prison where they will be locked up forever. And at the time when they will burn and die, those who collaborated with them will be bound together with them from henceforth unto the end of all generations."

    2 Peter 2.4: For if God did not spare the angels when they sinned, but cast them into hell and committed them to chains of deepest darkness to be kept until the judgment.

11. **10.11–15:** And to Michael God said, "Make known to Semyaza and the others who are with him, who fornicated with the women, that they will die together with them in all their defilement. And when they and all their children have battled with each other, and when they have seen the destruction of their beloved ones, bind them for seventy generations underneath the rocks of the ground until the day of their judgment and of their consummation, until the eternal judgment is concluded. In those days they will lead them into the bottom of the

fire—and in torment—in the prison where they will be locked up forever. And at the time when they will burn and die, those who collaborated with them will be bound together with them from henceforth unto the end of all generations. And destroy all the souls of pleasure and the children of the Watchers, for they have done injustice to man."
1 Peter 3.19: in which also he went and made a proclamation to the spirits in prison.

12. **12.4:** At that moment, the Watchers were calling me. And they said to me, "Enoch, scribe of righteousness, go and make known to the Watchers of heaven who have abandoned the high heaven, the holy eternal place, and have defiled themselves with women, as their deeds move the children of the world, and have taken unto themselves wives: They have defiled themselves with great defilement upon the earth."
    Jude 6: And the angels who did not keep their own position, but left their proper dwelling, he has kept in eternal chains in deepest darkness for the judgment of the great day.

13. **14.19:** and from beneath the throne were issuing streams of flaming fire. It was difficult to look at it.
    Revelation 22.1: Then the angel showed me the river of the water of life, bright as crystal, flowing from the throne of God and of the Lamb.

14. **14.22:** The flaming fire was round about him, and a great fire stood before him. No one could come near unto him from among those that surrounded the tens of millions that stood before him.
    Revelation 5.11: Then I looked, and I heard the voice of many angels surrounding the throne and the living creatures and the elders; they numbered myriads of myriads and thousands of thousands.

15. **15.6–7:** Indeed, formerly you were spiritual, having eternal life, and immortal in all the generations of the world. That is why formerly I

did not make wives for you, for the dwelling of the spiritual beings of heaven is heaven.

Mark 12.25: For when they rise from the dead, they neither marry nor are given in marriage, but are like angels in heaven.

16. **16.1:** From the days of the slaughter and destruction, and the death of the giants and the spiritual beings of the spirit, and the flesh, from which they have proceeded forth, which will corrupt without incurring judgment, they will corrupt until the day of the great conclusion, until the great age is consummated, until everything is concluded (upon) the Watchers and the wicked ones.

     Matthew 13.39: and the enemy who sowed them is the devil; the harvest is the end of the age, and the reapers are angels.

17. **16.3:** You were once in heaven, but not all the mysteries of heaven are open to you, and you only knew the rejected mysteries. These ones you have broadcast to the women in the hardness of your hearts and by those mysteries the women and men multiply evil deeds upon the earth. Tell them, 'Therefore, you will have no peace!'

     1 Peter 1.12: It was revealed to them that they were serving not themselves but you, in regard to the things that have now been announced to you through those who brought you good news by the Holy Spirit sent from heaven—things into which angels long to look!

18. **18.13:** And I saw there the seven stars which were like great, burning mountains.

     Revelation 8.8: The second angel blew his trumpet, and something like a great mountain, burning with fire, was thrown into the sea.

19. **18.15–16:** And the stars which roll over upon the fire, they are the ones which have transgressed the commandments of God from the beginning of their rising because they did not arrive punctually. And

he was wroth with them and bound them until the time of the completion of their sin in the year of mystery.

Jude 13: wild waves of the sea, casting up the foam of their own shame; wandering stars, for whom the deepest darkness has been reserved forever.

20. **18.16:** And he was wroth with them and bound them until the time of the completion of their sin in the year of mystery.

Revelation 20.3: and threw him into the pit, and locked and sealed it over him, so that he would deceive the nations no more, until the thousand years were ended. After that he must be let out for a little while.

21. **21.3:** And there I saw seven stars bound together in it, like great mountains, and burning with fire.

Revelation 8.8: The second angel blew his trumpet, and something like a great mountain, burning with fire, was thrown into the sea.

Revelation 17.9: This calls for a mind that has wisdom: the seven heads are seven mountains on which the woman is seated; also, there are seven kings.

22. **21.5–6:** Then one of the holy angels, Uriel, who was with me, guiding me, spoke to me and said to me, "Enoch, for what reason are you asking and for what reason do you question and exhibit eagerness? These are among the stars of heaven which have transgressed the commandments of the Lord and are bound in this place until the completion of ten million years, according to the number of their sins."

Jude 13: wild waves of the sea, casting up the foam of their own shame; wandering stars, for whom the deepest darkness has been reserved forever.

23. **21.6:** These are among the stars of heaven which have transgressed the commandments of the Lord and are bound in this place until the completion of ten million years, according to the number of their sins.

Revelation 20.3: and threw him into the pit, and locked and sealed it over him, so that he would deceive the nations no more, until the thousand years were ended. After that he must be let out for a little while.

24. **22.9–10:** And he replied and said to me, "These three have been made in order that the spirits of the dead might be separated by this spring of water with light upon it, in like manner, the sinners are set apart when they die and are buried in the earth and judgment has not been executed upon them in their lifetime."
Hebrews 12.23: and to the assembly of the firstborn who are enrolled in heaven, and to God the judge of all, and to the spirits of the righteous made perfect.

25. **22.9–14:** And he replied and said to me, "These three have been made in order that the spirits of the dead might be separated by this spring of water with light upon it, in like manner, the sinners are set apart when they die and are buried in the earth and judgment has not been executed upon them in their lifetime, upon this great pain, until the great day of judgment—and to those who curse there will be plague and pain forever, and the retribution of their spirits. They will bind them there forever—even from the beginning of the world. And in this manner is a separation made for the souls of those who make the suit and those who disclose concerning destruction, as they were killed in the days of the sinners. Such has been made for the souls of the people who are not righteous, but sinners and perfect criminals; they shall be together with (other) criminals who are like them, whose souls will not be killed on the day of judgment but will not rise from there." At that moment I blessed the Lord of Glory and I said, "Blessed be my Lord, the Lord of righteousness who rules forever."
Luke 16.26: Besides all this, between you and us a great chasm has been fixed, so that those who might want to pass from here to you cannot do so, and no one can cross from there to us.

26. **22.11:** upon this great pain, until the great day of judgment—and to those who curse there will be plague and pain forever, and the retribution of their spirits. They will bind them there forever—even from the beginning of the world.

    Jude 6: And the angels who did not keep their own position, but left their proper dwelling, he has kept in eternal chains in deepest darkness for the judgment of the great day.

27. **[UBS4] 25.5:** This is for the righteous and the pious. And the elect will be presented with its fruit for life. He will plant it in the direction of the northeast, upon the holy place—in the direction of the house of the Lord, the Eternal King.

    Revelation 15.3: And they sing the song of Moses, the servant of God, and the song of the Lamb: "Great and amazing are your deeds, Lord God the Almighty! Just and true are your ways, King of the nations!"

28. **[UBS4] 27.3:** There will be upon them the spectacle of the righteous judgment, in the presence of the righteous forever. The merciful will bless the Lord of Glory, the Eternal King, all the day.

    Revelation 15.3: And they sing the song of Moses, the servant of God, and the song of the Lamb: "Great and amazing are your deeds, Lord God the Almighty! Just and true are your ways, King of the nations!"

    *1 Timothy 1.17: To the King of the ages, immortal, invisible, the only God, be honor and glory forever and ever. Amen.

29. **38.2:** and when the Righteous One shall appear before the face of the righteous, those elect ones, their deeds are hung upon the Lord of the Spirits, he shall reveal light to their righteous and the elect who dwell upon the earth, where will the dwelling of the sinners be, and where the resting place of those who denied the name of the Lord of the Spirits? It would have been far better for them not to have been born.

    Matthew 26.24: The Son of Man goes as it is written of him, but woe to that one by whom the Son of Man is betrayed! It would have been better for that one not to have been born.

30. **39.4:** Then I saw other dwelling places of the holy ones and their resting places too.
Luke 16.9: And I tell you, make friends for yourselves by means of dishonest wealth so that when it is gone, they may welcome you into the eternal homes.

31. **40.1:** And after that, I saw a hundred thousand times a hundred thousand, ten million times ten million, an innumerable and uncountable multitude who stand before the glory of the Lord of the Spirits.
Revelation 5.11: Then I looked, and I heard the voice of many angels surrounding the throne and the living creatures and the elders; they numbered myriads of myriads and thousands of thousands.

32. **46.3:** And he answered me and said to me, "This is the Son of Man, to whom belongs righteousness, and with whom righteousness dwells. And he will open all the hidden storerooms; for the Lord of the Spirits has chosen him, and he is destined to be victorious before the Lord of the Spirits in eternal uprightness."
Colossians 2.3: in whom are hidden all the treasures of wisdom and knowledge.

33. **48.7:** And he has revealed the wisdom of the Lord of the Spirits to the righteous and the holy ones, for he has preserved the portion of the righteous because they have hated and despised this world of oppression together with all its ways of life and its habits in the name of the Lord of the Spirits; and because they will be saved in his name and it is his good pleasure that they have life.
James 3.6: And the tongue is a fire. The tongue is placed among our

members as a world of iniquity; it stains the whole body, sets on fire
the cycle of nature, and is itself set on fire by hell.

34. **48.10:** On the day of their weariness, there shall be an obstacle on the
earth and they shall fall on their faces; and they shall not rise up again,
nor anyone be found who will take them with his hands and raise
them up. For they have denied the Lord of the Spirits and his Messiah.
Blessed be the name of the Lord of the Spirits!
Jude 4: For certain intruders have stolen in among you, people who
long ago were designated for this condemnation as ungodly, who per-
vert the grace of our God into licentiousness and deny our only Master and Lord, Jesus Christ.
Mark 8.29: He asked them, "But who do you say that I am?" Peter
answered him, "You are the Messiah."

35. **51.1:** In those days, Sheol will return all the deposits which she had
received and hell will give back all that which it owes.
Revelation 20.13: And the sea gave up the dead that were in it, Death
and Hades gave up the dead that were in them, and all were judged
according to what they had done.

36. **51.2:** And he shall choose the righteous and the holy ones from
among the risen dead, for the day when they shall be selected and
saved has arrived.
Luke 21.28: Now when these things begin to take place, stand up and
raise your heads, because your redemption is drawing near.

37. **51.4:** In those days, mountains shall dance like rams; and the hills shall
leap like kids satiated with milk. And the faces of all the angels in heaven
shall glow with joy, because on that day the Elect One has arisen.
Mark 12.25: For when they rise from the dead, they neither marry
nor are given in marriage, but are like angels in heaven.

38. **54.6:** Then Michael, Raphael, Gabriel, and Phanuel themselves shall seize them on that great day of judgment and cast them into the furnace of fire that is burning that day, so that the Lord of the Spirits may take vengeance on them on account of their oppressive deeds which (they performed) as messengers of Satan, leading astray those who dwell upon the earth.
Revelation 13.14: and by the signs that it is allowed to perform on behalf of the beast, it deceives the inhabitants of earth, telling them to make an image for the beast that had been wounded by the sword and yet lived.

39. **60.8:** and the other, a male called Behemoth, which holds his chest in an invisible desert whose name is Dundayin, east of the garden of Eden, wherein the elect and the righteous ones dwell, wherein my grandfather was taken, the seventh from Adam, the first man whom the Lord of the Spirits created.
Jude 14: It was also about these that Enoch, in the seventh generation from Adam, prophesied, saying, "See, the Lord is coming with ten thousands of his holy ones.

40. **61.5:** And these measurements shall reveal all the secrets of the depths of the earth, those who have been destroyed in the desert, those who have been devoured by the wild beasts, and those who have been eaten by the fish of the sea. So that they all will return and find hope in the day of the Elect One. For there is no one who perishes before the Lord of the Spirits, and no one who should perish.
Revelation 20.13: And the sea gave up the dead that were in it, Death and Hades gave up the dead that were in them, and all were judged according to what they had done.

41. **61.8:** He placed the Elect One on the throne of glory; and he shall judge all the works of the holy ones in heaven above, weighing in the balance of their deeds.

Matthew 25.31: When the Son of Man comes in his glory, and all the angels with him, then he will sit on the throne of his glory.

42. **62.2–3:** The Lord of the Spirits has sat down on the throne of his glory, and the spirit of righteousness has been poured out upon him. The word of his mouth will do the sinners in; and all the oppressors shall be eliminated from before his face. On the day of judgment, all the kings, the governors, the high officials, and the landlords shall see and recognize him—how he sits on the throne of his glory, and righteousness is judged before him, and that no nonsensical talk shall be uttered in his presence.

Matthew 25.31: When the Son of Man comes in his glory, and all the angels with him, then he will sit on the throne of his glory.

43. **62.4:** Then pain shall come upon them as on a woman in travail with birth pangs—when she is giving birth the child enters the mouth of the womb and she suffers from childbearing.

1 Thessalonians 5.3: When they say, "There is peace and security," then sudden destruction will come upon them, as labor pains come upon a pregnant woman, and there will be no escape!

44. **63.10:** Furthermore, at that time, you shall say, "Our souls are satiated with exploitation money which could not save us from being cast into the oppressive Sheol."

Luke 16.9: And his master commended the dishonest manager because he had acted shrewdly; for the children of this age are more shrewd in dealing with their own generation than are the children of light.

45. **66.2:** But the Lord of the Spirits gave an order to the angles who were on duty that they should not raise the water enclosures but guard them—for they were the angles who were in charge of the waters. Then I left from the presence of Enoch.

Revelation 16.5: And I heard the angel of the waters say, You are just, O Holy One, who are and were, for you have judged these things.

46. **69.27:** Then there came to them a great joy. And they blessed, glorified, and exalted the Lord on account of the fact that the name of that Son of Man was revealed to them. He shall never pass away or perish from before the face of the earth.
    Matthew 25.31: When the Son of Man comes in his glory, and all the angels with him, then he will sit on the throne of his glory.
    Matthew 26.64: Jesus said to him, "You have said so. But I tell you, From now on you will see the Son of Man seated at the right hand of Power and coming on the clouds of heaven."
    John 5.22: The Father judges no one but has given all judgment to the Son.

47. **[UBS4] 70.1–4:** And it happened after this that his living name was raised up before that Son of Man and to the Lord from among those who dwell upon the earth; it was lifted up in a wind chariot and it disappeared from among them. From that day on, I was not counted among them. But he placed me between two winds, between the northeast and the west, where the angels took a cord to measure for me the place for the elect and the righteous ones. And there I saw the first (human) ancestors and the righteous ones of old, dwelling in that place.
    Hebrews 11.5: By faith Enoch was taken so that he did not experience death; and "he was not found, because God had taken him." For it was attested before he was taken away that "he had pleased God."

48. **Books 72–82:** [The Book of Heavenly Luminaries]
    Galatians 4.10: You are observing special days, and months, and seasons, and years.

49. **83.3–5:** I was then sleeping in my grandfather Mahalalel's house, and I saw in a vision the sky being hurled down and snatched and falling upon the earth. When it fell upon the earth, I saw the earth being swallowed up in the great abyss, the mountains being suspended upon mountains, the hills sinking down upon the hills, and tall trees being uprooted and thrown and sinking into the deep abyss. Thereupon a word fell into my mouth, and I began crying aloud, saying, "The earth is being destroyed."
2 Peter 3.6: through which the world of that time was deluged with water and perished.

50. **86.1:** Again I saw (a vision) with my own eyes as I was sleeping, and saw the lofty heaven; and as I looked, behold, a star fell down from heaven but managed to rise and eat and to be pastured among those cows.
Revelation 8.10: The third angel blew his trumpet, and a great star fell from heaven, blazing like a torch, and it fell on a third of the rivers and on the springs of water.

51. **91.7:** When sin, oppression, blasphemy, and injustice increase, crime, iniquity, and uncleanliness shall be committed and increase likewise. Then a great plague shall take place from heaven upon all these; the holy Lord shall emerge with wrath and plague in order that he may execute judgment upon the earth.
Romans 1.18: For the wrath of God is revealed from heaven against all ungodliness and wickedness of those who by their wickedness suppress the truth.

52. **91.15:** Then, after this matter, on the tenth week in the seventh part, there shall be the eternal judgment; and it shall be executed by the angels of the eternal heaven—the great judgment which emanates from all of the angels.

2 Peter 2.4: For if God did not spare the angels when they sinned, but cast them into hell and committed them to chains of deepest darkness to be kept until the judgment.

53. **93.3:** He then began to recount from the books and said, I was born the seventh during the first week, during which time judgment and righteousness continued to endure.

Jude 14: It was also about these that Enoch, in the seventh generation from Adam, prophesied, saying, See, the Lord is coming with ten thousands of his holy ones.

54. **94.8:** Woe unto you, O rich people! For you have put your trust in your wealth. You shall ooze out of your riches, for you do not remember the Most High.

Luke 6.24: But woe to you who are rich, for you have received your consolation.

James 5.1: Come now, you rich people, weep and wail for the miseries that are coming to you.

55. **97.8–10:** Woe unto you who gain silver and gold by unjust means; you will then say, "We have grown rich and accumulated goods, we have acquired everything that we have desired. So now let us do whatever we like; for we have gathered silver, we have filled our treasuries with money like water. And many are the laborers in our houses. Your lies flow like water. For your wealth shall not endure but it shall take off from you quickly, for you have acquired it all unjustly, and you shall be given over to a great curse."

Luke 12.19: And I will say to my soul, "Soul, you have ample goods laid up for many years; relax, eat, drink, be merry."

James 4.13: Come now, you who say, "Today or tomorrow we will go to such and such a town and spend a year there, doing business and making money."

56. **98.4:** I have sworn to you, sinners: In the same manner that a mountain has never turned into a servant, nor shall a hill ever become a maidservant of a woman, likewise, neither has sin been exported into the world. It is the people who have themselves invented it. And those who commit it shall come under a great curse.
    James 1.14: But one is tempted by one's own desire, being lured and enticed by it.

57. **99.8:** They shall become wicked on account of the folly of their hearts; their eyes will be blindfolded on account of the fear of their hearts, the visions of their dreams.
    Romans 1.21: for though they knew God, they did not honor him as God or give thanks to him, but they became futile in their thinking, and their senseless minds were darkened.

58. **102.5:** Be not sad because your soul has gone down into Sheol in sorrow; or because your flesh fared not well the earthly existence in accordance with your goodness; indeed the time you happened to be in existence was a time of sinners, a time of curse and a time of plague.
    Colossians 1.22: he has now reconciled in his fleshly body through death, so as to present you holy and blameless and irreproachable before him.

59. **03.4:** The spirits of those who died in righteousness shall live and rejoice; their spirits shall not perish, nor their memorial from before the face of the Great One unto all the generations of the world. Therefore, do not worry about their humiliation.
    Matthew 26.13: Truly I tell you, wherever this good news is proclaimed in the whole world, what she has done will be told in remembrance of her.

60. **104.13:** So to them shall be given the Scriptures; and they shall believe them and be glad in them; and all the righteous ones who learn from them the ways of truth shall rejoice.

1 Corinthians 4.17: For this reason I sent you Timothy, who is my beloved and faithful child in the Lord, to remind you of my ways in Christ Jesus, as I teach them everywhere in every church.

4 EZRA

1. **3.21–26:** For the first Adam, burdened with an evil heart, transgressed and was overcome, as were also all who were descended from him. Thus the disease became permanent; the law was in the hearts of the people along with its evil root; but what was good departed, and the evil remained. So the time passed and the years were completed, and you raised up for yourself a servant, named David. You commanded him to build a city for your name, and there to offer you oblations from what is yours. This was done for many years; but the inhabitants of the city transgressed, in everything doing just as Adam and all his descendants had done, for they also had the evil heart.

   Romans 5.12: Therefore, just as sin came into the world through one man, and death came through sin, and so death spread to all because all have sinned.

   *****1 Corinthians 15.45:** Thus it is written, "The first man, Adam, became a living being"; the last Adam became a life-giving spirit.

2. **4.8:** perhaps you would have said to me, "I never went down into the deep, nor as yet into Hades, neither did I ever ascend into heaven."

   John 3.13: No one has ascended into heaven except the one who descended from heaven, the Son of Man.

   Romans 10.6: But the righteousness that comes from faith says, "Do not say in your heart, 'who will ascend into heaven?'" (that is, to bring Christ down)

3. **4.35–37:** Did not the souls of the righteous in their chambers ask about these matters, saying, "How long are we to remain here? And when will the harvest of our reward come?" And the archangel Jeremiel answered and said, "When the number of those like yourselves is completed; for he has weighed the age in the balance, and measured the times by measure, and numbered the times by number; and he will not move or arouse them until that measure is fulfilled."

    Romans 11.25: So that you may not claim to be wiser than you are, brothers and sisters, I want you to understand this mystery: a hardening has come upon part of Israel until the full number of the Gentiles has come in.

    *Revelation 6.9–11: When he opened the fifth seal, I saw under the altar the souls of those who had been slaughtered for the word of God and for the testimony they had given; they cried out with a loud voice, "Sovereign Lord, holy and true, how long will it be before you judge and avenge our blood on the inhabitants of the earth?" They were each given a white robe and told to rest a little longer, until the number would be complete both of their fellow servants and of their brothers and sisters, who were soon to be killed as they themselves had been killed.

4. **6.25:** It shall be that whoever remains after all that I have foretold to you shall be saved and shall see my salvation and the end of the world.

    Matthew 10.22: and you will be hated by all because of my name. But the one who endures to the end will be saved.

    Mark 13.13: and you will be hated by all because of my name. But the one who endures to the end will be saved.

5. **7.6–14:** Another example: There is a city built and set on a plain, and it is full of all good things; but the entrance to it is narrow and set in a precipitous place, so that there is fire on the right hand and deep water on the left. There is only one path lying between them, that is, between the fire and the water, so that only one person can walk on the path. If now the city is given to someone as an inheritance,

how will the heir receive the inheritance unless by passing through the appointed danger?

I said, "That is right, lord." He said to me, "So also is Israel's portion. For I made the world for their sake, and when Adam transgressed my statutes, what had been made was judged. And so the entrances of this world were made narrow and sorrowful and toilsome; they are few and evil, full of dangers and involved in great hardships. But the entrances of the greater world are broad and safe, and yield the fruit of immortality. Therefore unless the living pass through the difficult and futile experiences, they can never receive those things that have been reserved for them."

Matthew 7.13 (*–14): Enter through the narrow gate; for the gate is wide and the road is easy that leads to destruction, and there are many who take it. For the gate is narrow and the road is hard that leads to life, and there are few who find it.

6. **7.11:** For I made the world for their sake, and when Adam transgressed my statutes, what had been made was judged.
   Romans 8.19: For the creation waits with eager longing for the revealing of the children of God.

7. **7.14:** Therefore unless the living pass through the difficult and futile experiences, they can never receive those things that have been reserved for them.
   Matthew 5.11: Blessed are you when people revile you and persecute you and utter all kinds of evil against you falsely on my account.

8. **7.36:** The pit of torment shall appear, and opposite it shall be the place of rest; and the furnace of hell shall be disclosed, and opposite it the paradise of delight.
   Luke 16.26: Besides all this, between you and us a great chasm has been fixed, so that those who might want to pass from here to you cannot do so, and no one can cross from there to us.

*Luke 16.23: In Hades, where he was being tormented, he looked up and saw Abraham far away with Lazarus by his side.

9. 7.72: For this reason, therefore, those who live on earth shall be tormented, because though they had understanding, they committed iniquity; and though they received the commandments, they did not keep them; and though they obtained the law, they dealt unfaithfully with what they received.
    Romans 7.23: but I see in my members another law at war with the law of my mind, making me captive to the law of sin that dwells in my members.

10. 7.75: I answered and said, "If I have found favor in your sight, O Lord, show this also to your servant: whether after death, as soon as everyone of us yields up the soul, we shall be kept in rest until those times come when you will renew the creation, or whether we shall be tormented at once?"
    Romans 8.19: For the creation waits with eager longing for the revealing of the children of God.

11. 7.77: For you have a treasure of works stored up with the Most High, but it will not be shown to you until the last times.
    Matthew 6.20: but store up for yourselves treasures in heaven, where neither moth nor rust consumes and where thieves do not break in and steal.

12. 7.113: But the day of judgment will be the end of this age and the beginning of the immortal age to come, in which corruption has passed away,
    Matthew 13.39: and the enemy who sowed them is the devil; the harvest is the end of the age, and the reapers are angels.

13. **7.118–119:** O Adam, what have you done? For though it was you who sinned, the fall was not yours alone, but ours also who are your descendants. For what good is it to us, if an immortal time has been promised to us, but we have done deeds that bring death?

   Romans 5.16: And the free gift is not like the effect of the one man's sin. For the judgment following one trespass brought condemnation, but the free gift following many trespasses brings justification.

14. **8.3:** Many have been created, but only a few shall be saved.

   Matthew 22.14: For many are called, but few are chosen.

15. **8.41:** For just as the farmer sows many seeds in the ground and plants a multitude of seedlings, and yet not all that have been sown will come up in due season, and not all that were planted will take root; so also those who have been sown in the world will not all be saved.

   Matthew 13.3 (*–8; par Mark 4.3–8): And he told them many things in parables, saying: "Listen! A sower went out to sow. And as he sowed, some seeds fell on the path, and the birds came and ate them up. Other seeds fell on rocky ground, where they did not have much soil, and they sprang up quickly, since they had no depth of soil. But when the sun rose, they were scorched; and since they had no root, they withered away. Other seeds fell among thorns, and the thorns grew up and choked them. Other seeds fell on good soil and brought forth grain, some a hundredfold, some sixty, some thirty.

   Mark 4.14: The sower sows the word.

   Matthew 22.14: For many are called, but few are chosen.

16. **8.60:** but those who were created have themselves defiled the name of him who made them, and have been ungrateful to him who prepared life for them now.

   Romans 1.21: for though they knew God, they did not honor him as God or give thanks to him, but they became futile in their thinking, and their senseless minds were darkened.

17. **9.31–37:** For I sow my law in you, and it shall bring forth fruit in you, and you shall be glorified through it forever. But though our ancestors received the law, they did not keep it and did not observe the statutes; yet the fruit of the law did not perish–for it could not, because it was yours. Yet those who received it perished, because they did not keep what had been sown in them. Now this is the general rule that, when the ground has received seed, or the sea a ship, or any dish food or drink, and when it comes about that what was sown or what was launched or what was put in is destroyed, they are destroyed, but the things that held them remain; yet with us it has not been so. For we who have received the law and sinned will perish, as well as our hearts that received it; the law, however, does not perish but survives in its glory.

    Matthew 13.3 (*–8; par Mark 4.3–8): And he told them many things in parables, saying: "Listen! A sower went out to sow. And as he sowed, some seeds fell on the path, and the birds came and ate them up. Other seeds fell on rocky ground, where they did not have much soil, and they sprang up quickly, since they had no depth of soil. But when the sun rose, they were scorched; and since they had no root, they withered away. Other seeds fell among thorns, and the thorns grew up and choked them. Other seeds fell on good soil and brought forth grain, some a hundredfold, some sixty, some thirty."

    Mark 4.14: The sower sows the word.

18. **9.37:** the law, however, does not perish but survives in its glory.

    Romans 7.12: So the law is holy, and the commandment is holy and just and good.

19. **10.9:** Now ask the earth, and she will tell you that it is she who ought to mourn over so many who have come into being upon her.

    Romans 8.22: We know that the whole creation has been groaning in labor pains until now;

20. **12.42:** For of all the prophets you alone are left to us, like a cluster of grapes from the vintage, and like a lamp in a dark place, and like a haven for a ship saved from a storm.

    2 Peter 1.19: So we have the prophetic message more fully confirmed. You will do well to be attentive to this as to a lamp shining in a dark place, until the day dawns and the morning star rises in your hearts.

21. **13.30–32:** And bewilderment of mind shall come over those who inhabit the earth. They shall plan to make war against one another, city against city, place against place, people against people, and kingdom against kingdom. When these things take place and the signs occur that I showed you before, then my Son will be revealed, whom you saw as a man coming up from the sea.

    Mark 13.8: For nation will rise against nation, and kingdom against kingdom; there will be earthquakes in various places; there will be famines. This is but the beginning of the birth pangs.

3 MACCABEES

1. **2.3:** For you, the creator of all things and the governor of all, are a just Ruler, and you judge those who have done anything in insolence and arrogance.

    Ephesians 3.9: and to make everyone see what is the plan of the mystery hidden for ages in God who created all things;

    Revelation 4.11: You are worthy, our Lord and God, to receive glory and honor and power, for you created all things, and by your will they existed and were created.

2. **[UBS4] 2.5:** You consumed with fire and sulfur the people of Sodom who acted arrogantly, who were notorious for their vices; and you made them an example to those who should come afterward.

Revelation 14.10: They will also drink the wine of God's wrath, poured unmixed into the cup of his anger, and they will be tormented with fire and sulfur in the presence of the holy angels and in the presence of the Lamb.

Revelation 20.10: And the devil who had deceived them was thrown into the lake of fire and sulfur, where the beast and the false prophet were, and they will be tormented day and night forever and ever.

Revelation 21.8: But as for the cowardly, the faithless, the polluted, the murderers, the fornicators, the sorcerers, the idolaters, and all liars, their place will be in the lake that burns with fire and sulfur, which is the second death.

3. **2.13:** see now, O holy King, that because of our many and great sins we are crushed with suffering, subjected t our enemies, and overtaken by helplessness.

   2 Peter 2.7: and if he rescued Lot, a righteous man greatly distressed by the licentiousness of the lawless.

4. **2.29:** Those who are registered are also to be branded on their bodies by fire with the ivy-leaf symbol of Dionysus, and they shall also be reduced to their former limited status.

   Galatians 6.17: From now on, let no one make trouble for me; for I carry the marks of Jesus branded on my body.

5. **4.16:** The king was greatly and continually filled with joy, organizing feasts in honor of all his idols, with a mind alienated from truth and with a profane mouth, praising speechless things that are not able even to communicate or to come to one's help, and uttering improper words against the supreme God.

   Romans 1.28: And since they did not see fit to acknowledge God, God gave them up to a debased mind and to things that should not be done.

1 Corinthians 12.2: You know that when you were pagans, you were enticed and led astray to idols that could not speak.

6. **4.17:** But after the previously mentioned interval of time the scribes declared to the king that they were no longer able to take the census of the Jews because of their immense number.
    Acts 5.7: After an interval of about three hours his wife came in, not knowing what had happened.

7. **5.35:** Then the Jews, on hearing what the king had said, praised the manifest Lord God, King of kings, since this also was his aid that they had received.
    1 Timothy 6.15: which he will bring about at the right time—he who is the blessed and only Sovereign, the King of kings and Lord of lords.
    Revelation 17.14: they will make war on the Lamb, and the Lamb will conquer them, for he is Lord of lords and King of kings, and those with him are called and chosen and faithful.
    [UBS4] Revelation 19.16: On his robe and on his thigh he has a name inscribed, "King of kings and Lord of lords."

8. **6.9:** And now, you who hate insolence, all-merciful and protector of all, reveal yourself quickly to those of the nation of Israel–who are being outrageously treated by the abominable and lawless Gentiles.
    Titus 2.11: For the grace of God has appeared, bringing salvation to all.

4 MACCABEES

1. **1.11:** All people, even their torturers, marveled at their courage and endurance, and they became the cause of the downfall of tyranny over their nation. By their endurance they conquered the tyrant, and thus their native land was purified through them.

James 1.3: because you know that the testing of your faith produces endurance.

2. **1.26:** In the soul it is boastfulness, covetousness, thirst for honor, rivalry, and malice;
    Romans 1.29–31: They were filled with every kind of wickedness, evil, covetousness, malice. Full of envy, murder, strife, deceit, craftiness, they are gossips, slanderers, God-haters, insolent, haughty, boastful, inventors of evil, rebellious toward parents, foolish, faithless, heartless, ruthless.

3. **2.5–6:** Thus the law says, "You shall not covet your neighbor's wife or anything that is your neighbor's." In fact, since the law has told us not to covet, I could prove to you all the more that reason is able to control desires. Just so it is with the emotions that hinder one from justice.
    Romans 7.7: What then should we say? That the law is sin? By no means! Yet, if it had not been for the law, I would not have known sin. I would not have known what it is to covet if the law had not said, "You shall not covet."

4. **2.6:** In fact, since the law has told us not to covet, I could prove to you all the more that reason is able to control desires. Just so it is with the emotions that hinder one from justice.
    Romans 13.9: The commandments, "You shall not commit adultery; You shall not murder; You shall not steal; You shall not covet"; and any other commandment, are summed up in this word, "Love your neighbor as yourself."

5. **2.15:** It is evident that reason rules even the more violent emotions: lust for power, vainglory, boasting, arrogance, and malice.
    Romans 1.29–31: They were filled with every kind of wickedness, evil, covetousness, malice. Full of envy, murder, strife, deceit, crafti-

ness, they are gossips, slanderers, God-haters, insolent, haughty, boastful, inventors of evil, rebellious toward parents, foolish, faithless, heartless, ruthless.

6. **3.13–19:** Eluding the sentinels at the gates, they went searching throughout the enemy camp and found the spring, and from it boldly brought the king a drink. But David, though he was burning with thirst, considered it an altogether fearful danger to his soul to drink what was regarded as equivalent to blood. Therefore, opposing reason to desire, he poured out the drink as an offering to God. For the temperate mind can conquer the drives of the emotions and quench the flames of frenzied desires; it can overthrow bodily agonies even when they are extreme, and by nobility of reason spurn all domination by the emotions. The present occasion now invites us to a narrative demonstration of temperate reason.
Luke 6.12: Now during those days he went out to the mountain to pray; and he spent the night in prayer to God.

7. **4.1–14:** Now there was a certain Simon, a political opponent of the noble and good man, Onias, who then held the high priesthood for life. When despite all manner of slander he was unable to injure Onias in the eyes of the nation, he fled the country with the purpose of betraying it. So he came to Apollonius, governor of Syria, Phoenicia, and Cilicia, and said, "I have come here because I am loyal to the king's government, to report that in the Jerusalem treasuries there are deposited tens of thousands in private funds, which are not the property of the temple but belong to King Seleucus." When Apollonius learned the details of these things, he praised Simon for his service to the king and went up to Seleucus to inform him of the rich treasure. On receiving authority to deal with this matter, he proceeded quickly to our country accompanied by the accursed Simon and a very strong military force. He said that he had come with the king's authority to seize the private funds in the treasury. The people indignantly

protested his words, considering it outrageous that those who had committed deposits to the sacred treasury should be deprived of them, and did all that they could to prevent it. But, uttering threats, Apollonius went on to the temple. While the priests together with women and children were imploring God in the temple to shield the holy place that was being treated so contemptuously, and while Apollonius was going up with his armed forces to seize the money, angels on horseback with lightning flashing from their weapons appeared from heaven, instilling in them great fear and trembling. Then Apollonius fell down half dead in the temple area that was open to all, stretched out his hands toward heaven, and with tears begged the Hebrews to pray for him and propitiate the wrath of the heavenly army. For he said that he had committed a sin deserving of death, and that if he were spared he would praise the blessedness of the holy place before all people. Moved by these words, the high priest Onias, although otherwise he had scruples about doing so, prayed for him so that King Seleucus would not suppose that Apollonius had been overcome by human treachery and not by divine justice. So Apollonius, having been saved beyond all expectations, went away to report to the king what had happened to him.

Acts 9.1–29: Meanwhile Saul, still breathing threats and murder against the disciples of the Lord, went to the high priest and asked him for letters to the synagogues at Damascus, so that if he found any who belonged to the Way, men or women, he might bring them bound to Jerusalem. Now as he was going along and approaching Damascus, suddenly a light from heaven flashed around him. He fell to the ground and heard a voice saying to him, "Saul, Saul, why do you persecute me?" He asked, "Who are you, Lord?" The reply came, "I am Jesus, whom you are persecuting. But get up and enter the city, and you will be told what you are to do." The men who were traveling with him stood speechless because they heard the voice but saw no one. Saul got up from the ground, and though his eyes were open, he could see nothing; so they led him by the hand and brought him into Damascus. For three days he was without sight, and neither ate nor drank. Now there was a disciple in Damascus named Ananias. The Lord said to him in a vision, "Ananias." He answered, "Here I am, Lord." The Lord said to him, "Get up and go to the street called Straight, and at the house of Judas look for a man of Tarsus named Saul. At this moment he is praying, and he has seen in a vision a man named Ananias come in and lay his hands on him so that he might regain his sight." But Ananias answered, "Lord, I have heard from many about this man, how much evil he has done to your saints in Jerusalem; and here he has authority from the chief priests to bind all who invoke your name." But the Lord said to him, "Go, for he is an instrument whom I have chosen to bring my name before Gentiles and kings and before the people of Israel; I myself will show him how much he must suffer for the sake of my name." So Ananias went and entered the house. He laid his hands on Saul and said, "Brother Saul, the Lord Jesus, who appeared to you on your way here, has sent me so that you may regain your sight and be filled with the Holy Spirit." And immediately something like scales fell from his eyes, and his sight was restored. Then he got up and was baptized, and after taking some food, he regained his strength. For several days he was with the disciples in Damascus, and immediately he began to proclaim Jesus in the synagogues, saying, "He is the Son of God." All who heard him were amazed and said, "Is not this the man who made havoc in Jerusalem among those who invoked this name? And has he not come here for the purpose of bringing them bound before the chief priests?" Saul became increasingly more powerful and confounded the Jews who lived in Damascus by proving that Jesus was the Messiah. After some time had passed, the Jews plotted to kill him, but their plot became known to Saul. They were watching the gates day and night so that they might kill him; but his disciples took him by night and let him down through an opening in the wall, lowering him in a basket. When he had come to Jerusalem, he attempted to join the disciples; and they were all afraid of him, for they did not believe that he was a disciple. But Barnabas took him, brought him to the apostles, and described for them how on the road he had seen the Lord, who had spoken to him, and how in Damascus he had spoken boldly in the name of Jesus. So he went in and out among them in Jerusalem, speaking boldly in the name of the Lord. He spoke and argued with the Hellenists; but they were attempting to kill him.

8. **5.2:** ordered the guards to seize each and every Hebrew and to compel them to eat pork and food sacrificed to idols.
   Acts 15.29: that you abstain from what has been sacrificed to idols and from blood and from what is strangled and from fornication. If you keep yourselves from these, you will do well. Farewell.

9. **6.31:** Admittedly, then, devout reason is sovereign over the emotions.
   1 Timothy 3.16: Without any doubt, the mystery of our religion is great: He was revealed in flesh, vindicated in spirit, seen by angels, proclaimed among Gentiles, believed in throughout the world, taken up in glory.

10. **7.8:** Such should be those who are administrators of the law, shielding it with their own blood and noble sweat in sufferings even to death.
    Romans 15.16: to be a minister of Christ Jesus to the Gentiles in the priestly service of the gospel of God, so that the offering of the Gentiles may be acceptable, sanctified by the Holy Spirit.

11. **7.16:** If, therefore, because of piety an aged man despised tortures even to death, most certainly devout reason is governor of the emotions.
    1 Timothy 3.16: Without any doubt, the mystery of our religion is great: He was revealed in flesh, vindicated in spirit, seen by angels, proclaimed among Gentiles, believed in throughout the world, taken up in glory.

12. **7.19:** since they believe that they, like our patriarchs Abraham and Isaac and Jacob, do not die to God, but live to God.

Matthew 23.32: I am the God of Abraham, the God of Isaac, and the God of Jacob'? He is God not of the dead, but of the living.
Luke 20.37–38: And the fact that the dead are raised Moses himself showed, in the story about the bush, where he speaks of the Lord as the God of Abraham, the God of Isaac, and the God of Jacob. Now he is God not of the dead, but of the living; for to him all of them are alive."

13. **9.8:** For we, through this severe suffering and endurance, shall have the prize of virtue and shall be with God, on whose account we suffer;
    James 5.10: As an example of suffering and patience, beloved, take the prophets who spoke in the name of the Lord.

14. **12.13:** As a man, were you not ashamed, you most savage beast, to cut out the tongues of men who have feelings like yours and are made of the same elements as you, and to maltreat and torture them in this way?
    Acts 14.15: Friends, why are you doing this? We are mortals just like you, and we bring you good news, that you should turn from these worthless things to the living God, who made the heaven and the earth and the sea and all that is in them.

15. **12.17:** and I call on the God of our ancestors to be merciful to our nation.
    Acts 24.14: But this I admit to you, that according to the Way, which they call a sect, I worship the God of our ancestors, believing everything laid down according to the law or written in the prophets.

16. **13.14:** Let us not fear him who thinks he is killing us.
    Matthew 10.28: Do not fear those who kill the body but cannot kill the soul; rather fear him who can destroy both soul and body in hell.

17. **13.15:** for great is the struggle of the soul and the danger of eternal torment lying before those who transgress the commandment of God.
Luke 16.23: In Hades, where he was being tormented, he looked up and saw Abraham far away with Lazarus by his side.

18. **13.17:** For if we so die, Abraham and Isaac and Jacob will welcome us, and all the fathers will praise us.
Matthew 8.11: I tell you, many will come from east and west and will eat with Abraham and Isaac and Jacob in the kingdom of heaven,

19. **15.2:** Two courses were open to this mother, that of religion, and that of preserving her seven sons for a time, as the tyrant had promised.
Hebrews 11.25: choosing rather to share ill-treatment with the people of God than to enjoy the fleeting pleasures of sin.

20. **15.7:** and because of the many pains she suffered with each of them she had sympathy for them.
James 1.4: and let endurance have its full effect, so that you may be mature and complete, lacking in nothing.

21. **15.8:** yet because of the fear of God she disdained the temporary safety of her children.
Hebrews 11.25: choosing rather to share ill-treatment with the people of God than to enjoy the fleeting pleasures of sin.

22. **16.1:** If, then, a woman, advanced in years and mother of seven sons, endured seeing her children tortured to death, it must be admitted that devout reason is sovereign over the emotions.
1 Timothy 3.16: Without any doubt, the mystery of our religion is great: He was revealed in flesh, vindicated in spirit, seen by angels, proclaimed among Gentiles, believed in throughout the world, taken up in glory.

23. **16.12:** Yet that holy and God-fearing mother did not wail with such a lament for any of them, nor did she dissuade any of them from dying, nor did she grieve as they were dying.

    1 Thessalonians 1.8: For the word of the Lord has sounded forth from you not only in Macedonia and Achaia, but in every place your faith in God has become known, so that we have no need to speak about it.

24. **16.16:** My sons, noble is the contest to which you are called to bear witness for the nation. Fight zealously for our ancestral law.

    Hebrews 12.1: Therefore, since we are surrounded by so great a cloud of witnesses, let us also lay aside every weight and the sin that clings so closely, and let us run with perseverance the race that is set before us,

25. **16.25:** They knew also that those who die for the sake of God live to God, as do Abraham and Isaac and Jacob and all the patriarchs.

    Matthew 23.32: I am the God of Abraham, the God of Isaac, and the God of Jacob'? He is God not of the dead, but of the living.

    Luke 20.37(*–38): And the fact that the dead are raised Moses himself showed, in the story about the bush, where he speaks of the Lord as the God of Abraham, the God of Isaac, and the God of Jacob. Now he is God not of the dead, but of the living; for to him all of them are alive.

26. **17.4:** Take courage, therefore, O holy-minded mother, maintaining firm an enduring hope in God.

    1 Thessalonians 1.3: remembering before our God and Father your work of faith and labor of love and steadfastness of hope in our Lord Jesus Christ.

27. **17.10–15:** They vindicated their nation, looking to God and enduring torture even to death. Truly the contest in which they were engaged was divine, for on that day virtue gave the awards and tested them for their endurance. The prize was immortality in endless life. Eleazar was

the first contestant, the mother of the seven sons entered the competition, and the brothers contended. The tyrant was the antagonist, and the world and the human race were the spectators. Reverence for God was victor and gave the crown to its own athletes.

Hebrews 12.1: Therefore, since we are surrounded by so great a cloud of witnesses, let us also lay aside every weight and the sin that clings so closely, and let us run with perseverance the race that is set before us,

28. **17.20:** These, then, who have been consecrated for the sake of God, are honored, not only with this honor, but also by the fact that because of them our enemies did not rule over our nation,
    John 12.26: Whoever serves me must follow me, and where I am, there will my servant be also. Whoever serves me, the Father will honor.

29. **18.24:** to whom be glory forever and ever. Amen.
    Romans 16.27: to the only wise God, through Jesus Christ, to whom be the glory forever! Amen.
    Galatians 1.5: to whom be the glory forever and ever. Amen.

JUBILEES

1. **1.23:** But after this they will return to me in all unrighteousness and with all of (their) heart and soul. And I shall cut off the foreskin of their heart and the foreskin of the heart of their descendants. And I shall create for them a holy spirit, and I shall purify them so that they will not turn away from following me from that day and forever.
   Romans 2.29: Rather, a person is a Jew who is one inwardly, and real circumcision is a matter of the heart—it is spiritual and not literal. Such a person receives praise not from others but from God.

2. **2.19:** And he said to us, "Behold I shall separate for myself a people from among all the nations. And they will also keep the Sabbath. And

I will sanctify them for myself, and I will bless them. Just as I have sanctified and shall sanctify the Sabbath day for myself thus shall I bless them. And they will be my people and I will be their God."

Romans 9.24: including us whom he has called, not from the Jews only but also from the Gentiles?

3. **19.21, etc.:** Let your hands be strong and let your heart rejoice in your son, Jacob. Because I love him more than all of my sons. He will be blessed forever and his seed will be one which fills all of the earth.

   Romans 4.13: For the promise that he would inherit the world did not come to Abraham or to his descendants through the law but through the righteousness of faith.

PSALMS OF SOLOMON

1. **1.5:** They exalted themselves to the stars, they said they would never fall.

   Matthew 11.23: And you, Capernaum, will you be exalted to heaven? No, you will be brought down to Hades. For if the deeds of power done in you had been done in Sodom, it would have remained until this day.

2. **4.23:** Blessed are those who fear God in their innocence; the Lord shall save them from deceitful and sinful people and save us from every evil snare.

   2 Timothy 3.11: my persecutions, and my suffering the things that happened to me in Antioch, Iconium, and Lystra. What persecutions I endured! Yet the Lord rescued me from all of them.

3. **4.25, etc.:** Lord, let your mercy be upon all those who love you.

   Romans 8.28: We know that all things work together for good for those who love God, who are called according to his purpose.

4. **5.3:** For no one takes plunder away from a strong man, so who is going to take (anything) from all that you have done, unless you give (it)?

   Mark 3.27: But no one can enter a strong man's house and plunder his property without first tying up the strong man; then indeed the house can be plundered.

   [UBS4] Luke 11.21–22: But when one stronger than he attacks him and overpowers him, he takes away his armor in which he trusted and divides his plunder.

5. **5.9-11:** You feed the birds and the fish, as you send rain to the wilderness that the grass may sprout, to provide pasture in the wilderness for every living thing, and if they are hungry, they will lift up their face to you. You feed kings and rulers and peoples, O God, and who is the hope of the poor and the needy, if not you, Lord?

   Matthew 6.26: Look at the birds of the air; they neither sow nor reap nor gather into barns, and yet your heavenly Father feeds them. Are you not of more value than they?

6. **7.1:** Do not move away from us, O God, lest those who hate us without cause should attack us.

   John 15.25: It was to fulfill the word that is written in their law, "They hated me without a cause."

7. **7.6:** While your name lives among us, we shall receive mercy and the gentile will not overcome us.

   John 1.14: And the Word became flesh and lived among us, and we have seen his glory, the glory as of a father's only son, full of grace and truth.

8. **8.2:** The sound of many people as of a violent storm, as a raging fire storm sweeping through the wilderness.

   Revelation 19.1: After this I heard what seemed to be the loud voice of a great multitude in heaven, saying, "Hallelujah! Salvation and glory and power to our God."

9. **9.2:** Because of this God mixed them (a drink) of a wavering spirit, and gave them a cup of undiluted wine to make them drunk.
1 John 4.6: We are from God. Whoever knows God listens to us, and whoever is not from God does not listen to us. From this we know the spirit of truth and the spirit of error.

10. **8.15:** He brought someone from the end of the earth, one who attacks in strength; he declared war against Jerusalem and her land.
Acts 1.8: But you will receive power when the Holy Spirit has come upon you; and you will be my witnesses in Jerusalem, in all Judea and Samaria, and to the ends of the earth.

11. **8.28:** Bring together the dispersed of Israel with mercy and goodness, for your faithfulness is with us.
Romans 3.3: What if some were unfaithful? Will their faithlessness nullify the faithfulness of God?

12. **9.5:** The one who does what is right saves up life for himself with the Lord, and the one who does what is wrong causes his own life to be destroyed; for the Lord's righteous judgments are according to the individual and the household.
Romans 2.5: But by your hard and impenitent heart you are storing up wrath for yourself on the day of wrath, when God's righteous judgment will be revealed.

13. **10.2:** The one who prepares (his) back for the whip shall be purified, for the Lord is good to those who endure discipline.
Hebrews 12.7: Endure trials for the sake of discipline. God is treating you as children; for what child is there whom a parent does not discipline?

14. **12.6:** May the salvation of the Lord be upon Israel his servant forever; may the wicked perish once and for all from before the Lord. And may the Lord's devout inherit the Lord's promises.

Hebrews 6.12: so that you may not become sluggish, but imitators of those who through faith and patience inherit the promises.

15. **14.1:** The Lord is faithful to those who truly love him, to those who endure his discipline.

Romans 7.10: and I died, and the very commandment that promised life proved to be death to me.

16. **14.3:** The Lord's devout shall live by it forever; the Lord's paradise, the trees of life, are his devout ones.

Revelation 22.2: through the middle of the street of the city. On either side of the river is the tree of life with its twelve kinds of fruit, producing its fruit each month; and the leaves of the tree are for the healing of the nations.

17. **15.2–3:** For who, O God, is strong except he who confesses you in truth; and what person is powerful except he who confesses your name? A new psalm with song with a happy heart, the fruit of the lips with the tuned instrument of the tongue, the first fruits of the lips from a devout and righteous heart.

Hebrews 13.15: Through him, then, let us continually offer a sacrifice of praise to God, that is, the fruit of lips that confess his name.

18. **15.8:** But they shall pursue sinners and overtake them, for those who act lawlessly shall not escape the Lord's judgment.

Romans 2.3: Do you imagine, whoever you are, that when you judge those who do such things and yet do them yourself, you will escape the judgment of God?

19. **16.5:** I will give thanks to you, O God, who came to my aid for (my) salvation, and who did not count me with the sinners for (my) destruction.
Luke 22.37: For I tell you, this scripture must be fulfilled in me, "And he was counted among the lawless;" and indeed what is written about me is being fulfilled.

20. **17.1:** Lord, you are our king forevermore; for in you, O God, does our soul take pride.
Romans 2.17: But if you call yourself a Jew and rely on the law and boast of your relation to God.

21. **17.21:** See, Lord, and raise up for them their king, the son of David, to rule over your servant Israel in the time known to you, O God.
John 7.42: Has not the scripture said that the Messiah is descended from David and comes from Bethlehem, the village where David lived?
***Matthew 24.36:** But about that day and hour no one knows, neither the angels of heaven, nor the Son, but only the Father.

22. **17.23–24:** In wisdom and in righteousness to drive out the sinners from the inheritance; to smash the arrogance of sinners like a potter's jar; To shatter all their substance with an iron rod; to destroy the unlawful nations with the word of his mouth.
Revelation 2.27: to rule them with an iron rod, as when clay pots are shattered.

23. **17.25:** At his warning the nations will flee from his presence; and he will condemn sinners by the thoughts of their hearts.
Luke 21.24: they will fall by the edge of the sword and be taken away as captives among all nations; and Jerusalem will be trampled on by the Gentiles, until the times of the Gentiles are fulfilled.

24. **17.26, 29:** He will gather a holy people whom he will lead in righteousness; and he will judge the tribes of the people that have been made holy by the Lord their God.... He will judge peoples and nations in the wisdom of his righteousness. Pause.

    Matthew 19.28: Jesus said to them, "Truly I tell you, at the renewal of all things, when the Son of Man is seated on the throne of his glory, you who have followed me will also sit on twelve thrones, judging the twelve tribes of Israel."

25. **17.30:** And he will have gentile nations serving him under his yoke, and he will glorify the Lord in a place prominent above the whole earth. And he will purge Jerusalem and make it holy as it was even from the beginning.

    Matthew 21.12: Then Jesus entered the temple and drove out all who were selling and buying in the temple, and he overturned the tables of the money changers and the seats of those who sold doves.

26. **[UBS4] 17.31, 34:** for nations to come from the ends of the earth to see his glory, to bring as gifts her children who had been driven out, and to see the glory of the Lord with which God has glorified her.... The Lord himself is his king, the hope of the one who has a strong hope in God. He shall be compassionate to all the nations who reverently stand before him.

    Revelation 21.24, 26: The nations will walk by its light, and the kings of the earth will bring their glory into it.... People will bring into it the glory and the honor of the nations.

27. **17.32:** And he will be a righteous king over them, taught by God. There will be no unrighteousness among them in his days, for all shall be holy, and their king shall be the Lord Messiah.

    Luke 2.11: to you is born this day in the city of David a Savior, who is the Messiah, the Lord.

28. **17.36:** And he himself will be free from sin, in order to rule a great people. He will expose officials and drive out sinners by the strength of his word.
    Hebrews 4.15: For we do not have a high priest who is unable to sympathize with our weaknesses, but we have one who in every respect has been tested as we are, yet without sin.

29. **17.43:** His words will be purer than the finest gold, the best. He will judge the peoples in the assemblies, the tribes of the sanctified. His words will be as the words of the holy ones, among sanctified peoples.
    Revelation 3.18: Therefore I counsel you to buy from me gold refined by fire so that you may be rich; and white robes to clothe you and to keep the shame of your nakedness from being seen; and salve to anoint your eyes so that you may see.

30. **18.6–7:** Blessed are those born in those days, to see the good things of the Lord which he will do for the coming generation; which will be under the rod of discipline of the Lord Messiah, in the fear of his God, in wisdom of spirit, and of righteousness and of strength.
    Matthew 13.6 [?]: But when the sun rose, they were scorched; and since they had no root, they withered away.
    *Matthew 24.19: Woe to those who are pregnant and to those who are nursing infants in those days!
    18.10: Our God is great and glorious, living in the highest heavens, who arranges the stars into orbits to mark the time of the hours from day to day. And they have not deviated from their course, which he appointed them.
    Luke 2.14: "Glory to God in the highest heaven, and on earth peace among those whom he favors!"

2 BARUCH

1. **14.8-9:** O Lord, my Lord, who can understand your judgment? Or who can explore the depth of your way? Or who can discern the majesty of your path? Or who can discern your incomprehensible counsel? Or who of those who are born has ever discovered the beginning and the end of your wisdom?

    Romans 11.33: O the depth of the riches and wisdom and knowledge of God! How unsearchable are his judgments and how inscrutable his ways!

2. **14.13:** Therefore, they leave this world without fear and are confident of the world which you have promised to them with an expectation full of joy.

    Romans 4.13: For the promise that he would inherit the world did not come to Abraham or to his descendants through the law but through the righteousness of faith.

3. **15.8:** For this world is to them a struggle and an effort with much trouble. And that accordingly which shall come, a crown with great glory.

    Romans 8.18: I consider that the sufferings of this present time are not worth comparing with the glory about to be revealed to us.

4. **21.13:** For if only this life exists which everyone possesses here, nothing could be more bitter than this.

    1 Corinthians 15.19: If for this life only we have hoped in Christ, we are of all people most to be pitied.

5. **23.4:** For when Adam sinned and death was decreed against those who were to be born, the multitude of those who would be born was numbered. And for that number a place was prepared where the living ones might live and where the dead might be preserved.

Romans 5.12: Therefore, just as sin came into the world through one man, and death came through sin, and so death spread to all because all have sinned.

6. **32.6:** For greater than the two evils will be the trial when the Mighty One will renew his creation.
    Romans 8.18: I consider that the sufferings of this present time are not worth comparing with the glory about to be revealed to us.

7. **48.8:** With signs of fear and threat you command the flames, and they change into winds. And this the word you bring to life that which does not exist, and with great power you hold that which has not yet come.
    Romans 4.17: As it is written, "I have made you the father of many nations"—in the presence of the God in whom he believed, who gives life to the dead and calls into existence the things that do not exist.

8. **48.22:** In you we have put our trust, because, behold, your Law is with us, and we know that we do not fall as long as we keep your statutes.
    Romans 2.17: But if you call yourself a Jew and rely on the law and boast of your relation to God.

9. **51.3:** Also, as for the glory of those who proved to be righteous on account of my law, those who possessed intelligence in their life, and those who planted the root of wisdom in their heart—their splendor will then be glorified by transformations, and the shape of their face will be changed into the light of their beauty so that they may acquire and receive the undying world which is promised to them.
    Romans 4.13: For the promise that he would inherit the world did not come to Abraham or to his descendants through the law but through the righteousness of faith.
    54.10: Blessed is my mother among those who bear, and praised among women is she who bore me.

Luke 1.42: And exclaimed with a loud cry, "Blessed are you among women, and blessed is the fruit of your womb."

10. **54.15:** For although Adam sinned first and has brought death upon all who were not in his own time, yet each of them who has been born from him has prepared for himself the coming torment.
Romans 5.12: Therefore, just as sin came into the world through one man, and death came through sin, and so death spread to all because all have sinned.

11. **54.17–18:** But now, turn yourselves to destruction, you unrighteous ones who are living now, for you will be visited suddenly, since you have once rejected the understanding of the Most High. For his works have not taught you, nor has the artful work of his creation which has existed always persuaded you.
Romans 1.19: For what can be known about God is plain to them, because God has shown it to them.

12. **57.2:** For at that time the unwritten law was in force among them, and the works of the commandments were accomplished at that time, and the belief in the coming judgment was brought about, and the hope of the world which will be renewed was built at that time, and the promise of the life that will come later was planted.
Romans 2.15: They show that what the law requires is written on their hearts, to which their own conscience also bears witness; and their conflicting thoughts will accuse or perhaps excuse them.

13. **59.6:** The suppression of wrath, the abundance of long-suffering, the truth of judgment.
Romans 9.22: What if God, desiring to show his wrath and to make known his power, has endured with much patience the objects of wrath that are made for destruction.

TESTAMENT OF MOSES
(NA27: ASSUMPTION OF MOSES)

1. **3.11:** Is this not that which was made known to us in prophecies by Moses, who suffered many things in Egypt and at the Red Sea and in the wilderness for forty years.
   Acts 7.36: He led them out, having performed wonders and signs in Egypt, at the Red Sea, and in the wilderness for forty years.

2. **5.4:** For they will not follow the truth of God, but certain of them will pollute the high altar by [4–6 letters lost] the offerings which they place before the Lord. They are not truly priests at all, but slaves, yea sons of slaves.
   Romans 1.25: Because they exchanged the truth about God for a lie and worshiped and served the creature rather than the Creator, who is blessed forever! Amen.

3. **12.7:** Yet this is not on account of either my strength or weakness, it is simply that his mercies and long-suffering have lighted on me.
   Romans 9.16: So it depends not on human will or exertion, but on God who shows mercy.

4. **?:** See Clement of Alexandria, Origen, et al.
   Jude 9: But when the archangel Michael contended with the devil and disputed about the body of Moses, he did not dare to bring a condemnation of slander against him, but said, "The Lord rebuke you!"

TESTAMENT OF REUBEN

1. **4.3:** Even until now my conscience harasses me because of my impious act.
   Romans 2.15: They show that what the law requires is written on

their hearts, to which their own conscience also bears witness; and their conflicting thoughts will accuse or perhaps excuse them.

2. **5.5:** Accordingly, my children, flee from sexual promiscuity, and order your wives and daughters not to adorn their heads and their appearances so as to deceive man's sound minds. For every woman who schemes in these ways is destined for eternal punishment.
    1 Corinthians 6.18: Shun fornication! Every sin that a person commits is outside the body; but the fornicator sins against the body itself.

TESTAMENT OF LEVI

1. **Chapter 2:** [Levi passes through first heaven, into second, and is told he will enter the third, in which is the presence of the Lord.]
    2 Corinthians 12.2: I know a person in Christ who fourteen years ago was caught up to the third heaven—whether in the body or out of the body I do not know; God knows.

2. **3.2:** And contains fire, snow, and ice, ready for the day determined by God's righteous judgment. In it are all the spirits of those dispatched to achieve the punishment of mankind.
    Romans 2.5: But by your hard and impenitent heart you are storing up wrath for yourself on the day of wrath, when God's righteous judgment will be revealed.

3. **3.6:** They present to the Lord a pleasing odor, a rational and bloodless oblation.
    Romans 12.1: I appeal to you therefore, brothers and sisters, by the mercies of God, to present your bodies as a living sacrifice, holy and acceptable to God, which is your spiritual worship.

4. **14.4:** For what will all the nations do if you become darkened with impiety? You will bring down a curse on our nation, because you want to destroy the light of the Law which was granted to you for the enlightenment of every man, teaching commandments which are opposed to God's just ordinances.
    Romans 2.22: You say, "We know that God's judgment on those who do such things is in accordance with truth."

5. **18.7:** And the glory of the Most High shall burst forth upon him. And the spirit of understanding and sanctification shall rest upon him.
    Romans 1.4: And was declared to be Son of God with power according to the spirit of holiness by resurrection from the dead, Jesus Christ our Lord.

6. **18.9:** And in his priesthood the nations shall be multiplied in knowledge on the earth and they shall be illumined by the grace of the Lord, but Israel shall be diminished by her ignorance and darkened by her grief. In his priesthood sin shall cease and lawless men shall rest from their evil deeds, and righteous men shall find rest in him.
    Hebrews 9.26: For then he would have had to suffer again and again since the foundation of the world. But as it is, he has appeared once for all at the end of the age to remove sin by the sacrifice of himself.

TESTAMENT OF ZEBULON

1. **9.5–9:** In the writing of the fathers I came to know that in the last days you shall defect from the Lord, and you shall be divided in Israel, and you shall follow after two kings; you shall commit every abomination and worship every idol. Your enemies will take you captive and you shall reside among the gentiles with all sorts of sickness and tribulation and oppression of soul. And thereafter you will remember the Lord and repent, and he will turn you around because he is merciful and

compassionate; he does not bring a charge of wickedness against the sons of men, since they are flesh and the spirits of deceit lead them astray in all of their actions. And thereafter the Lord himself will arise upon you, the light of righteousness with healing and compassion in his wings. He will liberate every captive of the sons of men from Beliar, and every spirit of error will be trampled down. He will turn all nations to being zealous for him. And you shall see he whom the Lord will choose: Jerusalem is his name. You will provoke him to wrath by the wickedness of your works, and you will be rejected until the time of the end.

Romans 11.25: So that you may not claim to be wiser than you are, brothers and sisters, I want you to understand this mystery: a hardening has come upon part of Israel, until the full number of the Gentiles has come in.

TESTAMENT OF DAN

1. **5.2:** Each of you speak truth clearly to his neighbor, and do not fall into pleasure and troublemaking, but be at peace, holding to the God of peace. Thus no conflict will overwhelm you.

    Romans 15.33: The God of peace be with all of you. Amen.

2. **6.2:** Draw near to God and to the angel who intercedes for you, because he is the mediator between God and men for the peace of Israel. He shall stand in opposition to the kingdom of the enemy.

    James 4.8: Draw near to God, and he will draw near to you. Cleanse your hands, you sinners, and purify your hearts, you double-minded.

TESTAMENT OF NAPHTALI

1. **8.4:** If you achieve the good, my children, men and angels will bless you; and God will be glorified through you among the gentiles. The

devil will flee from you; wild animals will be afraid of you, and the angels will stand by you.

James 4.7: Submit yourselves therefore to God. Resist the devil, and he will flee from you.

TESTAMENT OF JOSEPH

1. **7.8:** For if anyone is subjected to the passion of desire and is enslaved by it, as she was, even when he hears something good bearing on that passion he receives it as aiding his wicked desire.

    Romans 1.26: For this reason God gave them up to degrading passions. Their women exchanged natural intercourse for unnatural.

2. **8.5:** When I was in fetters, the Egyptian woman was overtaken with grief. She came and heard the report how I gave thanks to the Lord and sang praise in the house of darkness, and how I rejoiced with cheerful voice, glorifying my God, because through her trumped-up charge I was set free from this Egyptian woman.

    Acts 16.23, 25: After they had given them a severe flogging, they threw them into prison and ordered the jailor to keep them securely…. About midnight Paul and Silas were praying and singing hymns to God, and the prisoners were listening to them.

3. **10.1:** So you see, my children, how great are the things that patience and prayer with fasting accomplish.

    Romans 5.3: And not only that, but we also boast in our sufferings, knowing that suffering produces endurance.

    James 1.3: because you know that the testing of your faith produces endurance.

Testament of Benjamin

1. **4.3:** And even if persons plot against him for evil ends, by doing good this man conquers evil, being watched over by God. He loves those who wrong him as he loves his own life.
   Romans 12.21: Do not be overcome by evil, but overcome evil with good.

Life of Adam and Eve

1. **9.1:** Eighteen days went by. Then Satan was angry and transformed himself into the brightness of angels and went away to the Tigris River to Eve and found her weeping.
   2 Corinthians 11.14: And no wonder! Even Satan disguises himself as an angel of light.

Ascension of Isaiah

1. **5.11–15:** And they seized Isaiah the son of Amoz and sawed him in half with a wood saw. And Manasseh, and Belkira, and the false prophets, and the princes, and the people and all stood by looking on. And to the prophets who were with him he said before he was sawed in half, "Go to the district of Tyre and Sidon, because for me alone the Lord has mixed the cup." And while Isaiah was being sawed in half, he did not cry out, or weep, but his mouth spoke with the Holy Spirit until he was sawed in two. Beliar did this to Isaiah through Belkira and through Manasseh, for Sammael was very angry with Isaiah from the days of Hezekiah, king of Judah, because of the things which he had seen concerning the Beloved.
   Hebrews 11.37: They were stoned to death, they were sawn in two, they were killed by the sword; they went about in skins of sheep and goats, destitute, persecuted, tormented.

APOCALYPSE OF ELIJAH

1. **?:** [According to Origen; cf. Isaiah 64.4]
   1 Corinthians 2.9: But, as it is written, "What no eye has seen, nor ear heard, nor the human heart conceived, what God has prepared for those who love him."

FROM GREEK WRITERS
("FRAGMENTS OF PSEUDO-GREEK POETS")

1. **Aratus, Phaenomena, 5:**
   Acts 17.28: For "In him we live and move and have our being;" as even some of your own poets have said, "For we too are his offspring."

2. **Epimenides of Crete? Posidonius?:**
   Acts 17.28: For "In him we live and move and have our being;" as even some of your own poets have said, "For we too are his offspring."

3. **Epimenides, De Oraculis/Peri Chrēsmōn:**
   Titus 1.12: It was one of them, their very own prophet, who said, "Cretans are always liars, vicious brutes, lazy gluttons."

4. **Euripides, Bacchae, 794:** If I were you, I would offer him a sacrifice, not rage and kick against the goad, a man defying God.
   Acts 26.14: When we had all fallen to the ground, I heard a voice saying to me in the Hebrew language, "Saul, Saul, why are you persecuting me? It hurts you to kick against the goads."

5. **Heraclitus: ?**
   2 Peter 2.22: It has happened to them according to the true proverb, "The dog turns back to its own vomit," and, "The sow is washed only to wallow in the mud."

6. **Julianus, orr 8.246b: ? [see also 3, above]**
   Acts 26.14: When we had all fallen to the ground, I heard a voice saying to me in the Hebrew language, "Saul, Saul, why are you persecuting me? It hurts you to kick against the goads."

7. **Menander, Thaïs, 218: ?**
   1 Corinthians 15.33: Do not be deceived: "Bad company ruins good morals."

8. **Thucydides, II 97.4:** For there was here established a custom opposite to that prevailing in the Persian kingdom, namely, of taking rather than giving; more disgrace being attached to not giving when asked than to asking and being refused; and although this prevailed elsewhere in Thrace, it was practised most extensively among the powerful Odrysians, it being impossible to get anything done without a present.
   Acts 20.35: In all this I have given you an example that by such work we must support the weak, remembering the words of the Lord Jesus, for he himself said, "It is more blessed to give than to receive."

APPENDIX V

THE ANCIENT ANTICHRIST PROFILE
JEW OR GENTILE?

In the Second Temple profile, the Antichrist figure is the great eschato-logical enemy of the Son of David/Messiah. The profile consistently portrays this figure as an evil tyrant, distinct from Satan/Belial, but in league with or empowered by Satan/Belial. There is no suggestion that Second Temple Jews understood this figure as a Jewish pseudo-messiah, that is, a figure that Jews would mistakenly *embrace* as the messianic son of David. Consequently, the Second Temple profile of the great end-times enemy, the one Christians would identify as the end-times Antichrist, points to a man who *opposes* the Messiah, not one who masquerades as the Messiah.[313]

This focus is why the pre-end-times figures who factor into the ancient Jewish profile of the enemy of the Messiah are consistently Gen-tiles (e.g., Goliath, Antiochus IV, Gog).[314] The early church fathers' sus-picion of Roman leaders as being Antichrist candidates also reflects the Gentile tyrant profile.

All end-times systems agree that Antiochus IV was at least the initial fulfillment of Daniel 11. The dispensationalist would see spectacular fulfillment of prophecy in Daniel 11 in the known historical activities of Antiochus IV through roughly verse 39, after which the end times is in view. The preterist, or someone who simply takes a second-century B.C. view of the authorship of Daniel, would see the text being written in real time during the terror of Antiochus IV. If we were supposed to be reading "Jew" in Daniel 11 (see the comments below on "God/gods of his fathers") no one would see Antiochus as having any relationship to the figure of Daniel 11. It is absolutely clear and certain that he wasn't a Jew.

Given the Second Temple Jewish profile discussed in chapter 10—and the Old Testament passages from which Jews derived it—it makes little sense that the Antichrist would be a Jew who deceives Jews into believing that he is the true Messiah. That is a modern conception that does not align with the ancient evidence. The idea of an individual masquerading as the Messiah to dupe people into believing he is the true Messiah is better conveyed by a different term (*pseudochristos*; "false Christ"), a word that appears twice in the New Testament (Matthew 24:24; Mark 13:22). In neither case is a *specific* eschatological adversary in view.

The term "antichrist" (Greek: *antichristos*) occurs five times in four New Testament passages (1 John 2:18, 22; 4:3; 2 John 7). In the three passages where the *antichristos* is described (1 John 2:22; 4:3; 2 John 7), John associates the Antichrist in his epistles with the denial of the incarnate person of Christ—the denial that the Christ has come in the flesh. This denial (and the deception of its contrarian claims) neither favors nor compels understanding the Antichrist as a Jew. Teaching against the incarnation is, of course, quite consistent with an "opposing" Antichrist, as opposed to "masquerading in place of." Passages such as 2 Thessalonians 2 also do nothing to support the idea that the deception associated with the "lawless one" (2 Thessalonians 2:8–12) is a ruse to present himself as a Jewish Messiah or the returned (Jewish) Jesus. The passage is clear that Satan empowers the "lawless one" to do signs and wonders that deceive, but the "strong delusion" that occurs in conjunction with his appearance does *not* come from Satan. Paul wrote clearly that it comes from God: "Therefore God sends them a strong delusion, so that they may believe what is false" (2 Thessalonians 2:11).

Given the Antiochus IV alignment to Daniel 11 in general, Daniel 11:37–38 should be translated: "He shall pay no attention to the gods of his fathers, or to the one beloved by women. He shall not pay attention to any other god, for he shall magnify himself above all. He shall honor the god of fortresses instead of these. A god whom his fathers did not know he shall honor with gold and silver, with precious stones and costly gifts."[315] The Antichrist figure rejects the (plural) gods of his fathers; his native orientation is thus Gentile polytheism. While it is true that the phrase can be translated "God of his fathers," since the passage emulates a Gentile (Antiochus IV) so closely, at least until verse 40, with its shift to "the time of the end," the singular translation makes little sense. The language of Daniel 11:37–38 essentially portrays the great enemy as an atheist who considers himself a god—in contrast to the worship of his ancestry—or as adopting yet another god unknown among the (plural) gods of his ancestors.

Many readers will presume that this new, strange god is "the god of fortresses" mentioned in Daniel 11:39. This entire phrase—and hence the interpretations built on it—may be a fiction. That is, "god of fortresses" may not reflect the original text. In any respect, this doesn't affect the identification of the Antichrist figure as a Gentile, not a Jew.

EXCURSUS: THE "GOD OF FORTRESSES" PROBLEM

Understanding this issue necessarily begins with the realization that the book of Daniel as we have it comes to us as a bilingual document. Daniel 1:1–2:4a and Daniel 8–12 are in Hebrew. In between those two portions, Daniel 2:4b–7:28 are in Aramaic. As John and Adela Collins note, scholars have struggled (and still do) with comprehending why this is so. In their detailed scholarly commentary on the book, they summarize four explanations that have been offered in the history of scholarship, none of which have won consensus:

1. A single author composed the work in two languages.
2. The entire book was composed in Hebrew. An Aramaic version was issued almost simultaneously, for the benefit of those who could not read Hebrew.
3. The entire book was originally composed in Aramaic.
4. The combination of languages results from the incorporation of older Aramaic material into a work whose final stage was composed in Hebrew.[316]

The debate factors into how scholars approach certain passages in the book. Daniel 11 is one such passage where one's view of the above language-composition issue matters.

The authors of the Anchor-Yale commentary on Daniel, Louis Hartman and Alexander Di Lella opt for the third view—that Daniel was originally written (and so, inspired) in Aramaic. They write:

> During the following generation, the four apocalypses of the second part of Daniel were added to the six midrashic narratives of the first part to form a single book which began to be regarded as Sacred Scripture. All twelve chapters had originally been composed in Aramaic. But in order to ensure that the book would receive canonical recognition, the beginning (1:1–2:4a) and end (chs. 8–12) were translated into Hebrew.[317]

The effect this has on Daniel 11 is dramatic. Below are the English Standard Version and the translation of Hartman and Di Lella for Daniel 11:36–39, with key differences underlined:

ESV	Hartman and Di Lella
[36] "And the king shall do as he wills. He shall exalt himself and magnify himself above every god, and shall speak astonishing things against the God of gods. He shall prosper till the indignation is accomplished; for what is decreed shall be done. [37] He shall pay no attention to the gods of his fathers, or to the one beloved by women. He shall not pay attention to any other god, for he shall magnify himself above all. [38] He shall honor the god of fortresses instead of these. A god whom his fathers did not know he shall honor with gold and silver, with precious stones and costly gifts. [39] He shall deal with the strongest fortresses with the help of a foreign god. Those who acknowledge him he shall load with honor. He shall make them rulers over many and shall divide the land for a price.	[36] "The king will do as he pleases. He will exalt himself and make himself greater than any god, and even against the God of gods he will speak arrogantly. He will succeed until the time of wrath is completed, for what is decreed must be done. [37] He will have no regard for the gods of his ancestors; toward the darling of women and toward every other god he will act disrespectfully, for he will make himself greater than all of them. [38] Even the God of the pious ones he will despise, and on that God's stand he will honor, with gold, silver, precious stones, and costly gifts, a god whom his ancestors did not know. [39] Into the fortresses of the pious ones he will bring over soldiers of a strange god. Whoever acknowledges him he will provide with great honor, making them rulers over the many and distributing the land as their wages.

To understand why Hartman and Di Lella translate the passage as they do, one must realize that the Hebrew term for "fortresses" in Daniel 11:38 ("god of fortresses") is *ma'uzzim* (root form: *ma'oz*; noun construct form: *ma'uzzê*). This word occurs *seven times* in Daniel 11. The first occurrence is Daniel 11:7. Presuming that the inspired original of Daniel was in Aramaic, they say the following about the first occurrence of this word in Daniel 11:7:

The strongholds. The original Aramaic for Hebrew *māʿuzzê* was most likely *ḥisnê*; so also in 11:10b, 12, 19 the translator rightly rendered the Aramaic root *ḥsn* by the Hebrew root *ʿwz* [*ʿoz*]. But this misled him in 11:31, 38, 39 to connect Aramaic *ḥsyn*, "the pious ones," with the same Hebrew root *ʿwz*.[319]

Their perspective is that the translator who put the original Aramaic of Daniel 11 into Hebrew got two Aramaic words confused:

חסני ("strongholds, fortresses [of …]") and חסינ ("pious ones")[320]

The visual difference is a slight alteration in letter sequence. If one presumes that the translator got confused, then the text of Daniel 11:39 as we have it (post-inspiration, according to Hartman and Di Lella) should not include the word "fortresses." It should be translated as they propose, "pious ones."

Hartman and Di Lella argue that their translation of Daniel 11:38–39 is a straightforward indictment of the Antichrist figure—one that parallels precisely what Antiochus IV actually did when he slaughtered a pig on the altar in the temple. Here is their translation once more with my editorial comments in brackets to explain their idea.

> Even the God of the pious ones [i.e., Yahweh] he will despise, and on that God's stand [i.e., his altar] he will honor, with gold, silver, precious stones, and costly gifts, a god whom his ancestors did not know. Into <u>the fortresses of the pious ones</u> he will bring over soldiers of a strange god. Whoever acknowledges him he will provide with great honor, making them rulers over the many and distributing the land as their wages.[321]

The translation of Hartman and Di Lella result in a cohesive parallelism between verses 38 and 39, where the verses describe a twin desecration of the holy place (temple) and the holy city (Jerusalem):

v. 38: The God of the pious ones (i.e., Yahweh) he will despise, and on that God's stand (i.e., his altar) he will honor…a god whom his ancestors did not know.

v. 39: Into the fortresses of the pious ones he will bring over soldiers of a strange god.

While this alternative translation makes good sense, its weakness is obvious—it's based on speculation that Daniel was originally composed in Aramaic. As such, it is of limited value for building an exegetical theology. That said, those who presume "God of fortresses" must recognize that the phrase isn't a secure argument for a number of ideas that are attached to it. It is possible that Daniel was composed originally in Aramaic, but we simply don't know if that's the case.

If you studied the Bible on its own terms, in its own context,

without creeds and denominational preferences,

WHAT WOULD YOU HAVE?

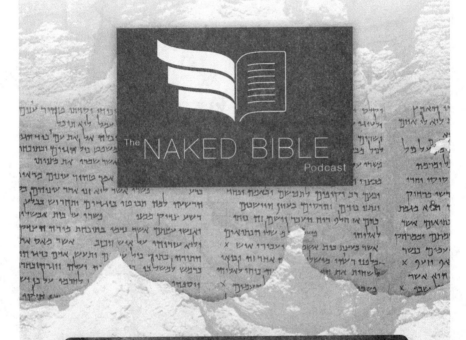

HOSTED BY DR. MICHAEL HEISER

WWW.NAKEDBIBLEPODCAST.COM

NOTES

1. The appellation "Book of Enoch" is incorrect since there are other (different) books of Enoch besides 1 Enoch. There is 2 Enoch (also called the *Slavonic Apocalypse of Enoch*), dated entirely to the late 1st century A.D., and 3 Enoch (also called the *Hebrew Apocalypse of Enoch*), which dates to fifth or sixth centuries A.D.
2. See appendix II for more detail.
3. Technically precise transliteration has not been used in this book. Transliteration of words from biblical Hebrew, Aramaic, and Greek, along with other ancient languages, has been simplified for English-only readers.
4. On the divine nature of the sons of God in Gen. 6:1–4, see the extended discussion in Michael S. Heiser, *The Unseen Realm: Recovering the Supernatural Worldview of the Bible* (Lexham Press, 2015) 93–109.
5. The material in the Book of Giants from Qumran overlaps with the content of 1 Enoch, most notably 1 Enoch 6–16, the expanded treatment of the episode of Gen. 6:1–4. This being the case, the present volume will include material from the Book of Giants in its discussion of the New Testament theme of "reversing Hermon." See appendix II.
6. See appendix I: "Reception of 1 Enoch in the Early Church."
7. R. Lopez, "Israelite Covenants in the Light of Ancient Near Eastern Covenants (Part 1 of 2)," *Chafer Theological Seminary Journal* 9:1 (2003): 97–102; idem, "Israelite Covenants in the Light of Ancient Near Eastern Covenants (Part 2 of 2)," *Chafer Theological Seminary Journal* 9:2 (2003): 92–111.
8. Norman L. Geisler and William E. Nix, *A General Introduction to the Bible* (Rev. and expanded; Chicago: Moody Press, 1986) 262.
9. See appendix I.

10. D. A. Carson, "Pseudonymity and Pseudepigraphy," ed. Craig A. Evans and Stanley E. Porter, *Dictionary of New Testament Background: A Compendium of Contemporary Biblical Scholarship* (Downers Grove, IL: InterVarsity Press, 2000) 858.

11. No such argument can be made on any grounds. For example, the oldest textual remains of 1 Enoch date (perhaps) to the third century B.C., long after the lifetime of the antediluvian figure for whom it is named and concerning whom it has much to say. See appendix II.

12. D. A. Carson, "Pseudonymity and Pseudepigraphy," 859; James H. Charlesworth, "Pseudonymity and Pseudepigraphy," ed. David Noel Freedman, *The Anchor Yale Bible Dictionary* (New York: Doubleday, 1992) 540.

13. See for example Helge S. Kvanvig, *Roots of Apocalyptic: the Mesopotamian Background of the Enoch Figure and of the Son of Man* (Neukirchener Verlag, 1988); idem, "The Watchers Story, Genesis and Atrahasis: A Triangular Reading." *Henoch* 24 (2002), 17–21; Siam Bhayro, "Noah's Library: Sources for *1 Enoch* 6–11," *Journal for the Study of the Pseudepigrapha* Vol 15.3 (2006): 163–177; James C. VanderKam, *Enoch and the Growth of an Apocalyptic Tradition,* Catholic Biblical Quarterly Monograph Series 16 (Washington, DC: Catholic Biblical Association of America, 1984); Loren T. Stuckenbruck, "Giant Mythology and Demonology: From the Ancient Near East to the Dead Sea Scrolls," in A. Lange, H. Lichtenberger and K.F. Diethard (eds.), *Demons: The Demonology of Israelite—Jewish and Early Christian Literature in Context of their Environment* (Tübingen: Mohr Siebeck, 2003) 318–38; Alan Lenzi, *Secrecy and the Gods: Secret Knowledge in Ancient Mesopotamia and Biblical Israel* (The Neo-Assyrian Text Corpus Project; State Archives of Assyria Studies XIX; Helsinki, 2008).

14. Material in this chapter is drawn from the author's much lengthier discussion in *The Unseen Realm: Recovering the Supernatural Worldview of the Bible* (Lexham Press, 2015) 92–109, 183–214. Overlaps in prose content here from that book are presented by permission.

15. The history of how Gen. 6:1–4 has been interpreted is chronicled in detail in two major studies: Annette Yoshiko Reed, *Fallen Angels and the History of Judaism and Christianity: The Reception of Enochic Literature* (Cambridge: Cambridge University Press, 2005); Archie J. Wright, *The Origin of Evil Spirits: The Reception of Genesis 6:1–4 in Early Jewish Literature*, Revised Edition (Fortress Press, 2015).

16. The verb form ("began") is third masculine singular. Since the word *'adam*, which is often rendered "mankind" or "humankind" in modern translations (e.g., Gen. 1:26), does not actually appear in the verse, the most natural rendering would be that *Seth* began to call on the name of the Lord. If this is the case, then the Sethite view needs to extrapolate Seth's faith to only *men* from that point on, since it is the "sons" of God who must be spiritually distinct from the "daughters" of humankind. One way around this is to argue that Gen. 6:1–4 describes godly Sethite men marrying ungodly non-Sethite women. The passage of course never says that, and it presumes that, by definition, the only godly women on the planet were those related to Seth. Those who insert "humankind" into the verse ("humankind began to call on the name of the Lord") undermine the Sethite view with that decision, as it would have humans from other lineages, not just that of Seth, calling on the name of the Lord.

17. It is also misguided to argue that the Sethite view is valid because the writers and editors of the Torah were living under the law. There are near-relation marriages in the Genesis story prior to the Sinai legislation. For example, Abraham and Sarah had the same father, but different mothers, a forbidden sexual relationship in the Torah (Gen. 20:12; cf. Lev. 18:9, 11; 20:17; Deut. 27:22). In other words, the later legal backdrop of Sinai isn't being presumed elsewhere in Genesis, so it cannot be presumed as the backdrop for Gen. 6:1–4. There simply is no support for condemned human intermarriage in the text.

18. On the incoherence of interpreting Hebrew *'elohim* in Psalm 82 as humans, see *Unseen Realm,* 23–27, and the scholarly sources found therein in footnotes. Several relevant essays can also be found on the author's website: http://www.thedivinecouncil.com.

19. The divinized kingship view is also defended by contending that there are no examples in ancient Near Eastern materials of divine beings "marrying" human women, while there are examples of kings claiming mixed ancestry from gods and humans. This wording deflects attention from the many references to sexual activity between divine beings and humans in ancient literature by suggesting that Gen. 6:1–4 must refer to matrimonial unions. This is playing word games, since the "marriage" idea derives from English translations. The word translated "wife" is simply the normal plural for "women" (*nashim*). The biblical euphemisms of "taking" (Gen. 6:2) or "going in to" a woman (Gen. 6:4) are not exclusively used for marriage. They are also used to describe the sexual act outside a marriage

bond. That is, "taking" a woman can describe an illicit sexual relationship (Gen. 38:2; Lev. 18:17; 20:17, 21; 21:7), as can "coming/going in to" (Gen. 38:2; 39:14; Lev. 21:11; Judg. 16:1; Amos 2:7). The point of the language of Gen. 6:1–4 is a sexual relationship, not matrimony. This objection is therefore a distinction without a difference. This view also fails logically. The objection about the lack of divine-human *marriages* is aimed at eliminating the divine element from Gen. 6:1–4, thus reducing the episode to purely human relationships (albeit with divine kings as focus). But on what logical basis would multiple marriages between kings and women bring the world into chaos, necessitating God's judgment in a catastrophic flood?

20. See, for example, Peter H. Davids, *The Letters of 2 Peter and Jude* (Pillar New Testament Commentary; Grand Rapids, MI: Eerdmans, 2006) 3; Michael Green, *2 Peter and Jude: An Introduction and Commentary* (Tyndale New Testament Commentaries 18; Downers Grove, IL: InterVarsity Press, 1987) 68; Jerome H. Neyrey, *2 Peter, Jude: A New Translation with Introduction and Commentary* (Anchor Yale Bible 37C; New Haven; London: Yale University Press, 2008) 120–22.

21. The word choice ("angels") comes from the Septuagint, which is the Old Testament used predominantly by New Testament writers.

22. Some interpreters imagine a pre-Fall rebellion of angels that might fit with 2 Peter. The Bible records no such event. The closest one comes to it is in Rev. 12:7–9. Not only was Revelation the last book of the New Testament to be written, which means it cannot be the referent of 2 Peter, but Rev. 12:7–9 associates the war in heaven with the first coming of the Messiah, not events before the Flood. There is no biblical evidence for a pre-Fall angelic rebellion. The idea comes from Milton's *Paradise Lost*, not the Bible.

23. The phrase "held captive in Tartarus" in 2 Pet. 2:4 is the translation of a verb lemma (ταρταρόω) that points to the term from classical Greek literature for the destination of the divine Titans, a term that is also used of their semi-divine offspring. See William Arndt, Frederick W. Danker, and Walter Bauer, *A Greek-English Lexicon of the New Testament and Other Early Christian Literature* (Chicago: University of Chicago Press, 2000) 991. The terminology clearly informs us that, for Peter and Jude, an antisupernaturalist interpretation of Gen. 6:1–4 was not in view. See G. Mussies, "Titans," in *Dictionary of Deities and Demons in the Bible*,

2nd ed. (ed. Karel van der Toorn, Bob Becking, and Pieter W. van der Horst; Leiden; Boston; Cologne; Grand Rapids, MI; Cambridge: Brill; Eerdmans, 1999) 872–874; G. Mussies, "Giants," in ibid., 343–345; David M. Johnson, "Hesiod's Descriptions of Tartarus (*Theogony* 721–819)," *The Phoenix* 53:1–2 (1999): 8–28; J. Daryl Charles, "The Angels under Reserve in 2 Peter and Jude," *Bulletin for Biblical Research* 15.1 (2005) 39–48.

24. This sort of thing is common in human experience. For example, anyone who has read John Calvin's thoughts on predestination or a dispensationalist's take on prophecy will find it next to impossible to eliminate that material from his or her thinking while reading, respectively, the book of Romans or Revelation. First Enoch and other works are part of the thinking of Peter and Jude because they were well known and taken seriously by contemporaries. The content of 1 Enoch shows up elsewhere in these epistles. It is obvious to those who study all these texts, especially in Greek, that Peter and Jude knew 1 Enoch very well. Scholars have devoted considerable attention to parallels between that book and the epistles of Peter and Jude. See George W. E. Nickelsburg, *1 Enoch: A Commentary on the Book of 1 Enoch 1–36, 81–108* (Minneapolis: Fortress, 2001) 83–87.

25. See the earlier cited study by A. Yoshiko Reed for the history of how the early church embraced and rejected the supernatural view of Gen. 6:1-4.

26. See chapter 3 of the present book for the Mesopotamian context of Gen. 6:1-4.

27. Plural forms of this lemma, depending on grammatical context, are *gigantes* and *gigantas*.

28. For a detailed discussion of the *Anakim* and other giant clans in the Old Testament, see *Unseen Realm,* 183–214.

29. The translation "fallen ones" is based on a characterization of the behavior of the giants, not on any passage that informs us this is what Nephilim means. One Dead Sea Scroll text says that the Watchers "fell" from right standing with God and that their offspring followed in their footsteps (CD [*Damascus Document*] II:1–19). Note that while the verb *naphal* appears in this verse, the word Nephilim does not. That is, the "fallen state" is not derivative of the name itself. The word Nephilim occurs only twice in the Dead Sea Scrolls. Neither instance makes a connection to any behavior. In fact, no explanation of the term is ever offered. Certain English translations of the

Dead Sea Scrolls will occasionally have this "fallen" language elsewhere, but such instances are bracketed—they have been supplied by translators but without any manuscript support (e.g., 4Q266 Frag. 2 ii:18). The most recent scholarly work on the Nephilim and the later giant clans is the recent Harvard dissertation by Brian Doak (published as *The Last of the Rephaim: Conquest and Cataclysm in the Heroic Ages of Ancient Israel*, Ilex Series 7 [Cambridge: Harvard University Press, 2013]). Despite its many merits, Doak's book on the giants fails with respect to the meaning of Nephilim. Annus's groundbreaking article (see chapter 3 of the present book) does not appear in either Doak's dissertation bibliography or that of his book.

30. As chapter 3 will make clear, a supernaturalist approach is the only approach consistent with the original Mesopotamian backstory to Gen. 6:1–4.

31. The result of the cohabitation (or some other form of divine intervention per the ensuing discussion) is also something that causes hesitation. The information obtainable from the text of Scripture and archaeology leads to the conclusion that neither the Nephilim nor their descendants were freakishly tall. The evidence points to the same range for unusually tall people today (the upper six-foot range to eight feet). There are two giants whose height is given to us in the biblical text. An unnamed Egyptian is said to have been five cubits tall in 1 Chronicles 11:23 (= 7.5 feet tall). Goliath is the other. The traditional (Masoretic) Hebrew text has him at "six cubits and a span" (1 Sam. 17:4), roughly nine feet, nine inches. The Dead Sea Scroll reading of 1 Sam. 17:4 disagrees and has Goliath at four cubits and a span, or six feet, six inches. Virtually all scholars consider the Dead Sea Scrolls reading superior and authentic. Archaeological work across the ancient Near East confirms that six and one-half feet tall was, by the standards of the day, a giant. To date, there is no human skeletal evidence from Syria-Palestine (Canaan) that shows extraordinary height. A number of amateur researchers and websites have asserted that two seven-foot female skeletons were found in a twelfth-century-B.C. cemetery at Tell es-Sa'idiyeh on the east bank of the Jordan. This assertion comes from a commentary on Deuteronomy written by Jeffrey Tigay of the University of Pennsylvania (J. Tigay, *Deuteronomy*, JPS Torah Commentary [Philadelphia: Jewish Publication Society, 1996], 17). Tigay gave the following footnote information after mentioning this alleged discovery: "The discovery in Jordan was reported by Jonathan Tubb of

the British Museum in a lecture at the University of Pennsylvania in 1995; see the British Museum's forthcoming *Excavations at Tell es-Sa'idiyeh III/2.*" As it turns out, this is *not* true. I wrote professor Tubb at the British Museum to ask if he had published a report on these two skeletons, and I mentioned Tigay's footnote. He replied (April 29, 2014): "I'm sorry to disappoint, but I'm afraid the footnote resulted from a misunderstood comment I made at a lecture on Sa'idiyeh I gave at Penn some time ago. We don't, in fact, have any unusually large skeletons from the Sa'idiyeh cemetery. We are in the last stages of preparing the final report on the graves, and all of the metrics will be contained in the volume." Readers can visit www.moreunseenrealm.com (ch. 25) for a screenshot of the original email. To date, there are no human skeletons from Canaan that show bizarre height. For documentation of these statements and scholarly bibliography, see my discussion (and footnotes) in *Unseen Realm,* 210–214. The size of Og's bed (Deut. 3:11) cannot be taken as a precise indication of Og's own dimensions. First, the most immediate link back to the Babylonian polemic is Og's bed (Hebrew: *'eres*). Its dimensions (9 × 4 cubits) are precisely those of the cultic bed in the ziggurat called Etemenanki—which is the ziggurat most archaeologists identify as the Tower of Babel referred to in the Bible.[10] Ziggurats were part of temple complexes—divine houses. The unusually large bed at Etemenanki was housed in "the house of the bed" (*bit erši*). It was the place where the god Marduk and his divine wife, Zarpanitu, met annually for ritual lovemaking, the purpose of which was divine blessing upon the land. The ritual was also concerned with maintaining the cosmic order instituted by the gods. Consequently, a link between Og and Marduk via the matching bed dimensions telegraphed the idea that Og was the inheritor and perpetuator of the Babylonian knowledge and cosmic order from before the Flood. This ties Og directly back to Gen. 6:1–4 and its Apkallu polemic discussed in chapter 3 of the present book. What the dimensions don't do is give us Og's height—the numbers are very obviously given for a theological purpose, not a clinical one. On Marduk's bed and sacred marriage, See See Martti Nissinen, "Akkadian Rituals and Poetry of Divine Love," in *Mythology and Mythologies: Methodological Approaches to Intercultural Influences; Proceedings of the Second Annual Symposium of the Assyrian and Babylonian Intellectual Heritage Project Held in Paris, France, October 4–7, 1999*, Melammu Symposia 2 (ed. R. M. Whiting; Helsinki:

Neo-Assyrian Text Corpus Project, 2001) 93–136; Beate Pongratz-Leisten, "Sacred Marriage and the Transfer of Divine Knowledge: Alliances between the Gods and the King in Ancient Mesopotamia," in *Sacred Marriages: The Divine-Human Sexual Metaphor from Sumer to Early Christianity* (ed. Martti Nissinen and Risto Uro; Winona Lake, IN: Eisenbrauns, 2008) 43–72.

32. Sarah would have been well past the age of producing an egg for fertilization and the physical demands of bringing a child to term.

33. One scholar has recently put forth the idea that Yahweh is perceived as a "sexual deity" in the Old Testament: David E. Bokovoy, "Did Eve Acquire, Create, or Procreate with Yahweh? A Grammatical and Contextual Reassessment of קנה in Genesis 4:1," *Vetus Testamentum* 63 (2013) 19–35. I do not believe a phrase like "sexual deity" captures the semantic point of Gen. 4:1. Bokovoy argues that the verb in question in Gen. 4:1 (*qanah*) means to create or procreate. I would agree that the verb can certainly have this meaning. Bokovoy's argument is that the biblical writer believed God participated in the mystery of procreation. Although he doesn't state it, his assumption appears to be that the biblical writers attributed conception to the deity because, unlike us, they didn't know scientifically how human fertilization and what happens in the womb worked. I would also agree with that point. However, Bokovoy's conclusion, that Yahweh "actively participated" in Cain's procreation, needs qualifications that he does not include in his work. One can say that, in the perception of the biblical writer, and even Eve herself, God caused Eve's pregnancy. But what does that mean? The biblical writer wasn't ignorant of the man's (Adam's) involvement. The text of the first half of Gen. 4:1 says explicitly that Adam "knew Eve his wife, and she [subsequently] conceived." In other words, the biblical writer understood that sexual intercourse between a man and a woman led to pregnancy. There is no prerequisite for modern scientific understanding for grasping that point. In the second half of the verse Eve says (ESV), "I have gotten [lemma: *qanah*; form: *qanîtî*] a man with the LORD." But note that Eve is the grammatical subject of this "sexual" verb, *not* the object. Bokovoy's writing sounds as though Yahweh is the subject here, and that Yahweh is participating *sexually* with Eve. That isn't what the grammar of the text says. The author's wording lacks precision and is therefore misleading. Nevertheless, following Bokovoy for the sake of discussion, one could translate Eve's statement this way:

"I have procreated a man with YHWH." What would this mean since the writer clearly has Adam as the one having sexual relations with Eve? The answer is simple. This passage is akin to others in the Old Testament where the author narrates the fact that couples have sexual intercourse and then attributes the pregnancy (e.g., "opening of the womb") to Yahweh—i.e., God gets credit for the mystery of procreation (Gen. 18:9–14; 21:1–2; 25:21; 29:32–35; 30:16–24; 1 Sam. 1:19–20; Pss. 17:14; 127:3; Isa. 44:2, 24). This is neither complicated nor shocking, and it isn't proof that Yahweh was thought to participate sexually with anyone. The mystery of procreation and the act of intercourse are *distinguished* in Gen. 4:1 and other passages.

34. Reconciling the first view with what 2 Pet. 2:4–10 and Jude 6–7 say about "the angels who sinned" is straightforward, especially given the sexual nature of the events of Sodom and Gomorrah, which both writers use as analogous situations. The second approach doesn't question the sexual language; it considers it euphemistic. Peter and Jude's inclusion of sexual language is no surprise—it is present in the Old Testament. This approach would argue that there is no reason to insist that Peter and Jude did not also consider it euphemistic. In any respect, what cannot be coherently denied is that Peter and Jude have divine beings as the offenders, not mere humans.

35. Both phrases are regarded as late editorial glosses by many evangelical and non-confessional scholars. See, for example, Brian Doak, *The Last of the Rephaim: Conquest and Cataclysm in the Heroic Ages of Ancient Israel*, Ilex Series 7 [(Cambridge: Harvard University Press, 2013) 78; Claus Westermann, *Genesis 1–11: A Continental Commentary* (Minneapolis: Fortress, 1994) 378. That they are part of the final form of the biblical text means they must be included in the canonical material that was the product of the process of inspiration.

36. The Hebrew of the phrase in Num. 13:33 literally reads that the sons of (*beney*) *Anak* were "from" (*min*) the Nephilim. The meaning is either that the Anakim were lineal (biological) descendants or were viewed as part of a group that descended from the Nephilim. Some have argued that the preposition *min* suggests the Anakim were only "like" the Nephilim, but there is no clear instance in the Hebrew Bible for this semantic nuance. As Doak notes in his discussion of the phrase, "Whatever the case, the Anaqim here are most certainly thought to be the physical (and thus "moral" or "spiritual") descendants of the Nephilim" (Doak, *Last of the Rephaim*, 79).

37. The quandary of how anyone, including the giants, had survived the Flood led some Jewish writers to speculate that Noah himself had been fathered by a Watcher. One Dead Sea scroll, *The Genesis Apocryphon*, has Noah's father challenging his wife, the mother of Noah, about whether her pregnancy was the work of one of the Watchers (*Genesis Apocryphon* [=1QapGen] 1:1–5:27). She vehemently denies the charge.

38. The argument for a local flood proceeds along several trajectories aside from scientific arguments. For scientific discussion, see David F. Siemens Jr., "Some Relatively Non-Technical Problems with Flood Geology," *Perspectives on Science and the Christian Faith* 44.3 (1992) 169–74; Davis Young and Ralph Searley, *The Bible, Rocks and Time: Geological Evidence for the Age of the Earth* (Downers Grove, IL: IVP Academic, 2008) 224–40. Our concern is with the biblical text and its own evidence for a local flood. First, the phrases in the Flood narrative that suggest a global event occur a number of times in the Hebrew Bible where their context cannot be global or include all people on the planet. For example, the phrase "the whole earth" (*kol 'erets*) occurs in passages that clearly speak of localized geography (e.g., Gen. 13:9; 41:57; Lev. 25:9, 24; Judg. 6:37; 1 Sam. 13:3; 2 Sam. 24:8). In such cases, "whole land" or "all the people in the area" are better understandings. Those options produce a regional flood event if used in Gen. 6–8 where the phrase occurs. Second, the Gen. 9:19 clearly informs us that "the whole earth" was populated by the sons of Noah. Gen. 10 (see 10:1) gives us the list of the nations spawned by the sons of Noah—all of which are located in the regions of the ancient Near East, the Mediterranean, and the Aegean. The biblical writers knew nothing of nations in another hemisphere (the Americas) or places like India, China, or Australia. The language of Gen. 10 therefore allows Gen. 7:21 to be restricted to only (or even some) of the people groups listed in the Table of Nations. That interpretation is consistent with a localized flood. Third, the phrase "all humankind" (*kol 'adam*) used in Gen. 7:21 also appears in contexts that cannot speak to all humans everywhere (e.g., Jer. 32:20; Psa. 64:9 can only refer to people who had seen what God had done, not people on the other side of the world). Lastly, Psa. 104:9 appears to forbid a global flood, since it has God promising to never cover the earth with water *as had been the case at creation.*

39. Both supernatural approaches to Gen. 6:1–4 can accommodate a local flood. Both posit survivors (by whatever means) somewhere in the

Mediterranean or Aegean, the known biblical world. Those survivors (at least some of them) would have had to eventually migrate to Canaan. At least one of the giant lineages can be traced to the Aegean (see ch. 25). In like manner, positing a post-Flood origin for more Nephilim would require more divine intervention of the same (undescribed) type.

40. A translation of "when" takes the 'asher clause as temporal. According to Westermann, this is the view espoused by most commentators. He is, however, apathetic as to whether a temporal understanding or another possibility is more coherent: "It does not really matter whether אשר is understood as temporal (with most interpreters) or iterative (so E. König, W. H. Schmidt and others) or as causal (e.g., B. S. Childs; against, and correctly, W. H. Schmidt); רשא is an afterthought, its function being in fact only to link and so to subordinate" (Westermann, *Genesis 1–11*, 377). Wenham notes that some Hebrew scholars consider the use of the Hebrew imperfect in this clause to allow for repetition: " 'Whenever the sons of the gods went into the daughters of men, they bore them children.' Though it is not impossible to translate this as a simple past event—'When they went in...'—it is more natural (with Skinner, König, Gispen) to take the imperfect 'went' and perfect preceded by *waw* ('bore...children') as frequentative. To 'go in to' is a frequent euphemism for sexual intercourse (cf. Gen. 30:16; 38:16)" (Gordon J. Wenham, *Genesis 1–15*, Word Biblical Commentary 1 (Dallas: Word, 1998), 143. See also Friedrich Wilhelm Gesenius, *Gesenius' Hebrew Grammar*, 2nd English ed. (ed. E. Kautzsch and Sir Arthur Ernest Cowley; Oxford: Clarendon Press, 1910) 315 (sec. 107e). Gesenius includes Gen. 6:4 as an instance of this interpretive nuance.

41. On the meaning of "watcher" (Aramaic: עיר; *'îr*), Nickelsburg writes: "If the Aram. עיר was the chief designation for the heavenly beings, precisely what was the meaning of this word? .... A derivation from the root עור ("to be awake," "to be watchful") is usually presumed and is reflected in the Greek translation ἐγρήγορος (*egrēgoros*)... Murray develops an extensive argument for the meaning "guardian" and for an allusion to the old guardian gods of Semitic antiquity. Various passages in 1 Enoch appear to apply such a function to these heavenly beings, although it is perhaps more to the point to describe them as advocates or mediators of human prayer. Throughout the translation in this volume, I have retained the traditional rendering 'watchers,' presuming not the notion of watching per se, but the first dictionary definition of this noun, 'one that sits up or

continues awake at night.' I do so for two reasons. First, neither Fitzmyer nor Murray presents a compelling reason for seeking another translation. Second, alongside the ancient translation ἐγρήγοροι, precisely such an interpretation appears to be presumed in [1 Enoch] 39:12, 13; 40:2; 61:12; 71:7 ("those who sleep not"), and it may also be indicated at 14:23. In both cases, these heavenly beings are on twenty-four-hour duty attending God—whether to praise God or to function as a kind of bodyguard in the throne room." See George W. E. Nickelsburg, *1 Enoch: A Commentary on the Book of 1 Enoch* (ed. Klaus Baltzer; *Hermeneia—a Critical and Historical Commentary on the Bible*; Minneapolis, MN: Fortress, 2001), 140; R. Murray, "The Origin of Aramaic *'îr*, Angel," *Orientalia* 53:2 (1984) 303–17.

42. ESV correctly renders the Aramaic phrase עִיר וְקַדִּישׁ as "a watcher, a holy one," as opposed to "a watcher and a holy one." That the *waw* conjunction between the words should be understood as creating an appositional relationship between the terms is apparent from the context—only *one* heavenly being converses with Daniel in the passage (note the ensuing singular participles used for the heavenly figure's proclamation in Dan. 4:14).

43. See appendix II. Some scholars include 1 Enoch 93:1–10 in the Apocalypse of Weeks.

44. J. J. Collins, "Enoch, Books of," ed. Craig A. Evans and Stanley E. Porter, *Dictionary of New Testament Background: A Compendium of Contemporary Biblical Scholarship* (Downers Grove, IL: InterVarsity Press, 2000) 314. This last comment about the sin of Adam will be explored in the present book in several chapters. This perspective, as one can imagine, affects the reading of certain New Testament passages.

45. Ibid., 316.

46. Ibid., 315.

47. Ibid.

48. Ibid., 315–316.

49. Nickelsburg, *1 Enoch*, 8.

50. Ibid., 8.

51. Ibid., 174ff. For convenience, I have chosen to omit brackets in reconstructed words and names.

52. This description is found in the Ethiopic text but is not present in some Greek manuscripts.

53. The direct reference to Mount Hermon—something of importance for our own study—is corrupted in the Ethiopic text. Its authenticity is attested in the Aramaic material of 1 Enoch found among the Dead Sea Scrolls (the first six words of 4QEnᵃ), as well as some Greek manuscripts.

54. In Hebrew (and Aramaic) "Hermon" (זמרח; *ḥermōn*) is related to חרם which means (as a verb: *ḥāram*) "devote to destruction" and (as a noun), "[thing] devoted to destruction." These terms are prominent in the biblical conquest account. As I discussed in *The Unseen Realm* (183–214), the annihilation terminology of the conquest was directed at the Anakim, the descendants of th Nephilim. Nickelsburg (p. 177) notes that this wordplay "is an explicit and typical etymologizing on the name of Mount Hermon (cf. Gen. 4:17; 28:10–19; 31:46–49), possible in both Hebrew and Aramaic. The mutual anathematizing of the watchers (for the verb חרם see 4QEnᵃ 1 3:3) explains the name of the mountain on which it took place (חרמון). The long history of religious activity in the environs of Hermon is well documented."

55. The text as established by Nickelsburg for his translations produces three offspring: giants, Nephilim, and "Elioud." Each succeeding group produces the next. Nickelsburg (p. 184) writes: "The interpretation of this passage, and specifically the relationship between "the giants" (*něpîlîm*) and "the mighty ones" (*gibbôrîm*), has long been disputed. Ancient interpreters disagreed, although the varying interpretations may reflect knowledge of the Enochic form of the tradition. An identification of the two groups with one another is as old as the LXX, which translates both nouns with οἱ γίγαντες ("the giants").... Modern interpreters also differ on the referents of the two nouns, and these interpretations are often tied to one's understanding of the history of the tradition. According to Westermann, the two groups are most likely identified with one another in the present state of the Genesis text." Nickelsburg is citing Claus Westermann, *A Continental Commentary: Genesis 1–11* (Minneapolis, MN: Fortress Press, 1994) 378–379. Westermann notes that originally the two terms "did not designate the same object, because Nephilim is a name whereas גברים [*gibborim*] describes a group" (p. 379). I agree with Westermann (and others) on this issue. For our purposes (i.e., establishing the Watcher story for the sake of New Testament interpretation), the issue isn't important. The term "Elioud" is enigmatic (See Nickelsburg's short survey of options, p. 185). My preference is that the term may derive

from the common Semitic root עלי ('*ly*; "exalted") and mean something like "arrogant ones." See for example Ugaritic '*ly* (verb: "to rise up" or "attack"; adjective: "exalted" (Gregorio Del Olmo Lete and Joaquín Sanmartín, " '*ly*," *A Dictionary of the Ugaritic Language in the Alphabetic Tradition* [Leiden: E. J. Brill, 2003], vol 1:160–161).

56. Nickelsburg's preferred text (the Greek version of Syncellus) omits the reference to the height of the Nephilim. The Ethiopic text and some Greek manuscripts read either three thousand or three hundred cubits for their height. It should be obvious that, given Nickelsburg's texts have these giants producing successions of giant offspring (with human women apparently), the heights are absurd, making sexual intercourse impossible.

57. It is interesting to note that the Ethiopic text describes Asael as "the tenth of the archons."

58. This last line of 1 Enoch 8:2 is a good illustration of why Enoch scholars have determined that the account is a composite of sources and traditions. Nickelsburg writes: "According to the second clause, these women then led the holy watchers astray. That is, the sin of Shemihazah and his companions, described in chaps. 6–7, was caused ultimately by the instruction of Asael. This idea implies two other ideas not present in chaps. 6–7. First, the original angelic sinner and primary author of the evil under consideration was not Shemihazah but Asael. Second, the angels were seduced by the women" (Nickelsburg, *1 Enoch*, 195).

59. Annette Yoshiko Reed, *Fallen Angels and the History of Judaism and Christianity*, 46.

60. Loren T Stuckenbruck, "The Origins of Evil in Jewish Apocalyptic Tradition: The Interpretation of Genesis 6:1–4 in the Second and Third Centuries B.C.E.," in *The Fall of the Angels* (ed. Christoff Auffarth and Loren T. Stuckenbruck; Leiden: E. J. Brill, 2004) 103, n. 35.

61. D. R. Schultz, "The Origin of Sin in Irenaeus and Jewish Pseudepigraphical Literature," *Vigiliae Christianae* 32:3 (Sep., 1978) 168–169, 172–173.

62. Ibid., 179, citing Irenaeus, *Proof of the Apostolic Preaching,* 18.

63. Stuckenbruck notes that the scholarly literature establishing this fact "is considerable." This is an understatement. He offers a short list of the scholarship on this point in the first footnote of his essay, "The Origins of Evil in Jewish Apocalyptic Tradition" (p. 87). His list includes: Devorah Dimant, *"The Fallen Angels" in the Dead Sea Scrolls and in*

the Apocryphal and Pseudepigraphic Books Related to Them, Hebrew University: Ph.D. Thesis 1974 (in mod. Hebrew); P. Hanson, "Rebellion in Heaven, Azazel and Euhemeristic Heroes in 1 Enoch 6–11," *Journal of Biblical Literature* 96 (1977) 195–233; G. W. E. Nickelsburg, "Apocalyptic and Myth in 1 Enoch 6–11," *Journal of Biblical Literature* 96 (1977) 383–405; M. J. Davidson, *Angels at Qumran. A Comparative Study of 1 Enoch 1–36, 72–108 and Sectarian Writings from Qumran*, Sheffield 1992; P. S. Alexander, "Wrestling Against Wickedness in High Places: Magic in the Worldview of the Qumran Community," in S. E. Porter and C. A. Evans (eds.), *Qumran Fifty Years After*, Sheffield 1997, 319–30; idem, "The Demonology of the Dead Sea Scrolls," in P. Flint and J. C. VanderKam (eds.), *The Dead Sea Scrolls after Fifty Years. A Comprehensive Assessment*, Leiden/Boston/Köln 1999, vol. 2, 331–53; and A. M. Reimer, 'Rescuing the Fallen Angels: The Case of the Disappearing Angels at Qumran', *Dead Sea Discoveries* 7 (2000): 331–53.

64. Stuckenbruck, "The Origins of Evil in Jewish Apocalyptic Tradition," 87–88.

65. The single best study on the material presented in this chapter was published in 2010: Amar Annus, "On the Origin of the Watchers: A Comparative Study of the Antediluvian Wisdom in Mesopotamian and Jewish Traditions," *Journal for the Study of the Pseudepigrapha* 19.4 (2010) 277–320. The publication of this study was followed closely by David Melvin, "The Gilgamesh Traditions and the Pre-History of Genesis 6: 1–4," *Perspectives in Religious Studies* 38:1 (2011): 23–32; Ida Fröhlich, "Mesopotamian Elements and the Watchers Traditions," in *The Watchers in Jewish and Christian Traditions* (ed. Angela Kim Hawkins, Kelley Coblentz Bautch, and John C. Endres, S.J.; Fortress Press, 2014), 11–24; Henryk Drawnel, "The Mesopotamian Background of the Enochic Giants and Evil Spirits," *Dead Sea Discoveries* 21:1 (2014): 14–38; Helge Kvanvig, *Primeval History: Babylonian, Biblical, and Enochic: An Intertextual Reading* (Journal for the Study of Judaism Supplement 149; Leiden: E. J. Brill, 2011). Some of the material in this last source was published earlier in 2002, though Annus' article supersedes that work considerably: Helge Kvanvig, "Gen. 6: 1–4 as an antediluvian event," *Scandinavian Journal of the Old Testament* 16:1 (2002): 79–112.

66. The only place I know of where this material has been brought to light in a source generally accessible to the public is my book: *The Unseen Realm:*

Recovering the Supernatural Worldview of the Bible (Lexham Press, 2015) 92–109.

67. J. C. Greenfield, "Apkallu," in *Dictionary of Deities and Demons in the Bible* (ed. Karel van der Toorn, Bob Becking, and Pieter W. van der Horst: Leiden: E. J. Brill; Grand Rapids: Eerdmans, 1999) 72.

68. Annus (p. 302) notes: "The realm of Apsu is often confused with underworld in Mesopotamian literature. Evidence indicates that the reason for this was either a simple confusion, or Apsu itself was occasionally thought to be a netherworld inhabited by malevolent spirits. The second option seems more likely, as there are many literary references, which place underworld deities and demons in Apsu." See also Wayne Horowitz, *Mesopotamian Cosmic Geography* (Eisenbrauns, 1998) 342–343.

69. Kvanvig, *Roots of Apocalyptic*, 201.

70. Annus, 295.

71. Entire scholarly studies on such access to secret knowledge have been produced. The most recent and, arguably, the most thorough, is Alan Lenzi, *Secrecy and the Gods: Secret Knowledge in Ancient Mesopotamia and Biblical Israel* (The Neo-Assyrian Text Corpus Project; State Archives of Assyria Studies XIX; Helsinki, 2008).

72. For the concept of the divine council (cf. Psa. 82:1, 6; 89:5–8; 1 Kings 22:19–23), see Heiser, *Unseen Realm*, 23–37 or the papers at http://www.thedivinecouncil.com.

73. Lenzi, 106–107.

74. Ibid., 287–289.

75. Francesca Rochberg, *The Heavenly Writing: Divination, Horoscopy, and Astronomy in Mesopotamian Culture* (Cambridge University Press, 2004) 17.

76. Annus., 289. On this subject, see also the monograph by the great Sumerian-Akkadian scholar William Hallo, *Origins: The Ancient Near Eastern Background of Some Modern Western Institutions* (Leiden: E. J. Brill, 1996).

77. The Seleucid period is historically late, well after the Babylonian (or earlier) era. Nevertheless, as studies of the *apkallu* have confirmed, the ideas and names conveyed in this tablet have a much older history in Mesopotamian material. See Lenzi, 107–108.

78. The spellings and the list come from Lenzi, 108.

79. Anne Draffkorn Kilmer, "The Mesopotamian Counterparts of the Biblical Nephilim," in *Perspectives on Language and Text: Essays and Poems in*

Honor of Francis I. Andersen's 60th Birthday (ed. E. W. Conrad and E. G. Newing; Eisenbrauns, 1987) 39–40. On the cuneiform text from which this information derives, see Erica Reiner, "The Etiological Myth of the 'Seven Sages'," *Orientalia* 30 (1961) 1–11.

80. Kilmer, 40-41. More on this *apkallu* and this cuneiform text below.

81. Ibid., 40.

82. Wright (*Origin of Evil Spirits*, 146–147) notes: "The death of the giants reveals something about the nature of their spirits. They are considered evil spirits because they were born on the earth; they are a mixed product of a spiritual being (Watcher angel) and a physical, and a somewhat spiritually undefined human. The resulting entities are identified in I Enoch 15.8 as 'strong spirits,' 'evil spirits,' which come out of their bodies at their death.... [T]he Watchers [were necessarily] bound in Tartarus in order to halt their activity, while the spirits of the giants, following the death of their physical body, are allowed to roam freely upon the earth. The ability to roam about the earth links the nature of the evil spirits of the giants to the spiritual nature of the Watchers prior to their fall. What is not clear is why these beings are given that freedom."

83. Annus, 297–303. The characterization of the Apkallu as fish-men points to their origin in the watery abyss in Mesopotamian religion. Apkallu are also characterized as bird-men, a likely image associated with their divine ("heavenly") nature. The major study on the pictorial iconography of Apkallu is F. A. M. Wiggerman, *Mesopotamian Protective Spirits: The Ritual Texts* (Leiden: E. J. Brill, 1992).

84. Cited by Annus, 309.

85. Ibid., 309, 311.

86. Ibid., 311 and 293, in that order. On this point see also John C. Reeves, *Jewish Lore in Manichean Cosmology: Studies in the Book of the Giants* (Hebrew Union College Monographs 14; Hebrew Union College Press, 1995) 95; Simo Parpola, *Letters from Assyrian and Babylonian Scholars* (The Neo-Assyrian Text Corpus Project; State Archives of Assyria Studies X; Helsinki, 1993) xx.

87. On this text and its translation, see R. Borger, "The Incantation Series *bīt mēseri* and Enoch's Ascension to Heaven," in *I Studied Inscriptions from before the Flood: Ancient Near Eastern, Literary, and Linguistic Approaches to Genesis 1–11* (ed. Richard S. Hess and David T. Tsumura; Sources for Biblical and Theological Study 4; Winona Lake, IN: Eisenbrauns, 1994) 230–231.

88. Annus, 283, 296. On the description of Gilgamesh in the Book of Giants from Qumran, see Loren Stuckenbruck, *The Book of Giants from Qumran: Text, Translation, and Commentary* (Texte und Studien zum antiken Judentum 63; Tübingen: Mohr Siebeck, 1997) 329. On the cuneiform evidence for Gilgamesh's height, see the line references in the translation of Andrew R. George, *The Babylonian Gilgamesh Epic: Introduction, Critical Edition and Cuneiform Texts* (Oxford University Press, 2003). On the Ugaritic material he refers to, Annus adds a footnote on p. 296 that cites another source by Andrew R. George: "The passage describing the physical appearance of Gilgamesh can be reconstructed in five lines as follows: '[A giant(?)] in stature, eleven cubits [was his height, four cubits was] the width of [his chest,] a triple cubit his foot, half a rod his leg, six cubits was the length of his stride, [x] cubits the whiskers(?) of his cheeks'." See Andrew R. George, "The Gilgameš Epic at Ugarit," *Aula Orientalis* 25 (207): 237–54.

89. Greenfield, 73.

90. Annus, 304. As noted earlier, this characterization as bird-men is likely chosen to denote the divine ("heavenly") nature of Apkallu.

91. *Merriam-Webster's Collegiate Dictionary,* 11th ed. (Springfield, MA: Merriam-Webster, Inc., 2003).

92. Annus, 280.

93. On Deut. 32:8–9 and its importance for biblical theology, see Michael S. Heiser, *The Unseen Realm,* 110–122; Michael S. Heiser, "Deuteronomy 32:8 and the Sons of God," *Bibliotheca Sacra* 158 (January–March 2001) 52–74.

94. Annus, 282, 289.

95. Annus, 282–283, 295.

96. Annus, 283, 314–315. Annus adds (p. 315): "The Aramaic term for 'Watchers' (ʿyr) must have come about as an adaptation of Akkadian term *maṣṣaru*, the term which denoted specialized guards for gates, doors, walls, and so on, but also divine guardians and their representations in private houses and temples. The verbal root ʿwr in Hebrew means '(to be) awake', and Syriac ʿr, with participle ʿīr means '(to be) awake, watch'. Hence the Aramaic term means 'wakeful one'. The expression ʿyryn came to denote angelic beings, whether they are good or rebellious, or could be used neutrally to refer to angels in general (Stuckenbruck 1997: 84). The cognate verb in Akkadian is *êru*, 'to be awake' (*CAD* E 326)." Annus attributes some of this to Stuckenbruck, *Book of Giants*, 84. The *CAD* = *The Chicago Assyrian Dictionary*.

97. This thought may be new to some readers, but messianic prophecy was *intentionally* cryptic for precisely the reason Paul noted. Satan and demons knew very well *who* Jesus was. They could reason that the "Son of the Most High" had come to restore Eden. But they were unaware of the path—that the indispensable element to the plan of God was the death and resurrection of His Son. This was something that could only be discerned after the fact. See Heiser, *The Unseen Realm*, chapter 28. The lemma behind "rulers of this world" (*archōn*) is a term used elsewhere in the singular for Satan / the Devil (Matt. 12:24; John 12:31; Eph. 2:2). It is also used in the Septuagint for the *elohim* sons of God ("princes") over the nations (Dan. 10:13; see Theodotian's Greek text of Daniel). The lemma is closely related to *archē*, a lemma used in the plural for spiritual powers of darkness (Eph. 3:10; 6:12; Col. 1:16; 2:15). For a lengthy overview of Paul's adoption of this worldview, see Ronn Johnson, "The Old Testament Background for Paul's Principalities and Powers," (PhD diss., Dallas Theological Seminary, 2004). For brief discussions of *archōn* and *archē*, see D. G. Reid, "Principalities and Powers," in *Dictionary of Paul and His Letters*, 746–752.

98. My view is *not* that Paul was arguing the story of the cross was in the starry heavens, but that the stars communicated the arrival of a divine king. In that sense, Paul believes it was possible for the news about Jesus' coming to be known to everyone. His task in the Gospel was to explain what that coming meant (the "mystery" as Paul called the plan of salvation), particularly with respect to the cross. Several well-known Christian writers have attempted to argue that the starry sky, and specifically the zodiac, lays out every detail of the work of Christ and the Gospel. Those attempts, well-intentioned as they were, go too far. It is fallacious to presume that the starry heavens could actually explain the way of salvation to someone when Christ Himself sent the apostles into the world to preach the gospel. If looking at the heavens was sufficient for evangelism, why would Jesus send out the apostles? (The sky has far greater and more immediate coverage!) Moreover, the message of the traveling apostles was not how to read the heavens—it was the work of Christ on the cross. Finally, the notion that the gospel message could be understood through the stars conflicts with the fact that the disciples themselves didn't understand the cross event until after the ascension (e.g., Luke 24:45–49). The most well-known efforts to argue

that the plan of salvation is revealed in the stars are: E. W. Bullinger, *The Witness of the Stars* (reprint; Forgotten Books, 2009) and Joseph Augustus Seiss, *The Gospel in the Stars* (reprint; General Books, 2009). The famous evangelical preacher D. James Kennedy also espoused this idea (see http://www.djameskennedy.com/full-view-sermon/ djk18549a-the-gospel-in-the-stars).

99. The major work in this regard is Bruce J. Malina, *The Genre and Message of Revelation: Star Visions and Sky Journeys* (Hendrickson, 1995). Malina overstates his case at times, and neglects the role of the Old Testament and Second Temple Jewish literature for interpreting Revelation, but he marshals a good deal of evidence that Revelation (at least major sections of it) should be considered part of the astral prophecy genre.

100. See for example these studies: Jodi Magness, "Helios and the Zodiac Cycle in Ancient Palestinian Synagogues," *Dumbarton Oaks Papers* 59 (2005): 1–52; Rachel Hachlili, "The Zodiac in Ancient Jewish Art: Representation and Significance," *Bulletin of the American Schools of Oriental Research* 228 (Dec. 1977) 61–77; James H. Charlesworth, "Jewish Astrology in the Talmud, Pseudepigrapha, the Dead Sea Scrolls, and Early Palestinian Synagogues," *Harvard Theological Review* 70:3/4 (July-October 1977) 183–200.

101. A noteworthy exception is the work of Dr. Ernest L. Martin, *The Star That Astonished the World* (2nd ed., 1996). (Martin's book is available free at www.askelm.org). Readers are referred to Martin's book for his far more detailed treatment of the astronomy associated with Revelation 12 and the birth of Jesus. The astronomical material in the present chapter follows Martin's book closely (by permission), but only selectively. There are many more points of data that could be brought to bear. Martin's view has been endorsed by leading experts on biblical chronology and many astronomers in the United States and abroad. While I find Martin's view the most convincing and coherent explanation of the astronomical events associated with Jesus' birth, that approval is not an endorsement of all that Martin says in the book or his other publications. I differ with several of Martin's beliefs, disagreements that extend to those entrusted with disseminating his work and guarding his legacy.

102. It is equally clear that this passage is not describing any sort of *primeval* angelic/demonic rebellion. The "third of the stars" reference follows the

birth of the child, which is clearly Jesus. Despite its obvious nature, this passage is often referred to by Bible students in defense of some sort of angelic rebellion at the time of the creation preceding the creation of humankind. There actually is no such passage in the Bible for that idea.

103. G. K. Beale, *The Book of Revelation, The New International Greek Testament Commentary* (Grand Rapids: Eerdmans, 1999) 621. Beale's commentary is one of the leading scholarly resources on Revelation. It is far and away the best commentary on Revelation with respect to interaction with Second Temple Jewish thinking.

104. See 2 Kings 19:21; Isa. 37:21; Jer. 14:17; 18:13; 31:4, 21; Amos 5:2; Lam. 1:15; 2:13.

105. Beale (*The Book of Revelation*, 642–643) describes the imagery: "Verse 6 is saturated with a rich diversity of OT, Jewish, and early Christian background. The woman flees from the dragon after the deliverance of her son. She flees so that the dragon will not annihilate her. This is not a mere literal escape, whether of Christians fleeing the Roman siege of Jerusalem in A.D. 66 and going to Pella (Eusebius, *H.E.* 3.5) or of a remnant of Christian Jews being protected from the future Great Tribulation. As in vv 1 and 2, the woman represents the community of faith, though now it is not that of the OT epoch, but the messianic community after Christ's resurrection. The woman is now on earth and not in heaven because she now represents the true people of God on earth. She escapes into the wilderness for protection because 'there she has a place prepared *by* (ἀπό) God'… She has not only protection but also 'nourishment,' which enables her to continue to exist…. The flight into the wilderness is a collective allusion primarily both to Israel's exodus from Egypt and the anticipated end-time exodus, which was to occur during Israel's latter-day restoration from captivity. First, it refers to the time when Israel fled from Egypt into the wilderness and was protected and nourished by Yahweh (Exod. 16:32; Deut. 2:7; 8:3, 15–16; 29:5; 32:10; Josh. 24:7; Neh. 9:19, 21; Pss. 78:5, 15, 19; 136:16; Hos. 13:5). The same pattern of flight into the wilderness is observable in the case of Elijah (1 Kings 17; 19:3–8) and Moses (Exod. 2:15; Josephus, *Ant.2.256*), who symbolize the church in Rev. 11:5–6. Similarly, Isaiah and other prophets 'withdrew…to a desert place' because 'Israel went astray' 'in service to Satan' (*Asc. Isa.* 2:7–11; cf. *Assumption of Moses 9:1*, 6). The OT faithful were those who 'wandered in the wilderness'

(Heb. 11:38). Matt. 2:15 links the flight of Jesus' parents from Herod and their return to Israel to the exodus. Together with the exodus, these other parallel desert pilgrimages could also be echoed in Revelation 12. Nevertheless, the parallel of Rev. 12:14 with v 6 makes the exodus background explicit. The 'two wings of the eagle' on which the woman is borne into the wilderness (v 14) allude to God's care of Israel after the exodus during the wilderness sojourn. In Deuteronomy the 'wilderness' (ἔρημος) is the avenue on which God guides Israel to the 'place' (τόπος) of the Promised Land, where the divine presence is to dwell (Deut. 1:31; 9:7; 11:5)."

106.   Beale (*The Book of Revelation*, 625–626) has devoted considerable attention to the ancient Jewish and Old Testament context for the woman. He writes in part: "Verses 2–6 reveal that this woman is a picture of the faithful community, which existed both before and after the coming of Christ. This identification is based on the OT precedent in which the sun, the moon, and eleven stars represent Jacob, his wife, and the eleven tribes of Israel (Gen. 37:9; cf. *Testament of Naphtali* 5:3ff.), who bow down to Joseph, who represents the twelfth tribe. The depiction could also reflect the portrayal in Jewish writings of Abraham, Sarah, and their progeny as sun, moon, and stars (*Test. Abr.* B 7:4–16).... Jewish exegetes believed that the sons of Jacob were likened to stars in Genesis 37 to connote the indestructible nature of Israel: as stars appear far from earth and immune from destruction by any earthly force, so also (true?) Israel was ultimately indestructible (*Midr. Rab.* Gen. 9; *Targ. Neof.* Gen. 50:19–21).... The twelve stars represent the twelve tribes of Israel. The woman's appearance may also connote Israel's priestly character (cf. 1:6; 5:10), since Philo's and Josephus's explanations of Exodus 28 and 39 use the imagery of a crown, the sun, the moon, and twelve stars to describe the vestments of the Israelite high priests, since the priests represented the twelve tribes before Yahweh in the temple service (Josephus, *Ant.* 3.164–72, 179–87; Philo, *Vit. Mos.* 2.111–12, 122–24; *Spec. Leg.* 1.84–95). In fact, in these same texts the parts of the priestly garment represented by the heavenly bodies are explicitly said to symbolize the twelve tribes of Israel. Such dual imagery was meant to indicate that Israel on earth also had a heavenly identity. Indeed, later Jewish writings interpreted the twelve signs of the zodiac as representing the twelve tribes of Israel (*Midr. Rab.* Exod. 15.6; *Midr. Rab.* Num. 2.14; cf. *b. Berakoth*

32b). Therefore, the twelve stars surrounding the woman call to mind the twelve constellations, which connote the Israel of God viewed from the perspective of Israel's heavenly life or calling."

107. Martin notes that, "Interpreting astronomical signs dominated the thinking of most people in the 1st century, whether the people were Jews or Gentiles. Indeed, the word "sign" used by the author of the book of Revelation to describe this celestial display was the same one frequently used by the ancients to denote the zodiacal constellations." Cited from the text at: http://www.askelm.com/star/star006.htm. The Greek lemma translated "sign" is *sēmeion*. Martin's source is a solid one: Henry George Liddell et al., *A Greek-English Lexicon* (With a revised supplement, 1996; Rev. and augm. throughout; Oxford; New York: Clarendon Press; Oxford University Press, 1996), 1593. The entry in part reads: "*Sign from the gods, omen*, S.*OC* 94; τὰ ἀπὸ τῶν θεῶν σ. γενόμενα Antipho 5.81, cf. Pl.*Phdr*.244c, *Ap*.40b, X.*Cyr*.1.6.1; *wonder, portent*, Lxx Ex.4.8, al.; σ. καὶ τέρατα Plb.3.112.8, Ev.Matt.24.24, Ev.Jo.4.48, cf. *IPE* l.c., D.S.17.114; φόβηθρα καὶ σ. ἀπ' οὐρανοῦ Ev.Luc.21.11; esp. of *the constellations*, regarded as *signs*, δύεται σημεῖα E.*Rh*.529 (lyr.), cf. Ion.1157."

108. While the symbolism we will discuss in this chapter communicates, and is thus consistent with Paul's quotation of Psalm 19:4 from the Septuagint ("their *voice* goes out"), the Masoretic Text reading of Psalm 19:4 actually aligns much better with the notion of a constellation following the ecliptic. The Masoretic Text of Psalm 19:4 reads: "their *line* goes out"). The stars communicating via a "line" that goes out in the heavens is quite descriptive of the astronomical notion of a path or ecliptic.

109. Martin, chapter 5, cited from the text at: http://www.askelm.com/star/star006.htm.

110. See Malina, 155–160, for a brief sketch of those mother goddess figures.

111. For a good summary of chaos and the imagery of the sea monster, see the entries for "Dragon" and "Sea" in *Dictionary of Deities and Demons in the Bible*, as well as F. J. Mabie, "Chaos and Death," in *Dictionary of the Old Testament: Wisdom, Poetry & Writings* (Edited by Tremper Longman III and Peter Enns; Downers Grove, IL: Inter-Varsity Press, 2008) 41–54.

112. Grant R. Osborne, *Revelation* (Baker Exegetical Commentary on the New Testament; Grand Rapids, Mich.: Baker Academic, 2002) 459.

113. Malina, 160–161.

114. There are other astronomical events besides the additional ones shared here. They can be discovered in Martin's book.

115. "Sun, Moon, and Stars (Introductory)," *The Encyclopaedia of Religion and Ethics,* XII (ed. James Hastings; Edinburgh: T & T Clark, 1921), 51. See also Martin's text at: http://www.askelm.com/star/star006.htm.

116. As Martin details in chapter 5 of his book, reading Revelation 12 this way correlates precisely with the chronological testimony of Luke concerning the timing of the birth of John the Baptist and his father's (Zechariah) priestly duties at the temple, where the angel met him to announce John's birth. The primary objection to this date is that it violates the accepted date for Herod's death (4 B.C.), requiring that Herod die in 1 B.C. Despite the objections of many to the September 11, 3 B.C. date on these grounds, a 1 B.C. date for Herod's death is indeed possible—and actually quite plausible. For recent research into how a 1 B.C. date for the death of Herod is historically coherent, see Ormond Edwards, "Herodian Chronology," *Palestine Exploration Quarterly* 114:1 (1982): 29–42; Andrew Steinmann, "When Did Herod the Great Reign?" *Novum Testamentum* 51 (2009):1–29. The former article focuses on numismatic (coins) evidence for reconsidering how Herod's dates are calculated and understood. The latter casts a wider net for data leading to a 1 B.C. death while also chronicling problems with the 4 B.C. consensus.

117. See Martin, chapter 5 (at http://www.askelm.com/star/star006.htm) for the details on these other conjunctions.

118. See Matthew 2:11, where the child Jesus is referred to with the Greek term *paidion,* as opposed to *brephos* in Luke 1:41. While the former can be used of an infant or toddler, the latter is only used of newborn infants or children *in utero.* See G. Braumann, and C. Brown, "Παῖς," *New International Dictionary of New Testament Theology* (ed. Lothar Coenen, Erich Beyreuther, and Hans Bietenhard; Grand Rapids, MI: Zondervan Publishing House, 1986), vol. 1: 283. Martin (ch. 5) points out that the account in the New Testament said the magi saw the star *rising* above the eastern horizon. And in August 12, 3 B.C., Jupiter *rose* as a morning star which soon came into conjunction with Venus. If the Magi began their own journey toward Jerusalem near this time, this apparent westward motion of Jupiter each day could have indicated to the Magi to proceed in the same westward direction toward Jerusalem. Martin follows this by

noting that the Magi could have been "following" Jupiter in the example it was setting. The Bible says the star "went ahead of them." Upon reaching Jerusalem the Magi were told to look toward Bethlehem for the newborn king. This occurred when the New Testament says the "star" came to a halt in the heavens (Matt. 2:9). Jupiter stopped its motion and "stood over where the young child was." In a word, the celestial body became stationary. Martin references Kittel's theological dictionary for this point. In commenting on the passive form of the Greek word for the star's behavior (ἐστάθη) Kittel quotes from A. Schlatter's *Kommentar z. Matthäusev* (1929): "In distinction from ἔστη, ἐστάθη implies that the star is halted» (see Gerhard Kittel, Geoffrey W. Bromiley, and Gerhard Friedrich (eds.), *Theological Dictionary of the New Testament* [Grand Rapids, MI: Eerdmans, 1964–], vol. 7:648). Martin also references the scholarly article by F. Steinmetzer at this point ("The Star of the Wise Men," *Irish Theological Quarterly,* VII [1912], 61.). Martin comments: "The theologian F. Steinmetzer, back in 1912, wrote an article stating his belief that Matthew was referring to one of these normal 'stationary' positions of the planets. Indeed, Steinmetzer suggested that the planet that suited Matthew's account the best was Jupiter. This is true."

119. Beale, *The Book of Revelation*, 620; cp. *b. Rosh Hashanah* 16.

120. Edwin R. Thiele, *The Mysterious Numbers of the Hebrew Kings* (Kregel, 1994) 28, 31, 161, 163.

121. Theodor Gaster, *Festivals of the Jewish Year* (4th ed.; William Sloane Associates, 1968) 109.

122. See the website Judaism 101: http://www.jewfaq.org/holiday2.htm.

123. Sample dates for *Rosh Ha-Shanah* are as follows: Jewish Year 5778: sunset September 20, 2017 - nightfall September 22, 2017; Jewish Year 5779: sunset September 9, 2018 - nightfall September 11, 2018; Jewish Year 5780: sunset September 29, 2019 - nightfall October 1, 2019. Source: http://www.jewfaq.org/holiday2.htm.

124. What follows in the present chapter from this point is a distillation of certain points in Robbins' essay. The full citation for this source is: Ellen Robbins, "The Pleiades, the Flood, and the Jewish New Year," in *Ki Baruch Hu: Ancient Near Eastern, Biblical, and Judaic Studies in Honor of Baruch A. Levine* (ed. Robert Chazan, William W. Hallo, and Lawrence Schiffman; Winona Lake, Ind.: Eisenbrauns, 1999) 329–344.

125. See http://terpconnect.umd.edu/~tlaloc/archastro/ae25.html (the

archaeoastronomy page of the University of Maryland). Another source notes, "ancient astrologers gave particular emphasis to the heliacal rising and setting of stars since these could be used as reliable indicators to agricultural conditions" (http://www.skyscript.co.uk/gl/heliacal.html).

126. See for example: http://www.theoi.com/Gigante/GiganteOrion.html.

127. See the Comprehensive Aramaic Lexicon. *Targum Job from Qumran - 11QtgJob; 11Q10.* Hebrew Union College, 2005.

128. Heiser, *The Unseen Realm,* 105–107.

129. Hermann Hunger and David Pingree, *Astral Sciences in Mesopotamia* (Leiden: E. J. Brill, 1999) 67.

130. A. E. Hill, "History of Israel 3: United Monarchy: Ideology of Kingship," ed. Bill T. Arnold and H. G. M. Williamson, *Dictionary of the Old Testament: Historical Books* (Downers Grove, IL: InterVarsity Press, 2005) 450.

131 The material in this chapter is based primarily on a 2010 dissertation by Amy S. Richter completed at Marquette University: Amy S. Richter, "The Enochic Watchers' Template and the Gospel of Matthew," PhD dissertation, Marquette University, 2010. At the time of this writing, Richter's dissertation was freely accessible in its entirety at: http://epublications.marquette.edu/cgi/viewcontent.cgi?article=1044&context=dissertations_mu.

132. The identification of all four women as Gentiles is plausible and, therefore, possible, but the matter is not certain. As Luz notes, "Tamar is usually, but not always, regarded in the Jewish tradition as a proselyte. (Footnote: In *Jub.* 41.1–2 and *T. Jud.* 10.1 she is presumably regarded as a member of Abraham's family. According to Philo [*Virt.* 221] she is a proselyte [Syrian Palestinian]; likewise according to rabbinic tradition where she becomes the daughter of Melchizedek). Ruth is a Moabitess, Rahab a resident of Canaanite Jericho. There are no reports about Bathsheba. Is that why she is cited not by name but as the wife of Uriah, who, as is well known, was a Hittite (2 Sam. 11:3)? That is conceivable, but it is by no means the most obvious idea that the readers would associate with the name Uriah. Thus, this sense is clear only with Ruth and Rahab. With Tamar it is quite possible, and for Bathsheba it may be possible" (Ulrich Luz, *Matthew 1–7: A Commentary on Matthew 1–7* [ed. Helmut Koester; Rev. ed.; Hermeneia—a Critical and Historical Commentary on the Bible; Minneapolis, MN: Fortress Press, 2007] 84–85.

133. Luz, *Matthew 1–7*, 83.

134. Richter, abstract (p. 3 of the dissertation in PDF form).

135. Ibid., abstract, 25–26.

136. Ibid., 3. The point here is not that Mathew's Gospel shows literary dependence on 1 Enoch. No scholar would argue that trajectory for a simple reason: There is no clear instance of Matthew quoting 1 Enoch. Rather, the point is that Matthew deliberately utilizes and inverts elements of the Watchers story to show how the circumstances of Jesus' conception, birth, and bloodline counteract the sin of the Watchers and its effects. Richter (p. 3) comments in a footnote: "I am cautious throughout this dissertation not to make claims that Matthew had access to a text containing the Enochic material. He may have had, but the fact that there is little, if any evidence, of Matthew's quoting material from 1 Enoch advises against making such a claim. However, I find the volume of material—even in the first two chapters of Matthew's Gospel—that can be explained in light of Enochic material to be evidence that Matthew was aware of many of the same traditions as those that would be gathered as 1 Enoch." Later (p. 22) she adds: This dissertation makes no claims of direct dependency of the Gospel of Matthew on the text of 1 Enoch. However, when examining Matthew chapters 1–2 in light of motifs of the Enoch watchers' template, evidence of these motifs as background for the Gospel material is apparent. This evidence appears in the frequency with which Enochic motifs can be identified in connection with material in Matthew's Gospel. The evangelist does not replicate any large sections of 1 Enoch, nor, as mentioned above, does he quote from 1 Enoch, with the possible exception of Sim's example. However, again and again in Matthew's genealogy and infancy narrative one finds motifs and allusions to material that one also finds in 1 Enoch. The number of instances in which Enochic motifs occur, even within the first two chapters of Matthew's Gospel, is too great for Matthew not to have been familiar with the Enochic tradition and for these to appear as background material as the evangelist tells his version of the story of Jesus."

137. Ibid., 47–48.

138. The negative view toward cosmetics is a good example. Ancient writers condemned cosmetics because of the association with seduction, which hearkened back to the Watchers episode. Richter (p. 49) notes that early Christian writers drew upon the Enochian material in their condemnation of cosmetics: "Clement uses the example of the watchers to appeal to

men that they not be enticed by women's beauty and fall like the rebel angels did. Both Tertullian and Cyprian make use of the story of the watchers' illicit pedagogy in their appeal to Christian women to cease using cosmetics and other means of beautification which came from such a corrupted source." Richter's sources are: (1) Clement: *Paedagogus* 3.2: "the mind is carried away by pleasure; and the unsullied principle of reason, when not instructed by the Word, slides down into licentiousness, and gets a fall as the due reward of its transgression. An example of this is the angels, who renounced the beauty of God for a beauty which fades, and so fell from heaven to earth" (*The Ante-Nicene Fathers;* Edited by Alexander Roberts and James Donaldson, 1885–1887; Repr. Peabody, Mass.: Hendrickson, 1994, vol 2:274); (2) Tertullian: *On the Apparel of Women* 1.2. (*ANF* 4:15); *Tertullian: Disciplinary, Moral and Ascetical Works* (trans. Rudolph Arbesmann, Emily Joseph Daly, Edwin A. Quain; The Fathers of the Church 40: A New Translation; ed. Roy Joseph Deferrari; New York: Fathers of the Church, 1959), 118–21; *On the Veiling of Virgins* 3.7 (Ante-Nicene Fathers, 4:32). Richter adds (p. 49, n. 116): "Tertullian argues that virgins should be veiled on the basis of the illicit sexual relations between the fallen angels and women. He reasons that the women whom the angels desired and consequently married must have been virgins. Therefore, virgins should be veiled."

139. Shuah is a name we will encounter again when we discuss Bathsheba.
140. LXX is an abbreviation for the Septuagint, the ancient Greek translation of the Hebrew Old Testament.
141. Richter, 63–64.
142. Richter, 63–64. Underlining is mine. There are many more details to these connections and other links in Richter's actual dissertation. My goal is to offer noteworthy examples in this chapter.
143. See Ludwig Koehler et al., *The Hebrew and Aramaic Lexicon of the Old Testament* (Leiden: E.J. Brill, 1994–2000), 876. Richter cites Martin Noth, *Die israelitischen Personennamen im Rahmen der gemeinsemitischen Namengebung* (Hildesheim: Olms, repr. 1980), 228; William F. Albright, "The Egyptian Empire in Asia in the Twenty-First Century B.C.," *Journal of the Palestine Oriental Society* 8 (1928) 238.
144. Richter, 65.
145. See for example, Joan Goodrick Westenholz, "Tamar, Qedēšā, Qadištu, and Sacred Prostitution in Mesopotamia," *Harvard Theological Review* 82 (July 1989): 245–266.

146. Westenholz, 253. See also Philip Jones, "Embracing Inana: Legitimation and Mediation in the Ancient Mesopotamian Sacred Marriage Hymn Iddin-Dagan A," *Journal of the American Oriental Society* 123 (2003): 291–303; Mary K. Wakeman, "Sacred Marriage," *Journal for the Study of the Old Testament* 22 (1982) 21–31.

147. Richter, 69 and note 167. Indeed, the close relationship of the Tamar story to sacred prostitute motifs has led some scholars to posit that Genesis 38 is a re-crafting of a story originally about a Canaanite *qedēshah*. See Michael C. Astour, "Tamar the Hierodule: an Essay in the Method of Vestigal Motifs," *Journal of Biblical Literature* 85 (1966) 185–96.

148. Richter, 93.

149. See Heiser, *The Unseen Realm,* 183–214, for a discussion of the conquest and the giant clans.

150. For example, Israelite warriors under Joshua are labeled with the term (Josh. 6:2; 8:3), as is David (1 Sam. 16:18). Even God is called *gibbor* in Deut. 10:17.

151. A search in Logos Bible Software (version 6) via the "Bible Word Study" function using the Logos Septuagint (edition of Rahlfs) reveals this rendering occurs fifteen times. For instances where no scholar would argue giants in view, see Pss. 18:6; 32:16; Isa. 3:2; 13:3; 49:24, 25. Other instances are likely not referring to giants, though some scholars see a suggestion in those passages.

152. Because Rahab is connected to Boaz in Matt. 1:5, this same presumptive connection to giants is also true of Ruth due to her connection to Boaz. Ruth, of course, is one of the four women in Jesus' genealogy. See the ensuing discussion.

153. In Greek, two consecutive *gamma* letters have the sound "ng"—hence "angel," not "aggel" in English pronunciation.

154. Richter, 94. Transliteration and translations were added by this author.

155. Richter (pp. 96–99) notes several inter-textual connections in the Hebrew of the Rahab story and that of Lot's interaction with the angels in Sodom. Apparently, the writer of both texts deliberately intended them to echo one another in certain respects. She also discusses (100–101) connections between how Matthew's account of the angelic warning to Joseph, Mary, and the Magi echo Rahab's "hiding of the elect" (Israelites).

156. Richter, 114.

157. Ibid., 117–118.

158. Richter (199–120) notes that rabbinic tradition altered the meaning of

parts of the Ruth story to "clean up" Ruth's ancestry. See *Ruth Rabbah* (5:12; 6:4; 8:4) and Étan Levine, *The Aramaic Version of Ruth* (Analecta Biblica 58; Rome: Biblical Institute, 1973) 22.

159. David R. Jackson, *Enochic Judaism: Three Defining Paradigm Exemplars* (London: T&T Clark, 2004) 62. Richter (122, n. 275) cites this study and adds in a footnote: "Jackson gives the examples of רוממה in 4Q394 8 i.10; 4Q396 1.5; 4Q397 5; cf. also 4Q174i.21, 2, 4. The phrase 'the spirits of the bastards' appears in 4Q511 35.7; 48, 49, 51.2-3. In 4Q510 1.5 reference is made to 'the spirits of the ravaging angels and the bastard spirits.'"

160. The translation is that of Abraham Cohen, cited in Richter.

161. Richter, 132–133.

162. The direct reference to Mount Hermon is corrupted in the Ethiopic text. Its authenticity is attested in the Aramaic material of 1 Enoch found among the Dead Sea Scrolls (the first six words of 4QEnᵃ), as well as some Greek manuscripts.

163. The Hebrew phrase translated "mountain of God" is *har 'elohim*. The phrase could be rendered "divine mountain" or, taking *'elohim* as a superlative, "mighty mountain." As Goldingay notes (see the ensuing discussion) in a footnote in his own discussion of Psalm 68: "J. A. Emerton emphasizes that not least in a context such as the present one, it is unlikely that *'ĕlōhîm* is merely a way of expressing the superlative" (citing J. A. Emerton, "The 'Mountain of God' in Psalm 68:16," in *History and Traditions of Early Israel* (Eduard Nielsen Festschrift; ed. André Lemaire and Benedikyt Otzen; Vetus Testamentum Supplements 50; Leiden: Brill, 1993), 24–37 (esp. 29–30).

164. J. J. M. Roberts, "The End of War in the Zion Tradition: The Imperialistic Background of and Old Testament Vision of World Peace," *Horizons in Biblical Theology* 26:1 (June 2004): 2–22 (esp. p. 4)

165. John Goldingay, *Baker Commentary on the Old Testament: Psalms 42–89* (ed. Tremper Longman III; vol. 2; Grand Rapids, MI: Baker Academic, 2006) 323.

166. See my lengthy discussions of these associations in *The Unseen Realm*, pp. 183–232.

167. The use of "Amorite" in the Old Testament is indiscriminate. In some passages it's a label for the entire population of Canaan (Josh. 7:7). In that sense, "Amorites" and "Canaanites" are interchangeable, both denoting non-Israelite in the land of Canaan. In other passages its use is

more specific to one people group among several within Canaan (Gen. 15:19–21).

168. The dimensions of Og's bed are not the dimensions of his actual height. While the text is clear that he was the last of the Rephaim and that "Rephaim" was a term associated with the giant Anakim (Deut. 2:11) who were "from the nephilim" (Num. 13:32-33), the bed's dimensions are mytho-theological. That is, the dimensions are designed to take readers back to Mesopotamian religion, the original context for Gen. 6:1-4. I wrote: "First, the most immediate link back to the Babylonian polemic is Og's bed (Hebrew: *'eres*). Its dimensions (9 × 4 cubits) are precisely those of the cultic bed in the ziggurat called Etemenanki— which is the ziggurat most archaeologists identify as the Tower of Babel referred to in the Bible. Ziggurats functioned as temples and divine abodes. The unusually large bed at Etemenanki was housed in "the house of the bed" (*bit erši*). It was the place where the god Marduk and his divine wife, Zarpanitu, met annually for ritual lovemaking, the purpose of which was divine blessing upon the land" (*The Unseen Realm,* 199).

169. Joel C. Slayton, "Bashan (Place)," ed. David Noel Freedman, *The Anchor Yale Bible Dictionary* (New York: Doubleday, 1992) 624.

170. See G. del Olmo Lete, "Bashan," in *Dictionary of Deities and Demons in the Bible*, 2nd ed. (ed. Karel van der Toorn, Bob Becking, and Pieter W. van der Horst; Leiden; Boston; Cologne; Grand Rapids, MI; Cambridge: Brill; Eerdmans, 1999) 161–62.

171. Scholarly studies on the origin of demons as Watcher spirits of dead Nephilim include: Wright, *The Origin of Evil Spirits* (op. cit); Kevin Sullivan, "The Watchers Traditions in 1 Enoch 6–16: The Fall of Angels and the Rise of Demons," in *The Watchers in Jewish and Christian Traditions* (ed. Angela Kim Harkins, Kelley Coblentz Bautch, and John C. Endres; Augsburg Fortress Publishers, 2014), 91–103; Silviu N. Bunta, "Dreamy Angels and Demonic Giants: The Watchers Traditions and the Origin of Evil in Early Christian Demonology," in *The Watchers in Jewish and Christian Traditions* (ed. Angela Kim Harkins, Kelley Coblentz Bautch, and John C. Endres; Augsburg Fortress Publishers, 2014) 116–138.

172. Nickelsburg, *1 Enoch,* 267.

173. Material for this and the following section is drawn in part from chapter 32 of my book, *The Unseen Realm.*

174. 2 Kgs. 1:2, 3, 6, 16; Matt. 10:25; 12:24, 27; Luke 11:15, 18–19. See W. Herrmann, "Baal Zebub," in *Dictionary of Deities and Demons in the Bible*, 2nd ed. (ed. Karel van der Toorn, Bob Becking, and Pieter W. van der Horst; Leiden; Boston; Cologne; Grand Rapids, MI; Cambridge: Brill; Eerdmans, 1999) 154–156.

175. Brandon Ridley, "Mount Hermon," ed. John D. Barry et al., *The Lexham Bible Dictionary* (Bellingham, WA: Lexham Press, 2012, 2013, 2014, 2015). Nickelsburg demonstrates the identification of Hermon / Bashan / Galilee in his study, "Enoch, Levi, and Peter: Recipients of Revelation in Upper Galilee," *Journal of Biblical Literature* 100:4 (1981): 575–600. The book of 1 Enoch itself identifies Hermon with the region known in Jesus' day as Upper Galilee. When Enoch writes down the confessions and petitions of the Watchers—their pleas to God for forgiveness and clemency, he says, "And I went and sat down upon the waters of Dan—in Dan which is on the southwest of Hermon" (1 Enoch 13:7). Nickelsburg observes, "This is a clear reference to the immediate environs of Tell Dan in upper Galilee" (p. 582).

176. Heiser, *The Unseen Realm,* 292–294.

177. Joel C. Slayton, "Bashan (Place)," ed. David Noel Freedman, *The Anchor Yale Bible Dictionary* (New York: Doubleday, 1992) 623. That Mount Hermon is also included in the boundaries of the promised land has been established by careful studies of the boundary descriptions. See Zecharia Kallai, "The Patriarchal Boundaries, Canaan, and the Land of Israel: Patterns and Application in Biblical Historiography," *Israel Exploration Journal* 47:1–2 (1997) 69-82 (esp. 73); idem, "Conquest and Settlement of Trans-Jordan: A Historiographical Study," *Zeitschrift des Deutschen Palästina-Vereins (1953+)* 99 (1983):110–118.

178. See 4Q394 8 i.10; 4Q396 1.5; 4Q397 5; 4Q174i.21, 2, 4; 4Q511 35.7; 48, 49, 51.2–3. In 4Q510 1.5.

179. Some scholars believe that the Legion confrontation is a cryptic call for political liberation. The argument is made on a twofold basis: (1) the Greek term for Legion (*legiōn*) is a direct reference to Roman forces, and (2) the Greek word translated "herd" (*agelē*) was also used of Roman military recruits. The logic is dubious. The region of the Gerasenes was known as Gentile territory—that herdsmen were caring for pigs in the region makes that evident. Jews wouldn't have been earnestly seeing Roman expulsion from Gentile areas, so a cryptic endorsement of

political liberation isn't the point Mark wanted his readers to catch.

180. See my discussion of Deuteronomy 32 and cosmic geography in *The Unseen Realm,* 110–123.

181. The translation and associated transcriptional brackets are those of Florentino García Martínez and Eibert J. C. Tigchelaar, "The Dead Sea Scrolls Study Edition (translations)" (Leiden; New York: Brill, 1997–1998) 1177.

182. Miryam T. Brand, " 'At the Entrance Sin is Crouching': The Source of Sin and Its Nature as Portrayed in Second Temple Literature," Ph.D. Dissertation, New York University, 2011, 33. Brand's dissertation was later published under the title, *Evil Within and Without: The Source of Sin and Its Nature as Portrayed in Second Temple Literature* (Journal of Ancient Judaism Supplements 9; Göttingen: Vandenhoeck & Rupprecht, 2013). References in this chapter are to Brand's dissertation.

183. García Martínez and Tigchelaar, 159–161.

184. Brand, 71. Similar terms are applied to humankind in general in 1QH^a V.31-35.

185. Brand, 269. While we'll see her statement about the link between human sinfulness and demons (i.e., the fallen Watchers) is correct, Brand overstates the dichotomy between the two perspectives about sin. She elsewhere (p. 269) claims that, "The attribution of sin to demons renders moot the question of why humans were created with sinful desires." It doesn't. There is no reason to suspect that Second-Temple Jews didn't believe both explanations were true. She also fails to consider the transparent truth of the Genesis 3 narrative, that humans were created imperfect (lesser than God and without his nature). By definition, any being lacking the nature of God himself will sin.

186. Brand, 275–276.

187. Brand, 287–288.

188. Translation is from Nickelsburg, *1 Enoch*, 267.

189. Nickelsburg, *1 Enoch,* 270–273. It should be noted that Brand's discussion (and some of her sources), portrays the Enochian tradition as confused on these points, having multiple contradictory perspectives. This is because of the scholarly propensity to divide 1 Enoch in multiple sources and traditions. Some of that division is demonstrable, while some of it (in my view) stems from the imagination. For many scholars of ancient literature, when a book says two different things, they are

typically thought of as having derived from two different sources. The notion that a writer can say opposing things for a reason and then later have those things converge seldom occurs to textual scholars, conditioned as they are to see multiple sources everywhere. Scholars reflexively tend to need *every* element of a given topic spelled out in *every* textual passage to see sameness of source for a given passage. This exaggerated sensitivity is a bi-product of the source-critical methodology in which scholars are trained. For our purposes, the issue doesn't matter, as the final form of 1 Enoch puts forth the belief that the post-Flood "Watcher demons" continued to corrupt humanity.

190. Translation is from Nickelsburg, *1 Enoch*, 267.

191. García Martínez and Tigchelaar, 1027–1029.

192. Brand, 369.

193. Tyler A. Stewart, "Fallen Angels, Bastard Spirits, and the Birth of God's Son: An Enochic Etiology of Evil in Galatians 3:19–4:11," Paper read at the annual meeting of the Society of Biblical Literature, 2014, 1–2.

194. As Stewart details, there have been a number of studies on the Second Temple Jewish subordination of the law of Moses to the revelation to Enoch. Among the sources he cites are: Gabriele Boccaccini, *Beyond the Essene Hypothesis : The Parting of the Ways between Qumran and Enochic Judaism* (Grand Rapids: Eerdmans, 1998), 68–79; Philip S. Alexander, "From Son of Adam to Second God: Transformations of the Biblical Enoch," in *Biblical Figures Outside the Bible* (Harrisburg: Trinity International Press, 1998), 87–122, esp. 107–110; George W. E. Nickelsburg, "Enochic Wisdom: An Alternative to the Mosaic Torah?" in *Hesed Ve-Emet* (ed. Jodi Magness and Seymour Gitin; BJS 320; Atlanta: Scholars Press, 1998), 123–132; James C. VanderKam, "The Interpretation of Genesis in 1 Enoch," in *The Bible at Qumran* (eds. P. W. Flint and T. H. Kim; Grand Rapids: Eerdmans, 2000), 129–148, esp. 142–146; Andreas Bendenbender, "Traces of Enochic Judaism within the Hebrew Bible," *Henoch* 24 (2002): 39–48; Andrei A. Orlov, *The Enoch-Metatron Tradition* (Texte und Studien zum antiken Judentum 107; Tübingen: Mohr Siebeck, 2005), 254–260; John J. Collins, "How Distinctive was Enochic Judaism?" *Meghillot* 5–6 (2007): 17–34. Helge S. Kvanvig, "Enochic Judaism – a Judaism without the Torah and the Temple," in *Enoch and the Mosaic Torah: The Evidence of Jubilees* (eds. Gabriele Boccaccini and Giovanni Ibba; Grand Rapids: Eerdmans 2009), 163–177.

195. Stewart, 6.
196. I discussed the role of angels in the giving of the law and the identity of this intermediary as the Angel of Yahweh, God in human form, in *The Unseen Realm,* 163–170. We will not devote space to these items in the present chapter.
197. Stewart, 7–8, 12–13; emphasis (underlining) is mine. On scholarly challenges to the interpretation of Gal. 3:19 that has the law *producing* human transgressions, see David J. Lull, "'The Law Was Our Pedagogue': A Study in Galatians 3:19–25," *Journal of Biblical Literature* 105, no. 3 (1986): 481–498, esp. 483–485; Richard B. Hays, *The Letter to the Galatians* (pages 181–348 in NIB 11; Nashville: Abingdon Press, 2000) 266. Stewart elsewhere notes, "Consistently χάριν is translated as "because of" in contemporary translations including NRSV, ESV, NIV, NASB. The preposition appears only here in Paul's undisputed letters, but also occurs in Eph 3:1, 14; 1 Tim 5:14; Titus 1:5; Lk 7:47; 1 Jn 3:12; Jude 16; LXX 2 Chron 7:21; Dan 2:13. This preposition simply cannot carry the exegetical load to indicate that the law *produces* transgression" (footnote 20, page 7; emphasis mine).
198. Richard J. Bauckham, *2 Peter, Jude* (vol. 50; Word Biblical Commentary; Dallas: Word, Incorporated, 1998) 89.
199. Stewart, 15–16.
200. The major study on Irenaeus in this regard is D. R. Schultz, "The Origin of Sin in Irenaeus and Jewish Apocalyptic Literature," Ph.D. dissertation, McMaster University, 1972. An abbreviated form of this study is D. R. Schultz, "The Origin of Sin in Irenaeus and Jewish Pseudepigraphical Literature," *Vigiliae Christianae* 32 (1978): 161–190. Quotations in this chapter from Schultz come from this shorter article. However, in his dissertation (appendix I) Schultz includes a lengthy table comparing the wordings of specific passages in Irenaeus' writings to passages in 1 Enoch. The correlations are quite obvious when viewed side by side.
201. Schultz, 161, 168–169, 172–173.
202. Tertullian, *de virg. vel.* 7; *de idol.* 9; *de oratio* 22.
203. Loren T. Stuckenbruck, "Why Should Women Cover Their Heads Because of Angels?" *Stone-Campbell Journal* 4 (2001): 205–234.
204. Stuckenbruck notes that this view is preferred by: J. B. Lightfoot, *Home Hebraicae et Talmudicae* (Oxford: Oxford University Press, 1859) 4:238; A. Padget, "Paul on Women in Church: The Contradiction of Coiffure in

1 Cor 11:2-16?" *Journal for the Study of the New Testament* 20 (1984):
69-86; and J. Murphy-O'Connor, "1 Corinthians 11:2–16 Once Again,"
Catholic Biblical Quarterly 50 (1988): 268–269. The ancient church
father Ambrosiaster also took this view ("The veil signifies power, and
the angels are bishops"; *Corpus Scriptorum Ecclesiasticorum Latinorum*
81.3:122).

205. B. W. Winter, *After Paul Left Corinth: The Influence of Secular Ethics
and Social Change* (Grand Rapids: Eerdmans, 2001) 133–138. The
notion that the *angeloi* are hostile spies is not harmed by the criticisms of
this view that follow. It's lethal weakness is that the supporting context—
the rest of what Paul says in 1 Cor. 11:2–16—does not fit the idea of
human spies. As this chapter will demonstrate, the full content of Paul's
teaching makes the fourth option, that Paul has the transgression of the
Watchers in mind, the most likely.

206. As Stuckenbruck notes (222), this view is put forth by James Moffatt,
The First Epistle of Paul to the Corinthians (London: SPCK, 1947), 152,
and Charles H. Talbert, *Reading Corinthians: A Literary and Theological
Commentary on 1 and 2 Corinthians* (New York: Crossroad, 1987) 69.

207. The angels of the seven churches in Rev. 2–3 are another possible
reference to humans, though this is much disputed.

208. David E. Garland, *1 Corinthians* (Baker Exegetical Commentary on the
New Testament; Grand Rapids, MI: Baker Academic, 2003) 526.

209. Stuckenbruck, 222–223.

210. Joseph Fitzmyer, "A Feature of Qumran Angelology in 1 Cor. 11:10,"
in *Essays on the Semitic Background of the New Testament* (ed. Joseph
A. Fitzmyer; Grand Rapids, MI; William B. Eerdmans Publishing
Company) 187–201. See also H. J. Cadbury, "A Qumran Parallel to
Paul," *Harvard Theological Review* 51 (1958) 1–2. See the remainder of
this chapter in the present work for a coherent resolution to the passage.

211. Fitzmyer, 188, note 1.

212. Fitzmyer's article and subsequent postscripts list the following as
being relevant: 1QWar Rule vii, line 6; 1QSa=Rule of the Congregation
ii, lines 8-9; 4QFlorilegium fragment 1 i, lines 3-4; CD=Damascus
Document xv, lines 15–17; 4Q491=4QWar Rule fragments 1-3, line 10;
4QD=Damascus Document fr. 8 i, lines 6–9;

213. Stuckenbruck, 224–225. The word "cult" in scholarly discussion refers to
liturgy and ritual—religious ceremony.

214. Ibid., 225–226.

215. Ibid., 226–227.

216. Ibid., 227.

217. Tertullian is an example of an early church leader who made this same connection: "It is on account of the angels, he says, that the woman's head is to be covered, because the angels revolted from God on account of the daughters of men" (*On Prayer* 22.5).

218. Stuckenbruck, 228–230. Stuckenbruck marshals a number of primary sources in the course of articulating his defense of an Enochian connection on these grounds.

219. Troy W. Martin, "Paul's Argument from Nature for the Veil in 1 Cor. 11:13–15: A Testicle instead of a Head Covering," *JBL* 123:1 (2004): 75–8 (see 75–76). Martin's thesis was contested by a subsequent essay: Mark Goodacre, "Does περιβολαιον Mean 'Testicle' in 1 Cor. 11:15?" *JBL* 130:2 (2011): 391–396. Martin then produced a thorough response to Goodacre in defense of his original essay: Troy W. Martin, "Περιβολαιον as 'Testicle' in 1 Cor. 11:15: A Response to Mark Goodacre," *JBL* 132:2 (2013) 453–465.

220. Martin, "Paul's Argument from Nature," 76–77.

221. Martin, "Paul's Argument from Nature," 78–80. The text for the Hippocratic test for sterility is Hippocrates, *Aph.* 5.59.

222. On the term "feet" as a euphemism for genitalia in the Hebrew Bible, see Marvin H. Pope, "Bible, Euphemism and Dysphemism," *The Anchor Yale Bible Dictionary* (vol. I; ed. David Noel Freedman; New York: Doubleday, 1992) 720–725; E. Ullendorff, "The Bawdy Bible," *Bulletin of the School of Oriental and African Studies* 42 (1949): 425–456.

223. Martin, "Paul's Argument from Nature," 83–84.

224. Material in this chapter is drawn from the author's book, *The Unseen Realm: Recovering the Supernatural Worldview of the Bible* (Lexham Press, 2015) 335–339. Overlaps in prose content from that book are presented here by permission.

225. For example, see Tertullian: *On the Crown* 3: "When we are going to enter the water, but a little before, in the presence of the congregation and under the hand of the president, we solemnly profess that we disown the devil, and his pomp, and his angels. Hereupon we are thrice immersed, making a somewhat ampler pledge than the Lord has appointed in the Gospel. Then when we are taken up "as new-born children" (Source:

Tertullian, "The Chaplet, or *De Corona*," in *Latin Christianity: Its Founder, Tertullian* [ed. Alexander Roberts, James Donaldson, and A. Cleveland Coxe; vol. 3; The Ante-Nicene Fathers; Buffalo, NY: Christian Literature Company, 1885] 394. See also, Tertullian, *On the Shows* 4; *On the Soul* 35.3. For a discussion of this practice, see Ansgar Kelly, *The Devil at Baptism: Ritual, Theology, and Drama* (Ithaca, NY: Cornell University Press, 1985) 94–105.

226. The most recent exhaustive study of 1 Peter 3:14–22 and all debates, data, and associated passages concerning the matter of the imprisoned spirits is William Joseph Dalton, *Christ's Proclamation to the Spirits: A Study of 1 Peter 3:18–4:6* (vol. 23; Analecta Biblica; Roma: Editrice Pontificio Istituto Biblico, 1989). I am in agreement with Dalton that the imprisoned spirits are not the people who died in the Flood, and that 1 Peter is following the story of the sin of the Watchers from *1 Enoch*. Dalton notes (pp. 19, 21) that his understanding is not isolated. Well known and respected commentators before him rejected the human identification for the imprisoned spirits: "The great commentary of Selwyn seemed to move a long way towards a solution. He took in the wider context of Jewish tradition, particularly the First Book of Enoch, and saw in the 'spirits' to whom Christ made proclamation the wicked angels associated in this tradition with the flood and presented as the real instigators of human sin. I personally discovered that this understanding of the text, which at first sight appears forced, was well supported by further study of First Enoch and other related texts. In Selwyn's explanation Christ's proclamation was an announcement of his victory over his angelic adversaries. The whole presentation, despite its problems, had the advantage of understanding 1 Pet. 3:19 and its context as part of Christian tradition, typical of the whole approach of 1 Peter. The victory of Christ over the superhuman powers of evil is, in fact, a basic element in early Christian tradition…. J. N. D. Kelly published his commentary in 1969. It is difficult for me to assess this work with impartiality, since in all points of importance it agrees with my own views on 1 Pet. 3:19 and 4:6. I found it particularly gratifying that Kelly had come independently to such conclusions. This commentary has particular value, not only because of the exegetical wisdom of the author, but because of his acknowledged mastery of early Christian history."…. In 1971 E. Best published his commentary on 1 Peter. In this he accepted the view that the 'spirits' in

3:19 are fallen angels. Their 'prison' should be set in the underworld, since, according to Best, there is no evidence in the relevant literature for such a prison in the heavens (despite 2 Enoch 7:1, where the fallen angels in the second heaven are described as "prisoners under guard")." Best, however, also believed that Christ offered salvation to the fallen angels (1 Pet. 3:19). I don't follow this thinking since it would be an inconsistency in the Enochian typology followed in 1 Peter 3. See the second part of the present chapter.

227. The term can also refer to one's inner being, way of thinking, rationality, etc. See Louw, Johannes P., and Eugene Albert Nida, *Greek-English Lexicon of the New Testament: Based on Semantic Domains* (New York: United Bible Societies, 1996), vol. 2, p. 200, for semantic options.

228. Ibid., vol. 2, p. 266. See also Liddell, Henry George, Robert Scott, Henry Stuart Jones, and Roderick McKenzie, *A Greek-English Lexicon* (Oxford: Clarendon Press, 1996) 2026.

229. Note that in 1 Peter 4:6, the gospel was preached to "the dead" (Greek: *nekrois*), a term defined in the same verse as "people" (*anthropous*). This vocabulary makes sense in 1 Peter 4:6, but not in 1 Peter 3:19. As noted in our discussion, the vocabulary differentiation is the basic reason why it makes little sense to see 1 Peter 4:6 and 1 Peter 3:19 as referring to the same event and objects. It should be added that seeing disembodied human spirits in 1 Pet. 4:6 does not require endorsing the idea that the disembodied dead get another chance at faith in Christ. 1 Pet. 4:6 says: "For this is why the gospel was preached even to those who are dead, that though judged in the flesh the way people are, they might live in the spirit the way God does." It is nothing more than an *assumption* that this preaching was post-mortem—an assumption largely deriving from a second assumption that 1 Peter 3:19 is another reference to this preaching. The preaching could refer to proclamation that preceded death. For example, one could say of a deceased relative whom one presumes did not embrace the gospel, "I gave Grandma the gospel" after Grandma died to refer to the fact that she had heard the gospel. There is no necessary reason the language has to refer to contacting Grandma in the afterlife to give her the gospel. The "judgment in the flesh the way people are" could simply refer to the fact that people die. Applying this to 1 Pet. 4:6, we have: "I gave Grandma the gospel because she was going to die like all people do, so that she might live in the spirit [read: have

eternal life] the way God does." In other words, the gospel is preached to mortals so that they, like God, can escape the finality of death and have everlasting life with the Lord. There is nothing in 1 Pet. 4:6 that *requires* a post-mortem reading.

230. Dalton, *Christ's Proclamation to the Spirits*, 160–161.

231. J. Ramsey Michaels, *1 Peter* (vol. 49; Word Biblical Commentary; Dallas: Word, Incorporated, 1998) 207–208. Michaels unfortunately gets tripped up in his analysis on one point. In the second ellipsis of the above selection he also wrote: "If this passage is brought to bear on 1 Peter, then the 'spirits in refuge' are neither the souls of those who died in the flood nor precisely the angels whose sin brought the flood on the earth, but rather the 'evil spirits' who came from the angels—probably identified in Peter's mind with the 'evil' or 'unclean' spirits of the Gospel tradition." This is demonstrably incorrect from the Enochian material. The "spirits in prison" of 1 Peter 3:19 are not the Watcher-spirits of the dead Nephilim for the simple reason that those spirits are not the ones the Enochian material has imprisoned. As we saw in an earlier chapter, Enoch's Watcher story has only the original offending Watchers ("sons of God") bound and imprisoned. The spirits of their offspring, the giants, while also being called Watchers, are never described as being imprisoned until the time of the end. Rather—in concert with the New Testament Gospels— these Watcher spirits are allowed to roam the earth and harass humanity. They are clearly not bound. Michaels has unfortunately conflated the two.

232. William F. Arndt, F. W. Gingrich, Frederick W. Danker, and Walter Bauer, *A Greek-English Lexicon of the New Testament and Other Early Christian Literature* (=BDAG; Chicago: University of Chicago Press, 2000) 285.

233. Ibid., 967–968. BDAG glosses the lemma this way: "attentiveness to obligation, conscientiousness" (p. 968). The entry and the secondary scholarship it cites for this meaning point to 1 Tim. 1:5; 1 Cor. 10:25, 27–29; Heb. 9:9, 14 as New Testament examples. In these instances, it may be helpful to think of "conscience" as one's predilection or inner disposition in some behavioral direction (as opposed to a "moral gyroscope" that parses good and evil). Contemporary texts such as 1 Clement 2:4; 34:7 illustrate the former usage and meaning. See H. Osborne, "Συνείδησις," *Journal of Theological Studies* 32 (1931): 167–178; B. Reicke, *The Disobedient Spirits and Christian Baptism,*

174–182 (more external examples); Margaret E. Thrall, "The Pauline Use of Συνείδησις," *New Testament Studies* 14.1 (1967): 118–125; Paul W. Gooch, " 'Conscience' in 1 Corinthians 8 and 10," *New Testament Studies* 33.2 (1987): 244–254.

234. For a short survey of the historical scholarly "back and forth" as to whether the concept of Antichrist is solely Christian or has deep Jewish roots, see William Horbury, *Messianism among Jews and Christians: Twelve Biblical and Historical Studies* (London: T&T Clark, 2003) 328–330. Horbury notes, for example: "Antichrist seems as native to Christianity as the devil with horns and a tail. This impression receives learned support in much recent scholarship. Thus G. C. Jenks, C. E. Hill and L. J. Lietaert Peerbolte all contend that the figure of Antichrist is a Christian development. In earlier years, by contrast, it had been considered originally Jewish by Wilhelm Bousset, Moritz Friedländer, Louis Ginzberg and Israel Lévi. Then, however, Paul Billerbeck (1926), concisely summarizing a wealth of material, urged that, despite appearances, there was virtually no contact in substance between ancient Jewish literature and the New Testament on Antichrist; in Jewish sources the messiah had political opponents, but the Christian Antichrist was a religious figure. More recently Stefan Heid, in a book finished in 1990, accepted that Bousset was fundamentally right. A contrast between Christian and Jewish sources, in some ways recalling that drawn by Billerbeck, has nevertheless returned to prominence. For Jenks (1991), Hill (1995) and Lietaert Peerbolte (1996), the expectation of an enemy specifically opposed to the messiah first occurs among the earliest Christians, rather than among the non-Christian or pre-Christian Jews. Pre-Christian traditions, it is urged, refer to an eschatological tyrant, a final attack by evil powers, or the accompanying false prophecy, rather than a messianic opponent who can properly be termed Antichrist. Yet, just as Belial with horns now looms up hauntingly in Qumran texts (see 11Q Apocryphal Psalms[a], col. iv, lines 6–7), so it may be asked again, a hundred years after Bousset, whether Antichrist is not pre-Christian and Jewish as well as Christian. With regard to the Jews in the Roman empire this question frames itself more precisely. In the early empire, was Antichrist a Jewish counterpart of Greek and Roman notions concerning the great enemy of a savior king? If so, Jews and gentiles would have shared, in this as in many other respects, a broadly similar pattern of

hopes and fears for the future." As our own discussion will note, Horbury answered this last question in the affirmative. Jews, in reaction to their Roman overlords, did indeed describe a great tyrant who, logically, would seek to defend the empire against the messianic son of David. Select studies noted by Horbury in the above quotation are: G. C. Jenks, *The Origins and Early Development of the Antichrist Myth* (Beihefte zur *Zeitschrift für die neutestamentliche Wissenschaft und die Kunde der älteren Kirche* 59; Berlin and New York, 1991); L. J. Lietaert Peerbolte, *The Antecedents of Antichrist: a Traditio-historical study of the Earliest Christian Views on Eschatological Opponents* (Leiden, 1996); C. E. Hill, "Antichrist from the Tribe of Dan," *Journal of Theological Studies,* new series 46 (1995): 99–117. See also Geert Wouter Lorein, *The Antichrist Theme in the Intertestamental Period* (Library of Second Temple Studies 44. London: Bloomsbury T & T Clark, 2003).

235. Horbury, 330. We'll be considering the Gog material in chapter 11.

236. As Bauckham notes, "There is widespread agreement that Jude's source in v 9 was the lost ending of the [Testament of Moses]…preserved for us only in Latin translation." (Richard J. Bauckham, *2 Peter, Jude* [vol. 50; Word Biblical Commentary; Dallas: Word, Incorporated, 1998], 67). Bauckham includes a lengthy excursus in his commentary about other Second Temple texts from Qumran that informed Jude of the idea expressed in Jude 9 ("Excursus: The Background and Source of Jude 9," *2 Peter, Jude,* 65–76).

237. Translation is that of James H. Charlesworth, *The Old Testament Pseudepigrapha* (vol. 1; New Haven: Yale University Press, 1983) 930–931.

238. Horbury, 332–333.

239. The Second Temple Jewish profile of the great end-times enemy of Messiah consistently portrays this figure as an evil tyrant, distinct from Satan/Belial, but in league with or empowered by Satan/Belial. Jews of the period didn't understand this figure as a Jewish pseudo-messiah, that is, a figure which Jews would mistakenly *embrace* as the messianic son of David. The Second Temple profile of the great end times enemy, the one Christians would identify as the end-times Antichrist, points to a man who *opposes* the Messiah, not one who masquerades as Messiah. See Appendix V for more detail.

240. T. Elgvin, "Belial, Beliar, Devil, Satan," *Dictionary of New Testament*

Background: A Compendium of Contemporary Biblical Scholarship (ed. Craig A. Evans and Stanley E. Porter; Downers Grove, IL: InterVarsity Press, 2000) 153–154.

241. Ibid., 156.

242. The main texts in this regard are the *War Scroll* (1QM); *The War Rule* (4Q285 or 4QSM, also known as *4QSefer ha-Milhamah*).

243. As I have written elsewhere: "The *Sibylline Oracles* is a collection of prophetic utterances attributed to a female prophetess known as the sibyl, regularly described as an elderly woman or old hag. The sibyl is actually a legendary figure known from classical sources, most notably the Aeneid of Virgil. She had acquired her reputation well before Virgil's time, though. Roman sources at times list sibyls, and the Romans kept a record of their oracles for consultation in times of crisis. In the Hellenistic period, the period in which the *Sibylline Oracles* were composed, there were allegedly several sibyls…. [A distinctive Jewish element] in Book 3 [is the] reference to the final divine judgment when 'the sons of the great God will live peacefully around the temple' (702–3) and God 'will raise up a kingdom for all ages among men' (767–68)" (Ken Penner and Michael S. Heiser, "Old Testament Greek Pseudepigrapha with Morphology" [Bellingham, WA: Lexham Press, 2008]).

244. John J. Collins, "Sibylline Oracles," in James H. Charlesworth, *The Old Testament Pseudepigrapha* (vol. 1; New York; London: Yale University Press, 1983) 360.

245. David W. Baker, *Nahum, Habakkuk and Zephaniah: An Introduction and Commentary* (vol. 27; Tyndale Old Testament Commentaries; Downers Grove, IL: InterVarsity Press, 1988) 31.

246. Ibid., 775–777.

247. Geert Wouter Lorein, *The Antichrist Theme in the Intertestamental Period* (vol. 44; Journal for the Study of the Pseudepigrapha; London: T & T Clark International, 2003) 150.

248. The source for Irenaeus' speculation is *Against Heresies* 5.28–30. On *Teitan,* Alan Bandy notes: "the Titans were figures from pagan mythology. There has never been a ruler with the name Titan." See Alan Bandy, "The Hermeneutics of Symbolism: How to Interpret the Symbols of John's Apocalypse," *Southern Baptist Journal of Theology* 14:1 (2010): 53 (footnote 52). This article is accessible at: http://www.sbts.edu/wp-content/uploads/sites/5/2015/10/SBJT-V14-N.1-Bandy.pdf.

249. Horbury, *Messianism among Jews and Christians,* 343.
250. The literary history of the story of the Titans in ancient Greece is complex and, at times, contradictory. See Jan Bremmer, "Remember the Titans!" in *The Fall of the Angels* (ed. Christoff Auffarth and Loren T. Stuckenbruck; Leiden: E. J. Brill, 2004) 35–61.
251. Michael S. Heiser, "Giants—Greco-Roman Antiquity," in the *Encyclopedia of the Bible and Its Reception*, vol. 10 (Berlin: Verlag Walter de Gruyter, 2015). Given that both the Titans and the giants of the classical Greek myths both fought against divine authority and were imprisoned in Tartarus, it is easy to see how those two groups get conflated in later ancient material. For example, Euripedes: *Hec.* 472; *Iph. Taur.* 224; Virgil: *Aen.* iv.179; Horace: *Odes* iii.4, 42, etc. The two groups are clearly distinguished in older material, such as Hesiod (8th cent. B.C.) and Xenophanes (6th cent. B.C., *Xenophanes*, frg. 21.20).
252. As I have written elsewhere: "One contextual meaning of *repha'im* in the Hebrew Bible [is] spirits of the dead in the underworld. Several biblical texts employ *repha'im* in parallel to other words for the shadowy dead (e.g., *methim*; 'dead') or in contexts dealing with the grave (*qeber*; *she'ol*) or the underworld (*she'ol*). Psalm 88:10 (Heb. 88:11) asks: 'Do you work wonders for the dead (*methim*)? Do the departed (*repha'im*) rise up to praise you? Selah Is your steadfast love declared in the grave (*qeber*), or your faithfulness in Abaddon?' …[T]he second contextual meaning of *repha'im* in the Hebrew Bible [is] the giants encountered in Canaan during the conquest and the time of David. The term *repha'im* is linked to other terms for Old Testament giant clans in the Torah. The Israelites' first trek to the promised land under the leadership of Moses failed when the people lost faith after the spies sent into the land reported the presence of the unusually tall Anakim, also referred to as Nephilim (Num. 13:28–33; compare Gen. 6:4). The Anakim are mentioned in several passages in Deuteronomy as 'great and tall' enemies (Deut. 1:28; 2:10, 21; 9:2). In describing ancient inhabitants of Moab, the Emim, Deut. 2:10–11 specifically describes the Anakim as *repha'im*: '(The Emim formerly lived there, a people great and many, and tall as the Anakim. Like the Anakim they are also counted as Rephaim, but the Moabites call them Emim')…. The giant Og, the king of Bashan (e.g., Deut. 1:4; 3:10; Josh. 9:10), is partnered in Scripture with another king, Sihon of Heshbon. Together they are referred to as 'kings of the

Amorites' (Deut. 3:1–8; 4:46–47; 31:4; Josh. 2:10; 9:10). 'Amorite' is a term that can refer broadly to the inhabitants of Canaan (e.g., Gen. 15:16; Deut. 1:7). Its association with Sihon, Og, and the Rephaim makes Amos 2:9–10 especially interesting, as it describes the Amorites dispossessed in the conquest of Canaan as unusually tall ('I destroyed the Amorite before them…whose height was like the height of the cedars and who was as strong as the oaks')." See Michael S. Heiser, "Rephaim," *The Lexham Bible Dictionary* (ed. John D. Barry et al.; Bellingham, WA: Lexham Press, 2016). This is a digital resource, so there are no page numbers.

253. See Heiser, *The Unseen Realm,* 183–218.

254. Brook W. R. Pearson, "Resurrection and the Judgment of the Titans: ἡ γῆ τῶν ἀσεβῶν in LXX Isaiah 26:19," in *Resurrection* (ed. Stanley E. Porter, Michael A. Hayes, and David Tombs; London; New York: T&T Clark, 1999), 5–51 (esp. 36–37).

255. The translation is from R. Doran, "Pseudo-Eupolemus (Prior to the First Century B.C.)," in James H. Charlesworth, *The Old Testament Pseudepigrapha,* vol. 2 (New Haven: Yale University Press, 1985) 880–882. The passages in Eusebius are *Praeparatio Evangelica* 9.187.2–9 (lines 2–3, 9 cited); 9.18.2 (most of the passage cited). Lines not cited have Abraham tracing his lineage to the giants and learning astrology. Why a Second Temple text would connect Abraham with the giants and astrology is beyond the scope of the present book. For a discussion of the rhetorical strategies behind what Pseudo-Eupolemus says about Abraham (contrasting him with Nimrod and aligning him with favored Enoch), see K. van der Toorn and P. W. van der Horst, "Nimrod Before and After the Bible," *Harvard Theological Review* 83:1 (Jan. 1990): 1–29 (esp. 20–25). The idea of someone (even a giant) surviving the Flood apparently did not trouble a number of Jewish readers of the Flood account (nor the Jewish writer of Pseudo-Eupolemus). This may be due to the fact that phrases in the Flood narrative that to most modern readers require a global flood of exhaustive loss of life, elsewhere do not denote exhaustive totality. As I wrote in a footnote in *The Unseen Realm* (p. 189): "[T]he phrases in the flood narrative that suggest a global event occur a number of times in the Hebrew Bible where their context cannot be global or include all people on the planet. For example, the phrase 'the whole earth' (*kol 'erets*) occurs in passages that clearly speak of localized geography (e.g., Gen. 13:9; 41:57; Lev. 25:9, 24; Judg. 6:37; 1 Sam

13:3; 2 Sam. 24:8). In such cases, 'whole land' or 'all the people in the area' are better understandings. Those options produce a regional flood event if used in Gen 6–8 where the phrase occurs…. Gen. 9:19 clearly informs us that 'the whole earth' was populated by the sons of Noah. Gen. 10 (see 10:1) gives us the list of the nations spawned by the sons of Noah—all of which are located in the regions of the ancient Near East, the Mediterranean, and the Aegean. The biblical writers knew nothing of nations in another hemisphere (the Americas) or places like India, China, or Australia. The language of Gen. 10 therefore allows Gen. 7:21 to be restricted to only (or even some) of the people groups listed in the Table of Nations. That interpretation is consistent with a localized flood…. [T] he phrase 'all humankind' (*kol 'adam*) used in Gen. 7:21 also appears in contexts that cannot speak to all humans everywhere (e.g., Jer. 32:20; Psa. 64:9 can only refer to people who had seen what God had done, not people on the other side of the world). Lastly, Psa. 104:9 appears to forbid a global flood, since it has God promising to never cover the earth with water *as had been the case at creation*."

256. The Greek fragments behind "son of Kronos" reads ὃν εἶναι Κρόνον (literally, "who is Kronos"). This cannot be correct, as it would require Belos and Kronos to be the same figure, whereas the next verse has Kronos begetting Belos (and Canaan). Consequently, scholars emend the final Greek letter in the phrase from an accusative form to a genitive so that it reads ὃν εἶναι Κρόνου ("who is of/from Kronos"). See Doran, 881.

257. Van der Toorn and van der Horst, "Nimrod Before and After the Bible," 16, 18.

258. Ibid., 17.

259. The term *gibbor* does not inherently mean "giant," though it can in context. Joshua's men who fought against the Anakim are called *gibborim* (Josh 8:3); David is called a *gibbor* (1 Sam. 16:18), as is Gideon (Judg. 6:12). Even God is so described (Isa. 9:6).

260. Etemenanki = Esagil (Sumerian). See Andrew R. George, "The Tower of Babel: Archaeology, History, and Cuneiform Texts," *Archiv für Orientforschung* 51 (2005/2006): 75–95; John H. Walton, "The Mesopotamian Background of the Tower of Babel Account and Its Implications," *Bulletin for Biblical Research* 5 (1995) 155–75.

261. Michael S. Heiser, *The Unseen Realm,* 198–199. See Martti Nissinen, "Akkadian Rituals and Poetry of Divine Love," in *Mythology and*

Mythologies: Methodological Approaches to Intercultural Influences; Proceedings of the Second Annual Symposium of the Assyrian and Babylonian Intellectual Heritage Project Held in Paris, France, October 4–7, 1999, Melammu Symposia 2 (ed. R. M. Whiting; Helsinki: Neo-Assyrian Text Corpus Project, 2001) 93–136; Beate Pongratz-Leisten, "Sacred Marriage and the Transfer of Divine Knowledge: Alliances between the Gods and the King in Ancient Mesopotamia," in *Sacred Marriages: The Divine-Human Sexual Metaphor from Sumer to Early Christianity* (ed. Martti Nissinen and Risto Uro; Winona Lake, IN: Eisenbrauns, 2008) 43–72.

262. Parts of this chapter are drawn substantially from my book, *The Unseen Realm,* chapters 40 and 41.

263. Our coverage of the items in this chapter will be necessarily brief. A good deal more could be said in defense of certain ideas. While the same regret could be expressed with most everything else in this book, the topics in this chapter involve considerable detail in textual and literary analysis in the original languages to lay out a full case for them. Since that isn't possible here, readers are encouraged to study the sources cited for more detail.

264. The translation is Nickelsburg's. See also 1 Enoch 13:1; 14:5; Jubilees 5:6, 10; 10:7–11). I refer here to chapter 2 of the present study.

265. There is considerable debate about whether this "star," whom all agree is a divine being, is good or evil. Thompson argues for the former: "Most commentators, including Charles and Aune, assume that the key was given to the star, who, they then argue, was in fact a fallen angel. But this creates a problem when the star-angel of 9:1 is identified with the angel of 20:1... The *aggelos* in Rev. 9:1 and the *aggelos* in 20:1 have the same heavenly origin and the same responsibility-the key to the abyss.... While the angel keeper of the key of Sheol is not named in Revelation, he is elsewhere. The Greek version of 1 Enoch 20:2 attributes control of Sheol to 'Uriel, one of the holy angels, who is over the world and over Tartarus'.... Elsewhere the angel keeper of Sheol is given a title. In *Sibylline Oracles* book 8 there is an occurrence of the rare Greek *kleidophylax,* 'key-keeper.' Although the sentence is incomplete, the context allows it to refer to an otherwise unidentified key-bearer who is responsible for the enclosure where persons are retained before coming before the judgment seat of God in the final judgment. The concept

of the angel keeper(s) of *Sheol* flows into early Christian thinking
by use of the Greek term *tartarouchoi aggeloi,* 'angels who keep
Tartarus,' in *Apocalypse of Paul* 18; *Gospel of Bartholomew* 4:12; and
Hippolytus, *Commentary on Daniel* 2.29.11. The synonymous expression
temelouchos aggelos, "angel keeping Tartarus," is found in Clement of
Alexandria, *Prophetic Eclogue* 41.1." See Steven Thompson, "The End
of Satan," *Andrews University Seminary Studies* 37:2 (1999) 260–262.
Beale argues that the keeper is evil: "The main debate is whether this
is a good or evil being. It could be either the archangel Uriel, who was
chief 'over Tartarus,' or the archangel Saraqael, who was 'over...the
spirits, who sin in the spirit' (*1 En.19:1*; 20:1–6; 21:1–10; *Testament of
Solomon* 2). But *1 Enoch* never calls those figures 'fallen stars.' Instead,
this description is reserved exclusively for fallen angels under the
confinement of the archangels.... In addition to the resemblances with
falling star depictions elsewhere (mentioned above), the conclusion that
this is not a good angel but a fallen angel is also suggested by v 11. There
the 'angel of the abyss' is called 'king over' the demonic locusts and
is called 'Abaddon' ('Destruction') and 'Apollyon' ('Destroyer'). The
heavenly being who is sovereign over the abyss and the locusts in vv 1–3
is probably the one called their 'king' in v 11.... Therefore, the angel in v
1 is either Satan or one of his minions (the latter would be parallel with *2
En.* 42:1, which portrays 'those who hold the keys...of the gates of hell'
as 'like great serpents, and their faces like extinguished lamps, and their
eyes of fire, their sharp teeth')." See G. K. Beale, *The Book of Revelation:
A Commentary on the Greek Text* (New International Greek Testament
Commentary; Grand Rapids, MI: Eerdmans, 1999) 491, 493.

266. Thompson, "The End of Satan," 260.
267. Beale, *The Book of Revelation*, 493. Aune adds to the data: "The "star"
is obviously some kind of supernatural being, as this verse and the
following make clear.... While the key to the abyss is mentioned again
in 20:1, the notion of a shaft that could be locked and unlocked is implied
rather than explicitly stated. In the other two references, in Rev. 11:7
and 17:8, the abyss is the place from which the beast is said to ascend.
Papyri Graecae Magicae XIII.169–70, 481–83 indicates a belief in a
supernatural being who rules over the abyss: "a god appeared, he was
put in charge of the abyss".... It is sometimes synonymous with the
underworld, which is the abode of the dead (*Jos. As.* 15:12; Ps. 71:20;

Rom. 10:7; Diogenes Laertes 4.27 mentions "the abyss of Pluto" =
Hades) and the place where demons are imprisoned (Luke 8:31; *1 Enoch*
18–21; *Jub.* 10:7 [the Greek fragment reads "to cast them into the abyss
until the day of judgment"; see Denis, *Fragmenta*, 86])." See David E.
Aune, *Revelation 6–16* (vol. 52B; Word Biblical Commentary; Dallas:
Word, Incorporated, 1998) 525–526.

268. See Alexander Kulik, "How the Devil Got His Hooves and Horns: The
Origin of the Motif and the Implied Demonology of *3 Baruch*," *Numen*
60 (2013): 195-229 (esp. 215–216).

269. In other words, to impose modern war machinery on the passage violates
the contextualized intention of the writer. Below I argue that Gog is best
identified as an evil supernatural being, perhaps even Satan. As such, he
is not the *human* Antichrist, but the being personified by or empowering
the Antichrist. Since the final battle in Revelation and Second-Temple
Jewish sources (e.g., 1QM, the Qumran *War Scroll*) has both divine and
human combatants on either side, I consider the released Watchers to be
part of the enemies described as "Gog and Magog" in league with Satan.

270. See G. Del Olmo Lete, "Bashan," *Dictionary of Deities and Demons in
the Bible* (ed. Karel van der Toorn, Bob Becking, and Pieter W. van der
Horst; Leiden: E. J. Brill; Eerdmans, 1999) 161–163.

271. C. E. Hill, "Antichrist from the Tribe of Dan," *Journal of Theological
Studies (new series)* 46:1 (April 1995): 102–104. This perspective on
the tribe of Dan was not shared by rabbinic commentators. Hill writes
elsewhere in his study (pp. 111–113): "The strongest Old Testament
footing for a Danite Antichrist would have to be the mention in two
passages of a serpent or serpents in close proximity to the mention of
the name of Dan (Gen. 49:17; Jer. 8:17). Yet the latter passage does not
seem to have played any part in rabbinic comment on Dan, and Jewish
exegesis of Gen. 49:16–18, Jacob's blessing of Dan, turns out to be
overwhelmingly positive. Gen. 49:16–18 reads, 'Dan shall judge his
people as one of the tribes of Israel. Dan shall be a serpent in the way,
a viper by the path, that bites the horse's heels so that his rider falls
backward. I wait for thy salvation, O Lord.' The Jewish interpretation of
these verses centered virtually exclusively on the figure of Samson who,
with all his faults, was more a Christ than an Antichrist figure. Even the
comparison with the serpent is explained in terms of Samson's exploits
against the Philistines by Targum Onkelos, glorified by Philo through a

linking with Moses' healing brass serpent (*Allegoriarum* ii), and even when allusion is made to the serpent in Eden in *Genesis Rabbah* 98.14 there is no apparent disapproval: 'As the serpent is found among women, so was Samson the son of Manoah found among women. As a serpent is bound by an oath, so was Samson the son of Manoah bound by an oath [citing Judg. 15: 12]. Just as all the serpent's strength resides in his head, so it was with Samson'.... Samson, as the biblical text in Judges makes abundantly clear, was a Danite. His father, Manoah, was a Danite. But when Jacob says that Dan will judge his people 'like one of the tribes of Israel', the tribe he will judge 'like' is the pre-eminent tribe of Judah (*Num. Rabbah* 14. 9). And according to R. Joshua b. Nehemiah, although Samson's father was a Danite, Samson's mother was from the tribe of Judah. Thus in Samson were the two tribes united. In *Genesis Rabbah* Jacob is said to have been so impressed with Samson in his vision that he thought this prodigious warrior was the Messiah! 'But when he saw him dead he exclaimed, 'He too is dead! Then I wait for thy Salvation, O God'" (ibid. 98. 14). This assertion that Samson, the one great Danite, had a mother descended from Judah helps explain the saying of R. Hama b. R. Hanina, on Gen. 49: 9, Jacob's blessing of Judah: 'This alludes to Messiah the son of David who was descended from two tribes, his father being from Judah and his mother from Dan, in connection with both of which "lion" is written: Judah is a lion's whelp; Dan is a lion's whelp (Deut. xxxiii,22)', a saying which, however, cannot have been intended to refer to Samson, as the Messiah here is expressly the son of David. Thus in the claim of a royal, Judahite paternal descent and Danite maternal descent we finally have a Jewish exegetical warrant for, not an Antichrist to be sure, but a Christ from the tribe of Dan."

272. I have argued for a Gentile Antichrist template in several places in earlier chapters, but see appendix V as well.

273. Revelation 20:7–10 has "Gog and Magog" as the end-times enemies of Jerusalem as though the two were separate entities. This is not a necessary conclusion. If, as seems quite likely, Gog is a person and Magog a country or region, saying Gog and Magog were gathered for battle in Rev. 20:8 can semantically point to the figure of Gog leading his hordes, gathered from the four corners of the earth, against Jerusalem. One could refer to "Patton from the U.S." as an enemy of the Nazis and "Patton *and* the U.S." making war against the Nazis without changing

the meaning—Patton the general led an army of U.S. soldiers against the Nazis. Magog is a person in the Table of Nations of Genesis 10, but that passage is designed to explain the national geography deriving from the post-Flood family of Noah. Lust summarizes the evidence for Magog being a place, not a person: "Magog is mentioned in the table of nations in Gen 10:2, and in 1 Chr 1:5, as one of the seven sons of Japheth. Three of these sons occur in Ezekiel's Gog section as three countries or nations over which Gog is lording (Gomer, Tubal, Meshech: 38:3, 6; 39:1). In Gen 10:3, Togarmah is listed as a son of Gomer. His name returns in Ezek 38:6 as Beth-togarmah alongside with Gomer. See J. Lust, "Magog," *Dictionary of Deities and Demons in the Bible* (ed. Karel van der Toorn, Bob Becking, and Pieter W. van der Horst; Leiden: E. J. Brill; Eerdmans, 1999) 536.

274. J. Lust, "Gog," *Dictionary of Deities and Demons in the Bible* (ed. Karel van der Toorn, Bob Becking, and Pieter W. van der Horst; Leiden: E. J. Brill 1999) 373–374.

275. This perspective is found with some frequency among dispensationalist evangelicals. See Paul Tanner, "Daniel's 'King of the North': Do We Owe Russia an Apology?" *Journal of the Evangelical Theological Society* 35:3 [Sept 1992]: 315–328.

276. For example, there is no such place-name as *ro'sh* known in the ancient world. As Astour has noted, the closest geographical correlation that could be argued is "*Ra'shi* (or *Ara'shi*) of Neo-Assyrian records, a district on the border of Babylonia and Elam…which had nothing in common with Meshech and Tubal" (M. C. Astour, "Ezekiel's Prophecy of Gog and the Cuthean Legend of Naram-Sin," *Journal of Biblical Literature* 95 [1976]: 567, note 4). Further, the place-name "Rosh" would have had no meaning to an ancient Hebrew audience, since "the name *Rus* was first brought to the region of the Kiev by the Vikings in the Middle Ages" (E. Yamauchi, *Foes from the Northern Frontier: Invading Hordes from the Russian Steppes* [Wipf & Stock Publishers; 2003], 23). *Rus* and the longer *Russia* are of course Indo-European words, while Hebrew is from the Semitic language family. Consequently, a Rosh:Russia equation is a linguistic fallacy (false etymology). Additionally, aside from Genesis 10's placement of Meshech and Tubal in Anatolia, Ezekiel's own descriptions of those places in Ezek 27:12–15 have them located among nations adjacent to Anatolia. The place-names are thus not the Russian cities,

but ancient ethnic groups firmly situated in the ancient near eastern geographical reality of the Hebrew Bible.

277. Block argues for the first option in the second volume of his lengthy scholarly commentary on Ezekiel (see Daniel Isaac Block, *The Book of Ezekiel, Chapters 25–48* [The New International Commentary on the Old Testament; Grand Rapids, MI: Eerdmans, 1997–] 435). The latter position follows the explanation of Gesenius and Waltke-O'Connor, where the second noun in the Hebrew construct phrase (שְׁאָר) functions adjectivally, as an "adjectival genitive" (See B. Waltke and M. O'Connor, *Introduction to Biblical Hebrew Syntax* [Eisenbrauns, 1990], 148; Friedrich Wilhelm Gesenius, *Gesenius' Hebrew Grammar* [Edited by E. Kautzsch and Sir Arthur Ernest Cowley; 2d English ed.; Oxford: Clarendon Press, 1910], par. 127).

278. Lust "Gog," 373.

279. The LXX mistakes appear to be behind the supposition of Gressmann, mentioned by Zimmerli, that Gog was a mythological "locust giant after the manner of the scorpion man in the Gilgamesh Epic." See Walther Zimmerli, Frank Moore Cross, and Klaus Baltzer, *Ezekiel: A Commentary on the Book of the Prophet Ezekiel* (Hermeneia—a Critical and Historical Commentary on the Bible. Philadelphia: Fortress Press, 1979–) 300. Zimmerli cites H. Gressmann, *Der Messias* (FRLANT 6; Göttingen: Vandenhoeck & Ruprecht, 1929), p. 129 n. 1. Block includes reference to this same idea and source on p. 433, footnote 31. The idea is almost certainly a conflation of the Septuagint translation errors related to Gog: LXX Amos 7:1 and the swapping in of "Gog" for "Og" in certain LXX passages. While data such as these takes the reader's mind directly to the locust army of Revelation 9 released from the Abyss, it is unwise to consider such a move exegetically legitimate. Revelation 9 never identifies a leader and never cites Amos 7:1. Likewise it is tenuous to identify Gog as a giant given the transparent textual confusion in the Septuagint. Put simply, one cannot use the confusion of the translators as evidence for any identification of Gog.

280. As I wrote in *Unseen Realm* (pp. 359–360): "The Bible records a number of such incidents. But the most traumatic incursions into Canaan were always from the north. In 722 B.C. Assyria conquered the ten tribes of the northern Israelite kingdom and deported them to many corners of its empire. In a series of three invasions from 605 to 586 B.C., Babylon

destroyed the southern kingdom, comprising only two tribes, Judah and Benjamin. Both Assyria and Babylon invaded Canaan from the north, since they were both from the Mesopotamian region. The trauma of these invasions became the conceptual backdrop for descriptions of the final, eschatological judgment of the disinherited nations (Zeph 1:14–18; 2:4–15; Amos 1:13–15; Joel 3:11–12; Mic 5:15) and their divine overlords (Isa 34:1–4; Psa 82). It is hard to overstate the trauma of the Babylonian invasion. The northern tribes, too, had met an awful fate, the outcome of which was well known to the occupants of the kingdom of Judah. But Judah was David's tribe, and Jerusalem the home of Yahweh's temple. As such, the ground was holy and—or so the kingdom of Judah thought— would surely never be taken by the enemy. But Zion's inviolability turned out to be a myth. Jerusalem and its temple were destroyed by Nebuchadnezzar in 586 B.C. The incident brought not only physical desolation but psychological and theological devastation. The destruction of Yahweh's temple and, consequently, his throne, would have been cast against the backdrop of spiritual warfare by ancient people. The Babylonians and other civilizations would have presumed that the gods of Babylon had finally defeated Yahweh, the God of Israel. Many Israelites would have wondered the same thing—or that God had forsaken his covenant promises (e.g., Psa 89:38–52). Either God was weaker than Babylon's gods or else he had turned away from his promises."

281. Heiser, *The Unseen Realm,* 360–361.

282. Block (p. 433) cites one source for this possibility: P. Heinisch, *Das Buch Ezechiel übersetzt und erklärt* (Heilige Schrift des Alten Testaments 8; Bonn: Hanstein, 1923) 183.

283. Lust, for example, rejects it as "highly implausible," but offers no reasons why it ought to be dismissed.

284. Heiser, *The Unseen Realm,* 366. Whether Rev. 20:7–10 includes the Antichrist (and, so, the notion that Gog is the Antichrist) depends on the interpretive approach to the book of Revelation one adopts. Many who read Revelation as a linear chronology (the "futurist" view) also understand Gog of Ezekiel to be the Antichrist—yet they somehow miss the fact that the Antichrist's demise (in a linear futurist reading) *precedes* the Gog and Magog defeat of Rev. 20:7–10. The Beast is captured and thrown into the lake of fire in Rev. 19:20. This means that, for a futurist approach to Revelation's events, Gog can't be identified

with the Antichrist (Beast). Those who see recapitulation (recycling) in
what Revelation describes and not a linear chronology of events do not
have this problem, for the judgment at Armageddon in Rev. 17–19 and
the battle of Rev. 20:7–10 are viewed as the same event. This allows an
identification (whatever that might be) of Gog with the Beast. For the
evidence aligning Armageddon of Rev. 17–19 with Rev. 20:7–10, see
Meredith G. Kline, "Har Magedon: The End of the Millennium," *Journal
of the Evangelical Theological Society* 39:2 (June 1996) 207–222.

285. The term "Armageddon" has been fundamentally misunderstood by
most prophecy teachers and enthusiasts, who presume the term points
to a battle at Megiddo. As I wrote in *The Unseen Realm* (pp. 369–372):
"Anyone who has ever investigated the term has undoubtedly read that
it refers to a battle that will take place at or near Megiddo, the presumed
geographical namesake for the term Armageddon. Further research
would perhaps detect the fact that in Zechariah 12:11 the place name
'Megiddo' is spelled (in Hebrew) with an 'n' on the end, tightening the
association between that place and the term Armageddon. As coherent as
all that sounds, it's wrong. As we'll see in this chapter, an identification
of Armageddon with Megiddo is unsustainable. With respect to the
word itself, the scriptural description of the event, and the supernatural
concepts tied to both those elements, the normative understanding of
Armageddon is demonstrably flawed.... John, the author of Revelation,
tells us explicitly that 'Armageddon' is a *Hebrew* term. John does that
in part because the book of Revelation is written in Greek. There's
something about the Greek word 'Armageddon' that required, for Greek
readers, clarification that the term had been brought into the verse from
Hebrew. Those who can read Greek, or at least know the alphabet, will
notice that the Greek term (Ἁρμαγεδών) would be transliterated into
English characters as *h-a-r-m-a-g-e-d-o-n*. If you don't know Greek,
you'll wonder right away where the initial 'h' in the transliteration
comes from. The 'h' at the beginning of the term corresponds to the
superscripted apostrophe before the capital 'A' in the Greek letters—
what is known as a rough breathing mark in Greek. The Greek language
had no letter 'h' and so instead used this mark to convey that sound. As
a result, the correct (Hebrew) term John uses to describe the climactic
end-times battle is *harmagedon*. This spelling becomes significant when
we try to discern what this *Hebrew* term means. The first part of the term

(*har*) is easy. In Hebrew *har* means "mountain." Our term is therefore divisible into *har-magedon*, "Mount (of) *magedon*." The question is, what is *magedon*?" Megiddo, of course, is not a mountain, and so the idea that the battle of Armageddon will be at Megiddo is deeply flawed. The Greek term *har-magedon* retroverts back into Hebrew as *har mo'ed,* the "mount of assembly" at which Yahweh lives and where his divine council serves him. That mountain is Zion—Jerusalem. Armageddon is a battle for God's dominion over Jerusalem *at Jerusalem.*

286. J. W. van Henten, "Typhon," *Dictionary of Deities and Demons in the Bible* (ed. Karel van der Toorn, Bob Becking, and Pieter W. van der Horst; Leiden: E. J. Brill, 1999) 880.

287. J. W. van Henten, "Antiochus IV as a Typhonic Figure in Daniel 7," in *The Book of Daniel in the Light of New Findings* (ed. A. S. van der Woude; Bibliotheca Ephemeridum Theologicarum Lovaniensium 106; Leuven: Peeters Publishers, 1993) 223–243 (esp. pp. 228, This is the same scholar who produced the *DDD* entry. This work is a much more thorough treatment.

288. The translations come from Nickelsburg, *1 Enoch.*

289. The Enochian material recognizes that God's plan for humanity was violated in a series of rebellions, two of which have divine beings as the catalysts (Gen. 3, Gen. 6:1–4). It is understandable, then, that Second Temple writers would assume the first divine rebel had a hand in the second divine rebellion. The two rebellions would have been further associated by the underworld itself. The divine cherub of Eden is cast down to earth (*'erets*) in the biblical account. This term is used elsewhere in the Hebrew Bible for the underworld realm of the dead (Jonah 2:6). The Watchers were imprisoned in this place, and the Watcher-spirits were the source of demons. But there is no sense that the Enochian writer thought the leader of the Watchers was the serpent figure of Eden. There is also no need to presume, as many scholars do, that the New Testament writers are presuming that equation. The New Testament writers do apply what is said about the leader of the Watchers to Satan, but they aren't following an Enochian equation by doing so.

290. For a detailed survey of Second Temple Jewish literature referencing Enochian material, see George W. E. Nickelsburg, *1 Enoch: A Commentary on the Book of 1 Enoch* (ed. Klaus Baltzer; Hermeneia—a Critical and Historical Commentary on the Bible; Minneapolis, MN: Fortress, 2001) 71–82.

291. Ken Penner and Michael S. Heiser, "Old Testament Greek Pseudepigrapha with Morphology" (Bellingham, WA: Lexham Press, 2008).

292. Nickelsburg, *1 Enoch*, 72.

293. Ibid., 72.

294. Ibid., 77.

295. G. J. Brooke, "Pesharim," ed. Craig A. Evans and Stanley E. Porter, *Dictionary of New Testament Background: A Compendium of Contemporary Biblical Scholarship* (Downers Grove, IL: InterVarsity Press, 2000) 778.

296. Nickelsburg, *1 Enoch*, 77.

297. For a lengthier survey of Christian sources that utilize *1 Enoch,* see Nickelsburg, 87-95 and James C. VanderKam, "1 Enoch, Enochic Motifs, and Enoch in Early Christian Literature," in idem and William Adler, eds., *The Jewish Apocalyptic Heritage in Early Christianity* (Compendia rerum iudaicarum ad Novum Testamentum 3/4; Minneapolis: Fortress Press, 1996).

298. George W. E. Nickelsburg, *1 Enoch: A Commentary on the Book of 1 Enoch* (ed. Klaus Baltzer; Hermeneia—a Critical and Historical Commentary on the Bible; Minneapolis, MN: Fortress, 2001) 87.

299. Nickelsburg, *1 Enoch*, 87–88.

300. Irenaeus of Lyons, "Irenaeus against Heresies," in *The Apostolic Fathers with Justin Martyr and Irenaeus* (ed. Alexander Roberts, James Donaldson, and A. Cleveland Coxe; vol. 1; The Ante-Nicene Fathers; Buffalo, NY: Christian Literature Company, 1885) 1330–331.

301. VanderKam, "1 Enoch, Enochic Motifs, and Enoch in Early Christian Literature," 43.

302. Tertullian, "On the Apparel of Women," in *Fathers of the Third Century: Tertullian, Part Fourth; Minucius Felix; Commodian; Origen, Parts First and Second* (ed. Alexander Roberts, James Donaldson, and A. Cleveland Coxe; trans. S. Thelwall; vol. 4; The Ante-Nicene Fathers; Buffalo, NY: Christian Literature Company, 1885) 415–16.

303. Tertullian, "On Idolatry," in *Latin Christianity: Its Founder, Tertullian* (ed. Alexander Roberts, James Donaldson, and A. Cleveland Coxe; trans. S. Thelwall; vol. 3; The Ante-Nicene Fathers; Buffalo, NY: Christian Literature Company, 1885), 370–71.

304. VanderKam, "1 Enoch, Enochic Motifs, and Enoch in Early Christian Literature," 54.

305. Nickelsburg, *1 Enoch*, 90.

306. Ibid., 92.

307. Ken Penner and Michael S. Heiser, *Old Testament Greek Pseudepigrapha with Morphology* (Bellingham, WA: Lexham Press, 2008).

308. George W. E. Nickelsburg, *1 Enoch: A Commentary on the Book of 1 Enoch* (ed. Klaus Baltzer; Hermeneia—a Critical and Historical Commentary on the Bible; Minneapolis, MN: Fortress, 2001), 9. Nickelsburg's footnote at the end of this selection reads (in part) as follows: "Throughout his edition, Milik assumes that Aramaic was the original language (J. T. Milik, *The Books of Enoch: Aramaic Fragments of Qumrân Cave 4* (Oxford: Clarendon, 1976).... Michael A. Knibb (Knibb, *The Ethiopic Book of Enoch: A New Edition in the Light of the Aramaic Dead Sea Fragments*, vol. 2:6–7) also considers an Aramaic original 'most probable.'"

309. Ken Penner and Michael S. Heiser, "Old Testament Greek Pseudepigrapha with Morphology" (Bellingham, WA: Lexham Press, 2008).

310. George W. E. Nickelsburg, *1 Enoch*, 8.

311. Ibid., 173.

312. See http://www.bombaxo.com/blog/biblical-stuff/apocrypha-and-pseudepigrapha/new-testament-allusions-to-apocrypha-and-pseudepigrapha/ .

313. My point here is that the masquerade idea has little to no solid *exegetical* support. One could argue, though, that such a masquerade might be *tactical* on the part of the Antichrist.

314. Some would appeal to 1 Kings 10:14 to defend the idea that the profile is not exclusively Gentile. That verse tells us that Solomon had accumulated 666 talents of gold. Scholars have noticed the number, naturally, and it may well be behind what John was thinking in Revelation. Beale comments, for example: "The mention in 1 Kgs. 10:14 of 666 talents of gold accumulated by Solomon may also be in John's field of reference. The 666 talents are mentioned immediately after Solomon has reached the peak of his kingship. After telling of such greatness, 1 Kings immediately tells how Solomon broke a series of God's laws for kings (Deut. 17:14–17) by multiplying gold, horses, chariots, and foreign wives and by becoming involved in idolatry (1 Kgs. 10:14–11:13). Consequently, the 666 from 1 Kings would have served as an excellent candidate for a number to symbolize the perversion of kingship through idolatry and

economic evil" (G. K. Beale, *The Book of Revelation: A Commentary on the Greek Text* [New International Greek Testament Commentary; Grand Rapids, MI; Eerdmans, 1999] 727). Beale's point is well taken. If John was thinking of Solomon, *he was using the number to denigrate the tyrannical abuse of kingship*, something entirely consistent with the description of his beast in Revelation. He wasn't using the number to identify the beast as a Jew. As the only alternative against the consistent Gentile typology for the great eschatological enemy, the argument from 1 Kings 10:14 for a Jewish antichrist is extraordinarily weak.

315. Some argue that the Hebrew phrase here (*'elōhê 'abōtayw*; "God/ gods of his fathers") is always used (with other suffixes, like "your") to describe Yahweh ("God of his fathers") and therefore points to a Jew. This is a more coherent approach to a Jewish antichrist than an appeal to Solomon but is inconclusive since the phrases in question can be found in polytheistic religions. For example, "the god of your father" and "the god of our fathers" can be found in Old Assyrian texts, a letter from Mari from the eighteenth century BC, hieroglyphic Hittite texts, and (with less precision) Ugaritic texts (Frank Moore Cross, "Yahweh and the God of the Patriarchs," *Harvard Theological Review* 55:4 (1962): 225–259 [esp. 228]; J. Philip Hyatt, "Yahweh as 'the God of my Father'," *Vetus Testamentum* 5:2 (1955): 130-136 [esp. 131–132]). The point is that the writer of Daniel might be drawing on a similar conception of pagans with this wording if he has a Gentile in view.

316. John Joseph Collins, and Adela Yarbro Collins, *Daniel: A Commentary on the Book of Daniel* (Ed. Frank Moore Cross; Hermeneia—a Critical and Historical Commentary on the Bible; Minneapolis, MN: Fortress Press, 1993), 12–13.

317. Louis F. Hartman and Alexander A. Di Lella, *The Book of Daniel: A New Translation with Notes and Commentary on Chapters 1-9* (vol. 23; Anchor Yale Bible; New Haven; London: Yale University Press, 2008) 14.

318. Ibid., 260.

319. Ibid, 267.

320. I have not spelled this term with final *nun* so readers can better see the visual confusion Hartman and Di Lella presume.

321. Ibid., 260.